Providing Mental Health Services to Youth Where They Are

Providing Mental Health Services to Youth Where They Are:

School- and Community-Based Approaches

Edited by
Harinder S. Ghuman, M.D.,
Mark D. Weist, Ph.D.,
and Richard M. Sarles, M. D.

Routledge
Taylor & Francis Group
NEW YORK AND LONDON

Published in 2002 by
Routledge
711 Third Avenue,
New York, NY 10017

Published in Great Britain by
Routledge
27 Church Road
Hove, East Sussex, BN3 2FA

First issued in paperback 2014

Routledge is an imprint of the Taylor & Francis Group, an informa business

Library of Congress Cataloging-in-Publication Data

Providing mental health services to youth where they are : school and community-based approaches / Harinder S. Ghuman, Mark D. Weist, and Richard M. Sarles, eds.
p. ; cm.
Includes bibliographical references and index.
ISBN 1-58391-300-9 (hardcover)
1. Students—Mental health services. 2. School children—Mental health services. 3. Community mental health services. I. Ghuman, Harinder S. II. Weist, Mark D. III. Sarles, Richard M. (Richard Milford), 1935–
[DNLM: 1. Community Mental Health Services—organization & administration—Adolescence. 2. Community Mental Health Services—organization & administration—Child. 3. School Health Services. 4. Adolescent Health Services. 5. Child Health Services. WA 352 P969 2002]
RC454.4 .P747 2002
362.2'083—dc21

2001052572

ISBN 13: 978-1-58391-300-0 (hbk)
ISBN 13: 978-0-415-76345-5 (pbk)

This book is dedicated to the victims
of the tragedy of September 11, 2001,
and to all those who have helped
and are continuing to help move
the United States toward
healing and renewed vitality.

Contents

Foreword ix
Acknowledgments xi

Introduction Principles Behind the Proactive Delivery of Mental Health Services to Youth Where They Are 1
Mark D. Weist and Harinder S. Ghuman

Part 1: School-Based Approaches

Chapter 1 School-Based Mental Health in the United States: An Historical Perspective and Baltimore's Experience 17
Yu Ling Han, Kristin V. Christodulu, Bernice Rosenthal, Louise Fink, and Mark D. Weist

Chapter 2 An Elementary School Mental Health Program Serving Immigrant and Minority Children 39
Jennifer Oppenheim and Robert J. Evert

Chapter 3 Establishing Successful School Mental Health Programs: Guidelines and Recommendations 57
Olga M. Acosta, Nancy A. Tashman, Christine Prodente, and Eric Proescher

Chapter 4 Practical Issues in School Mental Health: Referral Procedures, Negotiating Special Education, and Confidentiality 75
Steven W. Evans, Jennifer L. Sapia, Jennifer Axelrod Lowie, and Nancy K. Glomb

Chapter 5 Evaluation and Quality Improvement in School Mental Health 95
Melissa Grady Ambrose, Mark D. Weist, Cindy Schaeffer, Laura A. Nabors, and Susan Hill

Part 2: Home- and Community-Based Approaches

Chapter 6 Home- and Community-Based Services: Historical Overview, Concepts, and Models 113
Harinder S. Ghuman

Chapter 7 Development and Implementation of Mobile Crisis Services for Emotionally Disturbed Youth 129
Paramjit T. Joshi, Mark E. Greenberg, and Michelle Leff

Chapter 8 Home- and Community-Based Treatment Programs for Severely Emotionally Disturbed Treatment-Resistant Youth and Their Families: The Child Mobile Team 149
Harinder S. Ghuman, Eileen Hastings, and Marsha Gorth

Chapter 9 Family-Driven Treatment: Families as Full Partners in the Care of Children with Psychiatric Illness 163
Ann Vander Stoep, Marilynn Williams, and Charles Huffine

Chapter 10 Institutional Treatment Transferred: Narrative Family Therapy Approach to Acute Services 191
Thomas Hebeisen and Michael Longo

Part 3: Special Issues

Chapter 11 Children's Mental Health: Partnering with the Faith Community 209
Christine A. Prodente, Mark A. Sander, Alvin C. Hathaway, Tom Sloane, and Mark D. Weist

Chapter 12 Children Are Newsworthy: Working Effectively with the Media to Improve Systems of Child and Adolescent Mental Health 225
Caroline S. Clauss-Ehlers and Mark D. Weist

Contributors 241
Index 245

Foreword

Lois T. Flaherty, M.D.

School- and community-based services are here, but have they come to stay? Other movements have come and gone, victims of economic crises, a short public attention span, or political winds of fortune.

The promise of the community mental health movement in the 1960s was to serve all people, along the lines of a public health model. The original model was flawed, conceptualizing that somehow community mental health centers (CMHCs) could treat ill communities rather than individuals in need of mental health services. Although the CMHC model was seen as bringing services into the community, in reality services were no more accessible than they had been in the traditional clinic models. In some cases, child guidance clinics were actually disbanded and their services folded into CMHCs, leading to a decrease in focus on specialized services for children and adolescents. Hospitals were closed or downsized with the rationale that the new community mental health centers would make them obsolete. The aftermath was an increase in the numbers of untreated mentally ill. At the same time, youth violence, substance abuse, and teen pregnancy rates were rising. The CMHC movement was widely seen as a failure.

The idea of a public health approach to mental health care was not without merit. The problem was that the original approach lacked the means to effectively translate the ideal into practice. These means are trained personnel, effective interventions, and sufficient administrative and financial support to maintain a full continuum of care, including psychiatric hospitalization when necessary.

Many things have changed. Some of the ideas that are new now include a vigorous and still-growing advocacy movement on the part of families, the recognition that specialized knowledge and skills are necessary to treat children and adolescents in community settings, and partnerships between educational and mental health systems and among professionals of various disciplines. Economic forces have changed the way services have been reimbursed, the child and adolescent population has changed demographically, and both the prevalence and recognition of psychosocial problems among young people have increased. At the same time, the knowledge base about mental health has expanded dramatically, with enhanced ability to diagnose and treat mental illness in children and adolescents. Not the least in importance is our current understanding of the significance of so-called subthreshold or subclinical conditions, which, although they may not meet strict criteria for a psychiatric diagnosis, are now known to be associated with considerable impairment in functioning and to presage more serious disorders in adulthood. This confluence of factors has brought about the development of innovative services in schools, communities, and homes described in this book.

The development of school- and community-based services described in the following pages represents not only a significant advance but also a return to the roots of the child guidance movement, which was born in the early part of the twentieth century out of concerns that children were ending up in the jails and on the streets without attention to their psychological and social problems. In addition, it represents the hope that the dream of the CMHC movement to provide services to everyone in need of them can actually come to pass. It is significant that the Baltimore programs were fostered by the Baltimore City Health Department, an agency whose mission is the health of the citizens of Baltimore. At the same time, new information is emerging about the degree to which children's and adolescents' mental health needs are underserved even as services seem to be expanding. It is fitting that we enter the twenty-first century with a new determination to help children and adolescents, renewed energy and resources to fulfill this commitment, and the means to make it a reality.

Acknowledgments

We wish to thank the wonderful staff in our community and school mental health programs at the University of Maryland School of Medicine for their dedication to working with youth and their families. We wish to express appreciation and gratitude to Drs. John Talbott, Anthony Lehman, Fred Osher, David Pruitt, Jill Rachbeisel, and Ms. Eileen Hastings and Marsha Gorth for providing leadership and support to our programs.

In the work on this book, Mark Weist was supported by cooperative agreement U93 MC 00174 from the Office of Adolescent Health, Maternal and Child Health Bureau (Title V, Social Security Act), Health Resources and Services Administration, with co-funding by the Center for Mental Health Services, Substance Abuse, and Mental Health Services Administration. He was also supported by Grant number RO3 HSO9542 from the Agency for Healthcare Research and Quality.

We are indebted to our contributors for their commitment to excellence and their tolerance for several editorial rewritings. Special feelings of gratitude and appreciation are extended to Ms. Bernadette Capelle, Mr. George Zimmar, Ms. Hope Breeman, and the staff at Brunner-Routledge. Finally, we are especially grateful to our teachers, friends, and family, especially our wives, Jaswinder Ghuman, Amber Weist, and Lois Sarles, and our children, Avniel Ghuman; Tyler, Nathan, Jackson, Kylee, and Shannon Weist; and Kristen and Karen Sarles, who continue to provide us unwavering support and inspiration.

Principles Behind the Proactive Delivery of Mental Health Services to Youth Where They Are

Mark D. Weist, Ph.D., and Harinder S. Ghuman, M.D.

The purpose of this book is to capture elements of what can best be described as a revolution in children's mental health. This revolution begins with an intensive analysis of the way we have provided mental health care to children and adolescents. In some areas, this analysis suggests that our approaches are on the mark; in other areas, it suggests that our approaches have been far off base. For example, there is increasing recognition that a passive service delivery approach, whereby mental health staff "wait" for "patients" to come to them, is less than optimal. Increasingly, we are realizing that by waiting for the youth and families, we are only seeing a small percentage of those in need, and for even these youth and families the success of our efforts is limited by problems such as appointment noncompliance. Further, our established mental health centers are generally seeing youth with the most serious problems, and are generally not engaged in any activities that could be described as preventing problems or addressing them early in their development. As leaders in children's mental health and other related arenas (e.g., education, juvenile justice, child welfare) become more aware of these problems, they are increasingly embracing approaches that move staff out of offices and into the natural environments of youth and families, in order to provide services that are more proactive, preventive, and empirically supported. That is the theme of this book—moving beyond paradigms and approaches that have limited efforts in children's mental health, and moving toward approaches that hold considerable promise for reducing the considerable gap between children's mental health needs and effective services for them. Please note that we are not arguing that there is no role for more traditional mental health centers for youth and their families. Instead, this book will make the case that in many communities the work of these centers needs to be refocused and enhanced to deliver major portions of services to children, adolescents, and their families in natural environments.

The book is divided into three parts. The first describes the progressive development and critical issues confronted by comprehensive mental health programs in schools in the United States. The second explains a range of innovative approaches to bring mental health care to youth and families in other community settings. The final part includes two papers that address cross-cutting issues in child and adolescent mental health: building connections with communities of faith, and raising public awareness of youth mental health issues through strategic relationships with the media.

Importantly, the revolution in children's mental health care is growing on a foundation of reform that was laid in the early 1980s, which saw the beginning of intensive analyses of the extent of behavioral and emotional problems in youth, their treatment needs, and how best to develop systems of care, especially for youth with more significant disturbances. In her highly influential book *Unclaimed Children* (1982), Jane Knitzer reported that two-thirds of the three million children in the U.S. with serious emotional disturbances were receiving no treatment at all and others were receiving inappropriately restrictive care due to a lack of community-based alternatives. These compelling findings were subsequently confirmed by Saxe et al. (1986) in a study for the Office of Technology Assessment of the United States Congress.

In 1984, the National Institute of Mental Health launched the Child and Adolescent Service System Program (CASSP) to help states and communities in the development of community-based systems of care for underserved emotionally disturbed youth and their families. In addition, the U.S. Congress amended Public Law 99-660, the State Comprehensive Mental Health Services Plan Act that required states to plan, establish, and implement community-based systems of care for youth with serious emotional disturbances and their families. Congress also passed legislation to create the Child Mental Health Service Program in 1992 to fund community-based services for youth. Paralleling these congressional initiatives, the Robert Wood Johnson Foundation in 1987 and the Annie E. Casey Foundation in 1992 launched major child mental health initiatives.

The CASSP developed "core values" for systems of care for children and adolescents with more severe emotional and behavioral disturbances (Stroul & Friedman, 1986). These emphasized that the system should be child-centered, family-focused, and community-based. The types and mix of services provided should depend upon the needs of the child/adolescent and family. The locus of services as well as management and decision-making responsibility should be at the community level. The CASSP promoted the following ten guiding principles for communities to use in developing their systems of care. Youth with severe emotional and behavioral disturbances should:

1. Have access to a comprehensive array of services addressing their physical, educational, psychological, and social needs.
2. Receive individualized services congruent with their unique needs and strengths.
3. Be served in the least restrictive and most normative clinically appropriate environment.
4. Receive services that are family-centered; that is, involving the family in all aspects of their planning and delivery, with families treated as *collaborators, not recipients* of care.
5. Receive services that are linked and integrated with other child-serving agencies and programs.
6. Be provided with case management to ensure that multiple services are delivered in a coordinated and therapeutic manner and to enable easy movement through the system of services depending upon their changing needs.
7. Have their problems identified and responded to as early as possible to increase the likelihood of positive outcomes.
8. Be ensured a smooth transition to the adult service system (if indicated) as they mature.
9. Have their rights protected and have access to effective advocacy programs.
10. Receive culturally competent services, provided without regard to race, religion, physical disability, or other characteristics.

The reforms reviewed above have been associated with significant improvements in mental health care for youth and families in diverse communities around the United States. The Center for Mental Health Services of the Substance Abuse and Mental Health Services Administration has played a major role in increasing the impact of the CASSP initiative by providing significant grant support and leadership to communities in creating and sustaining systems of care for youth that are built on the above principles. The CASSP movement was also influential in the national movement toward school-based mental health programs, which began in earnest in the late 1980s. This was related to the fact that leaders in children's education and health in communities were reading reports and articles from the CASSP initiative, which helped to raise awareness about the significant problems in systems of mental health care for children and adolescents. In Baltimore and Maryland, CASSP-related reports had a direct effect on planning for the establishment of more comprehensive mental health programs for youth in schools. As these programs in schools began to grow, there was also a growing realization among people who worked in school mental health that CASSP initiatives provided support only for programs offering tertiary care to youth with more severe problems. Hence, while ideas related to reform assisted in expanding mental health programs in the schools, such support did not translate into increased resources for doing so. This led to the realization that the system was not really a true system of care, since only youth with the most severe problems were able to access help. Yu Ling Han and colleagues, in the opening chapter, capture this history in Baltimore, which reflects the national experience.

The 1990s witnessed the progressive development of more comprehensive mental health programs in schools. As programs have developed beyond the early stages, so has advocacy for broad systems of care that are for *all youth*, involving prevention, mental health promotion, and care for youth with more established problems. Key aspects of the school mental health movement, and the evolution of this broader system of care are reviewed in the following.

SCHOOL-BASED MENTAL HEALTH

As mentioned, more comprehensive mental health care for youth in schools began in earnest in the late 1980s. The general atmosphere of reform and improvement of children's mental health care helped to propel the movement, as did efforts to influence decision makers in schools and communities about the connection between emotional and behavioral problems in youth and barriers to student learning. In this regard, the work of Howard Adelman and Linda Taylor in Los Angeles has been particularly influential. Adelman and Taylor have developed an approach to build awareness in schools and communities that youth who are depressed, anxious, acting out, or coping with conditions of risk or stress (e.g., violence, crime) have difficulty learning. If schools want to achieve desired academic outcomes, it is incumbent on them to have sufficient resources in place to develop comprehensive programs that serve to remove and reduce barriers to student learning. In contrast with the token level of staff that most school systems pay for to do this work, Adelman and Taylor argue that *one-third* of a school system's resources should be allocated to *enable* student learning. Based on their long-standing and evolving work on this approach, it is being embraced by many school systems around the country. This has been related to the explicit policy framework the initiative is placed in, with the barriers-to-learning concept resonating for school districts that are dealing with increasing accountability pressures related to student academic performance and test scores (Adelman & Taylor, 1993, 1997, 1999).

Developing in conjunction with the evolution and refinement of school-owned programs that are embracing the barriers-to-learning framework are expanded school mental health (ESMH) programs. These programs represent a partnership between schools and community agencies to improve school-based services toward a full continuum of care (assessment, treatment, case management, prevention) for youth in both general and regular education (Weist, 1997). ESMH programs are compatible with efforts by schools to restructure and enhance resources to address barriers to student learning, as most schools will acknowledge that they do not have adequate resources to address learning, emotional, and behavioral problems among their students. And, because mental health services available to youth in outside agencies tend to be limited in many communities, schools have been characterized as the *de facto provider* of mental health care for them. This serves to increase stress on schools and school systems and drain their resources.

Consider this scenario: An eight year-old boy—"Joe"—is referred for special education placement related to acting-out behaviors. Learning problems are not apparent, but for him to be seen in the local mental health center takes seven weeks. An evaluation by the school's special education team can occur sooner, so he is referred there. Even though initial special education evaluation does not reveal learning problems, Joe is placed in special education, receiving a comprehensive evaluation and some classroom-based consultation. However, the school psychologist only works in the school one day a week, and has many pressures on her to do evaluations of other children for special education. She is a highly skilled therapist, and specializes in cognitive behavioral therapy and working with families. But, because of the demands of her job, and very limited time, she is unable to provide therapeutic services for Joe and his family. Referrals for such services in the community are made, but these all fail. Over time, Joe's problems become much worse, and ultimately he requires out-of-state residential treatment that costs $125,000 per year. Who pays? The *school system*. In the meantime, the public mental health system observes this happening. Is this appropriate? Most would agree that it is not. The point is that systems of education and health/mental health both have responsibilities for youth in school; ESMH programs acknowledge this responsibility, and merge the resources of systems of education, of mental health, and, whenever possible, of other systems such as child welfare, juvenile justice, and public health.

Expanded school mental health programs are inherently collaborative since they represent the joining of education and other community systems to improve mental health care for youth. In schools themselves, they also are highly collaborative, with mental health staff from community agencies working closely with school-hired mental health professionals (e.g., school counselors, social workers, and psychologists), school health staff (school nurses, consulting physicians), and education staff (teachers, school administrators). The term *expanded* is used to convey that these programs are building on, or augmenting, the framework for mental health that already exists in almost all schools; ESMH programs in no way threaten or supplant mental health programs that are directly supported by systems of education. Chapters by Olga Acosta and colleagues at the University of Maryland, and Steven Evans and colleagues at James Madison University, describe the merging of resources in schools and community agencies to develop ESMH programs, and provide hands-on, pragmatic strategies to ensure their success.

The third major development in mental health in schools is the already large and growing knowledge base on effective prevention programs. An increasing number of comprehensive prevention programs are documenting significant impacts on the psychosocial functioning of students; for example, leading to improved grades, decreased behavioral problems, and decreased risk behavior (e.g., sexual involvement, use/abuse of tobacco, alcohol, and drugs) (Cowen et al., 1996; Durlak, 1995; Elias & Clabby, 1992; Weissberg & Greenberg, 1998). However, these prevention programs are not broadly institutionalized, and there is a significant need to build bridges between the research and practice communities to promote their widespread adoption (Weist & Christodulu, 2000). Fortunately, in the context of increasing education-based programs to address barriers to learning (Adelman & Taylor, 1993, 1997, 1999), and expanded school mental health programs that are joining school and community resources (Armbruster, Gerstein, & Fallon, 1997; Catron & Weiss, 1994; Evans, 1999; Flaherty & Weist, 1999; Weist, 1997), more and more connections are being made to bring empirically supported prevention strategies to schools (Tashman et al., 2000; Weist & Christodulu, 2000). Together these developments constitute a national movement toward mental health promotion and intervention in the most universal natural setting—the schools.

The development and progression of this movement has been spurred by numerous factors, including: (1) an increasing awareness of the limitations of mental health care for youth in educational, health, and mental health systems (Adelman & Taylor, 1997; Burns & Friedman, 1990; Hoagwood, Jensen, Petti, & Burns, 1996; Knoff, 1996; Leaf et al., 1996; Weist & Christodulu, 2000; Weisz, Weiss, & Donenberg, 1992); (2) a growing recognition of the many advantages of school-based programs (Acosta et al. [chapter 3 in this book], Adelman & Taylor, 1993; Armbruster et al., 1997; Evans, 1999; Illback, Kalafat, & Sanders, 1997; Nabors, Weist, Tashman, & Myers, 1999; Oppenheim & Evert [chapter 2 in this book]); (3) the powerful impact of school-based health centers in highlighting unmet mental health needs in youth (Anglin, Naylor, & Kaplan, 1996; Lear, Gleicher, St. Germaine, & Porter, 1991); (4) organized and effective advocacy (Weist & Schlitt, 1998); and (5) increasing support from diverse sources, with progress in each area related to important policy changes that are occurring in community and state systems of mental health and education (Adelman & Taylor, 1999; Adelman et al., 1999; Dryfoos, 1994, 1998; Knoff, 1996).

Notably, funding sources for mental health programs in schools have increased dramatically in recent years. This support is coming at federal, state, and local levels. For example, at the federal level, the Maternal and Child Health Bureau of the Health Resources and Services Administration, U.S. Department of Health and Human Services (DHHS) has funded two national technical assistance centers (at the University of California, Los Angeles [UCLA], and the University of Maryland, Baltimore) and five states (Kentucky, Maine, Minnesota, New Mexico, and South Carolina) to develop, expand, and improve mental health programs in schools (Adelman et al., 1999). The Centers for Disease Control and Prevention is funding twenty-three states to improve coordinated school health programs in schools, which include a major emphasis on mental health care. The U.S. Department of Education is providing significant support to the development of mental health programs for youth in special and regular education; for example, through its departments of Special Education, and Safe and Drug Free Schools.

It is also noteworthy that the development of ESMH programs in the U.S. has been facilitated by the increasing focus on violence and youth, and strategies to prevent youth from being violent (Weist & Cooley-Quille, 2001). The unfortunate tragedies involving school shootings in Jonesboro, Arkansas; Paducah, Kentucky; and Littleton, Colorado (among other places), have served to provide additional evidence that in general, schools do not have sufficient resources to monitor and provide mental health assessment, treatment, and prevention services to their students. This has led to widespread support for the development of violence prevention programs in schools, embedded in the context of broader mental health programs. Exemplifying this support is the Safe Schools Healthy Students Initiative, involving over $100 million in funding per year beginning in 1999 to develop programs that provide mental health care and address and prevent violence-related issues among youth in schools. This program represents a significant collaboration between three federal agencies—the

Substance Abuse and Mental Health Services Administration of DHHS, the Department of Education, and the Office of Juvenile Justice and Delinquency Prevention. In addition, other federal partners, including the departments of Agriculture and Labor, will be joining this initiative, which represents an unprecedented level of collaboration at the federal level, as it grows in the next few years.

These developments are propelling the exchange of knowledge and best practice, and in some cases are leading to paradigmatic change. As movements and disciplines come together, there is a growing consensus on what constitute the essential elements of any community-change effort. These include: (1) involving stakeholders (e.g., youth, families, teachers, community leaders, clergy) in all facets of program planning, development, and evaluation; (2) assessing the needs of youth and available resources to identify gaps and point to priority areas for attention; (3) closely planning and coordinating the program with others that exist in the school, and with programs that exist in the community; (4) focusing program services on youth strengths and assets, and building them on empirically supported factors; (5) paying significant attention to the development and ongoing refinement of systems of quality improvement and program evaluation; (6) developing an increasingly sophisticated advocacy agenda; and (7) diversifying funding sources to enable a broad approach to care that emphasizes prevention and does not rely overly on fee-for-service. Two chapters capture critical dimensions of this work: Jennifer Oppenheim and Robert Evert of Linkages to Learning describe the development of a culturally competent and responsive program for elementary-aged youth; and Melissa Ambrose and colleagues at the University of Maryland review evaluation and quality improvement strategies for a large ESMH program in Baltimore.

MENTAL HEALTH PROGRAMS IN HOMES AND OTHER COMMUNITY SETTINGS

Home- and community-based mental health services are not just an important component of community-based systems of care but can also serve as a backbone to the whole system if the principles described above are properly applied. There is a long history and tradition of providing home-based health services in general medicine and psychiatry. However, psychiatric services for youth have always lagged behind, with adult-focused systems in psychiatry much better developed in most communities in the United States. Over the past two decades, mental health professionals working with youth have tried to clarify and define what is required and helpful in providing high-quality and effective home- and community-based programs. Chapter 6 by Harinder Ghuman of the University of Maryland describes the historical background and various models and concepts of home-based treatment for youth.

Most, if not all, communities, especially in inner cities, have been struggling to understand how to best care for youth and their families in psychiatric crisis. Commonly, emergency room staff are overwhelmed by a large number of youth waiting to be evaluated, and then struggle to find disposition options for them when the evaluation is completed. Far too often, youth requiring hospitalization have to wait in emergency rooms for hours if not days before being transferred to an inpatient facility (Christodulu, Lichenstein, Shafer, & Weist, in press). And it is also too common for youth to be transferred out of town and sometimes out of state to inpatient facilities due to a lack of beds in the home community. One can only imagine the trauma that these events have on children, adolescents, and their families; sadly, to date, it appears that the impact of such system failures has not been adequately studied.

It is equally difficult to arrange adequate follow-up care for youth who are not considered to be in need of inpatient hospitalization. Thus, the next crisis results in another visit to the emergency room and the cycle repeats itself. Amplifying on the CASSP principles reviewed earlier, a guiding theme in all systems of care should be that services are delivered in a timely fashion and in a way that matches with the presenting problems of families (i.e., no more intrusive than necessary). The chapter by Paramjit Joshi and colleagues describes the development and implementation of a home-based mobile crisis service in an inner city in an attempt to avoid the many problems with emergency room care and the psychiatric hospitalization of youth in need.

The majority of home- and community-based mental health programs are either developed for youth in crisis or for those characterized as a *special population;* for example, youth in the juvenile justice system or having substance abuse problems. These programs are often labor-intensive and time-limited, and unfortunately are only reaching a very small percentage of the youth who would benefit from them. Further, there is a large group of children and adolescents who are suffering from chronic mental disorders with acute and sub-acute episodes. If these youth do not enter into a full-blown *crisis*, they may *never* receive appropriate care. Complicating the picture is that many youth with intensive mental health needs come from families who also have intensive mental health needs, as well as needs for services in other systems (e.g., social services, specialized health care). For youth with more severe problems living in families facing multiple challenges, a principle of care should be that home-based services are provided for as long as necessary without a preconceived and arbitrary time limitation. VanDenBerg (1989) described how individualized unconditional care and wraparound services with flexible funds can be helpful in reducing the rate of referral for inpatient hospitalization for children and adolescents. Chapter 8 of this book, by Ghuman and colleagues of the University of Maryland, describes a home- and community-based treatment program that is attempting to care for these hard-to-reach populations while providing individualized and flexible services that are not time-limited.

Child and adolescent psychiatry has always considered the role of the family to be paramount in the development and treatment of the child. All chapters in part 2 of the book reflect that theme; that is, treating families as collaborators who have the key role in deciding on courses of treatment and action for their children. This principle is among the most important in the CASSP guidelines; however, common practice will usually reveal significant problems related to its adherence, with story after story recounted by families about curt and disrespectful care they have received from mental health professionals, often after waiting many weeks or months for an appointment (United States Public Health Service, 2000). The chapter by Ann Vander Stoep and colleagues from the University of Washington describes a project based on the assumption that families can manage their children's care with the support of community-based teams and provides important recommendations for empowering families to function effectively in this role.

Over the last two decades, there has been a massive shift in how mental health care is delivered to youth (Ghuman & Sarles, 1998). This change in service delivery has been driven primarily by escalating mental health costs. During the 1970s and early 1980s, some if not all hospitals were capitalizing on the burgeoning child and adolescent market, which no doubt led to many unnecessary hospitalizations of youth. During the latter 1980s and 1990s, state and federal policies for inpatient treatment and reimbursement followed the insurance industry and managed care organizations in restricting access to, and limiting the length of, hospital stays. In this scenario of restricted care, home- and community-based programs began to grow of necessity, in some communities without adequate consideration of whether the youth and families being treated by them were ready for such a transition. Youth, their families, and treating professionals were caught unprepared in this sudden shift. Writing about this phenomenon, Anthony (1994) stated, "If some were unqualified for admission (to the hospital) when admitted, there were others who were unfit for discharge. None of this was in accordance with the Hippocratic tradition aimed at helping and doing no harm" (p. xiii). The chapter by Thomas Hebeisen and Michael Longo at the Terry Children's Psychiatric Center describes how an institutional program was successfully transformed to a community-based program using an innovative *narrative therapy* approach.

CROSS-CUTTING ISSUES

This book concludes with discussions of two cross-cutting issues affecting mental health care for youth in all settings. Christine Prodente and colleagues provide background to the movement toward increased collaborations between the faith and mental health communities. They review both the promises and challenges of such collaborations, and present examples of faith–mental health partnerships. This chapter highlights that while there have been relatively few examples of such partnerships, they should increase considerably in the future because of their mutual benefits and due to supportive national developments (e.g., the establishment of the Office of Faith-Based and Community Initiatives of President Bush).

The final chapter in the book is an intriguing contribution led by Caroline Clauss-Ehlers, a media consultant and psychologist, on a topic that receives very little attention in children's mental health—strategically working with the media. Since the American public is generally not knowledgeable about major issues in child and adolescent mental health, raising public awareness and dialogue about the issues (e.g., the gap between needs and resources, the movement toward evidence-based care in natural settings) is fundamental to policy improvement and much-needed capacity building.

ONWARD

The revolution to improve mental health care for our nation's children and adolescents is achieving momentum, as underscored by the U.S. Surgeon General's Report on Mental Health in 1999. This report represents a call to action for the American public to pay more attention to mental health, legitimizes it as an issue that touches every citizen, and underscores significant problems within our mental health systems, especially the child and adolescent mental health system. Importantly, the report does not represent a beginning, but is instead a touchstone event in at least two decades of significant activity aimed at reforming and improving children's mental health care. In the fall of 2000, the Surgeon General further focused the nation's attention on children's mental health through a consensus conference that emphasized many of the themes that you will find in this book.

Moreover, due to advancing communication mechanisms and interest, international dialogue on improving mental health promotion and care for children and adolescents is escalating. The late fall of 2000 witnessed the inaugural World Conference on Mental Health Promotion, in which innovative child and adolescent programs focusing on promoting mental wellness in natural settings received prominent attention. In the summer of 2001 there were major international meetings on youth mental health promotion held in Alberta, Canada, and Paris, France, and numerous international meetings on this topic are planned for the coming years. In this increasing international dialogue on youth mental health promotion, countries are exchanging lessons learned and findings that are facilitating reforms and movements toward enhanced prevention, mental health promotion, and best practice across the spectrum of intervention.

In combination, reforms and improvements in child and adolescent mental health in the U.S. and abroad are transforming the landscape—toward programs in natural settings, that focus on promoting mental health, that emphasize continuous quality improvement and evidenced-based approaches, and that view youth and families as collaborators. The chapters in this book attempt to capture the zeitgeist of this child mental health system transformation that is reaching a new plateau of activity in this new decade, century, and millennium.

Our challenge is not only to continue but to escalate this pace of positive change. In order to do so, there is a need for increasing action at local, state, national, and international levels on policy, advocacy, program development, training, and research fronts. In this work, people from different disciplines and agencies will need to come together with youth, families, and community members in the development and advancement of coalitions that seek to analyze child mental health needs and programs, and build capacity through expanding and improving health-promoting, preventive, and treatment programs. One essential need is for broad, interdisciplinary training of mental health providers to ensure that practice increasingly reflects the vision portrayed in the chapters of this book and diverse recent literature. A second important need is for purposeful efforts to connect training, clinical practice, and research agendas on child and adolescent mental health in school and other community settings. It is our sincere hope that this book contributes to progress in advancing action agendas and in addressing both of these critical needs.

References

Adelman, H. S., & Taylor, L. (1993). School-based mental health: Toward a comprehensive approach. *Journal of Mental Health Administration, 20,* 32–45.

Adelman, H. S., & Taylor, L. (1997). Addressing barriers to learning: Beyond school-linked services and full-service schools. *American Journal of Orthopsychiatry, 67,* 408–421.

Adelman, H. S., & Taylor, L. (1999). Mental health in schools and systems restructuring. *Clinical Psychology Review, 19,* 137–163.

Adelman, H. S., Taylor, L., Weist, M. D., Adelsheim, S., Freeman, B., Kapp, L., Lahti, M., & Mawn, D. (1999). Mental health in schools: A federal initiative. *Children's Services: Social Policy, Research, and Practice, 2,* 95–115.

Anglin, T. M., Naylor, K. E., & Kaplan, D. W. (1996). Comprehensive school-based health care: High school students' use of medical, mental health, and substance abuse services. *Pediatrics, 97,* 318–330.

Anthony, E. J. (1994). Foreword. In H. S. Ghuman & R. M. Sarles (Eds.), *Handbook of adolescent inpatient psychiatric treatment.* New York: Brunner/Mazel.

Armbruster, P., Gerstein, S. H., & Fallon, T. (1997). Bridging the gap between service need and service utilization: A school-based mental health program. *Community Mental Health Journal, 33,* 199–211.

Burns, B. J., & Friedman, R. M. (1990). Examining the research base for child mental health services and policy. *Journal of Mental Health Administration, 17,* 87–97.

Catron, T., & Weiss, B. (1994). The Vanderbilt school-based therapy program: An interagency, primary-care model of mental health services. *Journal of Emotional and Behavioral Disorders, 2,* 247–253.

Christodulu, K. V., Lichenstein, R., Shafer, M., & Weist, M. D. (in press). Pediatric emergency medicine: Emerging trends and a review of psychiatric admissions.

Cowen, E. L., Hightower, A. D., Pedro-Carroll, J. L., Work, W. C., Wyman, P. A., & Haffey, W. G. (1996). *School-based prevention for children at risk.* Washington, DC: American Psychological Association.

Dryfoos, J. G. (1994). *Full Service Schools: A revolution in health and social services for children, youth, and families.* San Francisco: Jossey-Bass.

Dryfoos, J. G. (1998). School-based health centers in the context of education reform. *Journal of School Health, 68,* 404–408.

Durlak, J. A. (1995). *School-based prevention programs for children and adolescents.* Thousand Oaks, CA: Sage.

Elias, M. J., & Clabby, J. F. (1992). *Building social problem solving skills: Guidelines from a school-based program.* San Francisco: Jossey-Bass.

Evans, S. W. (1999). Mental health services in schools: Utilization, effectiveness, and consent. *Clinical Psychology Review, 19,* 165–178.

Flaherty, L. T., & Weist, M. D. (1999). School-based mental health services: The Baltimore models. *Psychology in the Schools, 36,* 379–389.

Ghuman, H. S., & Sarles, R. M. (1998). Ambulatory Services: Clinical, administrative and training issues. In H. S. Ghuman & R. M. Sarles (Eds.), *Handbook of child and adolescent outpatient, day treatment and community psychiatry.* Philadelphia: Brunner/Mazel.

Hoagwood, K., Jensen, P. S., Petti, T., & Burns, B. J. (1996). Outcomes of mental health care for children and adolescents: A comprehensive conceptual model. *Journal of the American Academy of Child and Adolescent Psychiatry, 35,* 1055–1063.

Illback, R. J., Cobb, C. T., & Joseph, H. M. (1997). *Integrated services for children and families: Opportunities for psychological practice.* Washington, DC: American Psychological Association.

Knitzer, J (1982). *Unclaimed children: The failure of public responsibility to children and adolescents in need of mental health services.* Washington, DC: Children's Defense Fund.

Knoff, H. M. (1996). The interface of school, community, and health care reform: Organizational directions toward effective services for children and youth. *School Psychology Review, 25,* 446–464.

Leaf, P. J., Alegria, M., Cohen, P., Goodman, S. H., Horowitz, S. M., Hoven, C. W., Narrow, W. E., Vaden-Kierman, M., & Reiger, D. A. (1996). Mental health service use in the community and schools: Results from the four-community MECA study. *Journal of the American Academy of Child and Adolescent Psychiatry, 35,* 889–897.

Lear, J. G., Gleicher, H. B., St. Germaine, A., & Porter, P. J. (1991). Reorganizing health care for adolescents: The experience of a school-based adolescent health care program. *Journal of Adolescent Health, 12,* 450–458.

Nabors, L. A., Weist, M. D., Tashman, N., & Myers, C. P. (1999). Quality assurance and school-based mental health services. *Psychology in the Schools, 36,* 485–493.

Saxe, L., Cross, T., Silverman, N., Batchelor, W., & Daugherty, D. (1986). *Children's mental health: Problems and services.* Durham, NC: Duke University Press.

Stroul, B. A., & Friedman, R. M. (1986). *A system of care for severely emotionally disturbed children and youth.* Washington, DC: Georgetown University Child Development Center, CASSP Technical Assistance Center.

Tashman, N. T., Weist, M. D., Acosta, O., et al. (2000). Toward the integration of prevention research and expanded school mental health programs. *Children's Services: Social Policy, Research, and Practice, 3,* 97–116.

United States Public Health Service. (2000). *Report of the Surgeon General's Conference on Children's Mental Health: A National Action Agenda.* Washington, DC: United States Government Printing Office.

VanDenBerg, J. (1989). *Alaska youth initiative: Program background.* Juneau, AK: Alaska Department of Health and Social Services, Division of Mental Health and Developmental Disabilities.

Weissberg, R. P., & Greenberg, M. T. (1998). Social and community competence-enhancement and prevention programs. In W. Damon, I. E. Sigel, & K. A. Renninger (Eds.), *Handbook of child psychology, Volume 5: Child psychology in practice* (pp. 877–954). New York: John Wiley & Sons.

Weist, M. D. (1997). Expanded school mental health services: A national movement in progress. In T. H. Ollendick & R. J. Prinz (Eds.), *Advances in clinical child psychology* (Vol. 19, pp. 319–352). New York: Plenum.

Weist, M .D., & Christodulu, K. V. (2000). Expanded school mental health programs: Advancing reform and closing the gap between research and practice. *Journal of School Health, 70,* 195–200.

Weist, M. D., & Cooley-Quille, M. (2001). Advancing efforts related to violence and youth. *Journal of Clinical Child Psychology, 30,* 147–151.

Weist, M. D., & Schlitt, J. J. (1998). Alliances and school-based health care. *Journal of School Health, 68,* 401–403.

Weisz, J. R., Weiss, B., & Donenberg, G. R. (1992). The lab vs. the clinic. *American Psychologist, 47,* 1578–1595.

PART ONE

School-Based Approaches

CHAPTER ONE

School-Based Mental Health in the United States: An Historical Perspective and Baltimore's Experience

Yu Ling Han, Ph.D., Kristin V. Christodulu, Ph.D., Bernice Rosenthal, M.P.H., Louise Fink, M.Ed., and Mark D. Weist, Ph.D.

Since the late 1980s, a full range of mental health services has been progressively developed in schools across the United States. These "expanded" school mental health (ESMH) programs augment assessment and administrative services for youth in special education by offering evaluative *and* treatment services (e.g., individual, group, and family therapies) to *all* youth in schools, including those in regular education. A national movement is under way to develop or improve ESMH programs in diverse communities in the United States. This movement has largely been a response to an increasing recognition of the limitations of community mental health centers (CMHCs) and private practitioners in meeting young people's mental health needs. ESMH programs were designed to overcome many of the barriers constraining the provision of mental health services in these traditional sites (Flaherty, Weist, & Warner, 1996; Weist, 1997).

ESMH programs owe part of their success to the preexisting and more established school-based health centers (SBHCs). Because the mission of SBHCs was to provide comprehensive health programs (Baltimore City Health Department, 1995; Juszczak, Fisher, Lear, & Friedman, 1995), they constituted a legitimate framework within which to set up mental health services. Additionally, SBHCs provided convenient access points for youth in schools to utilize these services. Indeed, it is within the context of SBHCs that the need for mental health services in schools has gained increasing recognition (Weist, 1997). Essentially, as SBHCs have expanded to more than 1,200 nationwide (Lear & Schlitt, 1998; National Assembly on School-Based Health Care, 1998), they have spurred the development of ESMH programs by underscoring tremendous mental health needs in youth. Over time, ESMH programs have gained sufficient recognition and legitimacy of their own to expand in school systems independent of the SBHCs.

Despite the national growth of these ESMH programs, little is known about the activities that facilitated their establishment, operation, and legitimization. A review of the literature showed minimal published information on how ESMH programs have developed (Flaherty et al., 1996). Because Baltimore has been recognized regionally and nationally as a leading city in the development of these programs, other cities may benefit from knowledge of the Baltimore experience. In this chapter, we provide relevant background to the development of ESMH programs nationally, and provide an historical account of the Baltimore programs from their inception to the current program operation.

THE NEED FOR EXPANDED SCHOOL MENTAL HEALTH PROGRAMS

The problems of children and their families, particularly those living in urban areas, have been well documented (e.g., Feigelman, Stanton, & Ricardo, 1993; Lear, Gleicher, St. Germaine, & Porter, 1991; Warner & Weist, 1996). These include poverty, exposure to crime and violence, frequent abuse and neglect, substance abuse, drug trafficking, family breakdown, illegitimacy, teen pregnancy, truancy, runaways, and juvenile delinquency (Baltimore City Children and Youth Task Force [Task Force], 1987). In 1991, the Congressional Office of Technology Assessment reported that up to 20 percent of youth under the age of twenty exhibit psychosocial problems severe enough to warrant intervention, but less than one-third of these youth actually receive mental health services.

Youth from inner cities such as Baltimore are particularly at risk for experiencing significant levels of life stressors. These include increased levels of crime and violence, poverty, substance abuse, and a greater occurrence of neglect and physical and sexual abuse. A 1986 estimate indicated that 15 percent (32,000) of the children and adolescents in Baltimore were in need of mental health treatment (Task Force, 1987).

Although these problems had existed for some time, the Task Force (1987) cited several factors that led bureaucratic agencies at the national, state, and local levels to address them. The first impetus came from the publication of research during the early- to mid-1980s documenting the scope and prevalence of emotional and behavioral problems among youth. Particularly influential in setting the policy direction regarding systems of care for children and adolescents was Jane Knitzer's *Unclaimed Children* (1982). The culmination of policy-related analyses during the next three years led to another influential work entitled *A System of Care for Severely Emotionally Disturbed Children and Youth* (Stroul & Friedman, 1986). Stroul and Friedman's goal was to outline a comprehensive interagency model of service for severely disturbed youth based on inputs from local community agencies. Given that their research was within a federal policy framework, this book became a primer in providing a detailed report on one of the biggest federal mental health programs for youth, the Child and Adolescent Service System Program (CASSP). The CASSP, a tertiary intervention model of systems of care, became so successful that this federal program had a significant impact on how the states organized their service delivery system.

Second, advocacy groups (e.g., Children's Defense Fund; Mental Health Association; Baltimore Mayor's Office for Children and Youth) placed the issue of children's mental health at the top of their agenda, and succeeded in making a profound impact on the general public and on state legislatures. In fact, these advocacy groups were seen by the Task Force as critical players in mobilizing community resources and promoting alternative services, including ESMH programs, for children and youth.

Third, a number of newspaper articles published in the *Baltimore Sun* (October 24, 1986; November 24, 1986; January 15, 1987) and the *New York Times* (September 6, 1987) increased awareness during 1986–87 of the mental health problems experienced by children and adolescents. Such coverage not only heightened public awareness but also underscored the deficiencies of governmental agencies in addressing these problems.

Fourth, in spite of budget cuts in social programs, in 1986 the federal government provided funds to twenty-six states to strengthen and widen the mental health services to children and youth offered by its CASSP. Tom Merrick of the Maryland State Department of Health and Mental Hygiene (DHMH) considered the CASSP to be a watershed federal program with a mission to move a significant proportion of mental health services from CMHCs to the school setting. That is, as states began to endorse this successful CASSP model for their most severely disturbed youth, greater recognition was given to the need for intervention as well as prevention. Thus mental health services would be available to all youth in need, not just those with severe emotional disturbance.

Baltimore's response to the increase in published studies, reports, and recommendations was to establish a Task Force on Mental Health Services for Children and Youth. The Task Force, created in April 1986 under the auspices of its local health department, adopted the CASSP and Caplan prevention (1964) models as their guiding principles. As in the CASSP model, the Task Force called into action a system of care that was "to be child-centered and community-based . . . non-residential" (Task Force, 1987, p. 27). Drawing from the Caplan model, the Task Force fostered the integration of programs offered by various agencies so as to achieve a comprehensive system of care that included: (1) primary prevention that would also reduce the likelihood of problems to occur; (2) secondary treatment that would address problems in the incipient stage; and (3) tertiary treatment to respond to problems that were already well established. With these principles as guideposts, the Task Force established a network of linkages among several lead agencies. It is from the collaborative work of these public and private organizations, such as the Baltimore City Health Department (BCHD), the Baltimore City Public Schools (BCPS), the State of Maryland DHMH, Johns Hopkins University (JHU), the University of Maryland, Baltimore (UMB), the Department of Social Services (DSS), the Juvenile Services Administration (JSA), and the Mayor's Office for Children and Youth, that the ESMH programs have been crystallized from an idea on the drawing board into a national presence.

AN HISTORICAL PERSPECTIVE

The emergence of more comprehensive mental health services in schools was part of a broader movement to establish a package of social services, including mental and physical health, social welfare, and vocational preparation programs, in elementary and secondary schools (Sedlak, 1997). The early history of this movement was associated with the changing role of formal education in America, especially at the secondary level.

During the late nineteenth and early twentieth centuries, secondary schools transformed their mission from teaching disciplinary knowledge to privileged students to preparing the majority of children for life by enhancing their vocational skills, improving the efficiency of their occupational choices, preventing social maladjustment, and ensuring adequate levels of personal hygiene and public health. Accordingly, schools were obligated to offer more than traditional classes in history, science, mathematics, and languages (Dryfoos, 1994; Levine & Levine, 1992).

While school administrators and teachers welcomed the movement, the catalyst for establishing and maintaining most initiatives came from outside the schools. Private-sector groups and public service organizations launched efforts to organize mental health and social services for schoolchildren.

Among the earliest, but also among the smallest, were programs designed to investigate and attempt to treat emotional and mental problems among schoolchildren, especially those from immigrant families. More prevalent were programs that provided direct relief from poverty and unemployment so that children would be able to attend school. In addition, specialists in guidance and counseling joined school faculties at the intermediate and secondary levels in an effort to help adolescents connect with higher education or the labor market.

Capitalizing on efforts to engage schools in the medical care of children, psychologists in the United States determined that the captive audience provided by compulsory attendance policies provided a ripe opportunity to apply their science to understanding and treating "special" children. During the late 1890s, in Philadelphia and a small number of other urban centers, psychological clinics were established by universities and medical institutions in partnership with public schools. The initial purpose of these clinics was to help schools manage "blind, deaf, feeble-minded and delinquent children" (Levine & Levine, 1992, p. 28), many of whom were suffering from "mental and moral retardation" (p. 32), and who were emerging in greater numbers in regular classrooms (Levine & Levine, 1992).

After 1906, at approximately the same time that the psychological clinics were becoming reinvigorated, private organizations and public schools in several large cities began to perform well-defined social welfare functions such as addressing truancy and delinquency, rehabilitating poor and disorganized families, and encouraging the "Americanization" of the immigrant population. The focus early on was to intervene on the behalf of students whose attendance and behavior problems stemmed from poverty, unemployment, sickness, or the inability to negotiate urban bureaucracies. Individuals who worked most directly in this area called themselves "visiting teachers." Visiting teachers saw an opportunity to gain access to the families of schoolchildren and to work on strengthening their values and habits.

Guidance and counseling professionals similarly worked in partnership with private-sector organizations, primarily to help adolescents and their families understand and participate in their local economies. Early activists, such as Frank Spaulding, claimed the right to exercise considerable control over students (Sedlak, 1997). Accordingly, guidance counselors soon established themselves as a group with responsibility for minimizing or preventing many of the social maladies they attributed to the improper alignment of youth and occupations. Targeting the processes through which children and youth selected and prepared for their careers, guidance counselors assisted young people in making course selections appropriate to certain occupations.

Regarding the more general evolution of the helping professions, the school-based social and mental health service initiatives became increasingly professionalized following World War I. The release in 1918 of the National Education Association's *Cardinal Principles of Secondary Education* provided an influential, systematic, and coherent justification for school-based social services. Originating in environmental and social reform, the mental health movement turned rapidly toward individual case management and away from attempting to remedy broader social and economic conditions. As such, the mental health professionals focused more on problems grounded in family dynamics or internal psychological conflict and less on those rooted in social and economic deprivation. Scientific principles and diagnosis penetrated the field of psychology, and school-based clinics began to utilize contemporary measurement and evaluation procedures.

With the professionalization of perspective and technique came two major shifts in the domain of the mental health field. First, psychiatric or psychoanalytic casework began to focus more narrowly on the "inner psychological problems of individuals" (Levine & Levine, 1992, p. 89). Second, practitioners moved away from working only with immigrant, working-class, and disadvantaged children to working with clients from the middle and upper classes.

One of the most enterprising youth-oriented initiatives of the 1920s demonstrated these changes. The Commonwealth Fund of New York City launched juvenile delinquency intervention programs in thirty urban, small-town, and rural communities in 1921. The Commonwealth Fund's professional approach to the prevention of juvenile delinquency drew upon the insights provided by the mental hygiene movement. Essentially, the mental hygiene movement reflected the efforts of social service workers to move away from working exclusively with the most intractable, disruptive, and delinquent children to engaging all children, especially middle-class adolescents with emotional and adjustment problems.

Economic difficulties present in the 1930s halted most school-based social services. It was not until after World War II in the mid-1940s that counselors and social workers were able to offer their services to middle-class children and adolescents in some schools.

Several national policy studies that examined the status of children and youth and the potential for school-based social services to counteract growth in delinquency among middle-class adolescents contributed to the rebuilding during the late 1930s and the 1940s. The reports called for schools to accept responsibility for providing physical and mental health programs and a full complement of guidance, counseling, and occupational-adjustment services for all children. Professional social work and mental health practitioners abandoned traditional social reform activities and refocused their efforts toward providing therapeutic, clinical, and personality adjustment services on an individual, case-by-case basis. Social and mental health professionals became committed to strengthening interpersonal relationships between children and their peers, their parents, and their teachers.

Social service staff were joined by professionals affiliated with state departments of education to lobby legislators to encourage investment in social and psychological services in schools. State officials began to provide special funding to school districts to identify and treat emotionally disturbed children.

By the late 1950s, mental health services had expanded notably. This trend was accelerated by professional aspirations to serve a broader clientele than the urban poor, state mandates to serve emotionally disturbed and delinquent youths, and increasing federal funds for counseling, guidance, special education, and social welfare services. From the Smith-Hughes Act passed during World War I to the National Defense Education Act of the Cold War, the federal government became continually more immersed in shaping and financing school-based guidance and counseling programs in districts serving families of all income levels.

The professionalization of mental health and social welfare services and the infusion of federal and state funds shaped the provision of services for the next several decades. Unlike efforts in the 1950s to "universalize" services by expanding markets to include middle- and upper-class students, many practitioners in the 1960s concentrated on disadvantaged populations. While school systems willingly received programs that were accompanied by state and federal reimbursement funds during the 1960s and 1970s, administrators and school board members found that the levels of external support were not sufficient to cover the costs of delivering the services. This resulted in the resistance and defection of many educational administrators.

Despite the growth of social service investments during the 1960s, little effort was made to fully integrate many of the programs. In addition, financial support for social services during the 1960s and 1970s influenced the delivery of school-based services. In order to get funds, boards of education were required to demonstrate that "community" interests were represented, which resulted in the formation of community councils that advised school personnel on local and neighborhood matters.

During the 1970s and 1980s, at local, state, and national levels, government policy and court interpretations resulted in a series of mandates and investments in coordinated services for children. The Education for

All Handicapped Children Act of 1976 (Public Law 94-142), and the Individuals with Disabilities Education Act of 1990 (IDEA) (PL 101-476), for the first time required states and districts to provide comparatively comprehensive social welfare, mental health, physical therapy, medical, and other services related to, or supportive of, academic education as entitlements to children ruled eligible under the laws. Unfortunately, mandating that states provide such a diverse range of services without providing adequate funding resulted in substantial ambivalence and discord (Gallagher, 1996).

In addition, school-based clinicians did not escape the general assault on the helping professions that swept through Europe and America after 1965. Teachers and counselors were accused by social critics of misusing a variety of diagnostic instruments in placing African-American children in lower academic tracks or in special classrooms for disruptive children. Therefore, it was not surprising that many educational professionals began to adopt a more passive role with their clients. For example, during the 1980s, counselors throughout the nation redefined their professional responsibilities and retreated from attempting to shape career and educational choices and began to focus more on individual, personal counseling. It should be noted, however, that schools have generally refused to fully integrate guidance and counseling with other mental health professionals. The role of passivity and neutrality among mental health, social welfare, and academic leaders can be detrimental to the well-being of the children and families these professions are meant to serve.

PRELIMINARY STAGES OF BALTIMORE CITY SCHOOL MENTAL HEALTH PROGRAMS

While the previous section described the development of ESMH programs nationally, the following provides an historical account of the Baltimore programs.

As mentioned earlier, the ESMH programs in Baltimore City have been nationally regarded as exemplary in the number, scope, and quality of services offered. To give a sense of the dramatic increase in the number of programs over the last fourteen years, in 1987 three schools in Baltimore City had ESMH programs; this rose to thirty in 1994, sixty in 1996, and over eighty in 2001, representing almost half the schools in Baltimore.

With regard to scope, Baltimore City's ESMH programs have been notable for their ability to encompass the spectrum of services, from primary prevention to tertiary care interventions. Additionally, Baltimore, with fiscal and policy support from the State of Maryland, has been highly respected for the ability of its programs to reach a broad student population that is not confined to students in special education. Due to reimbursement restrictions, many states and localities have had to limit their school-based mental health services to those students in special education. More specifically, a component of Public Law 94-142 mandated that government funds would cover only those mental health services targeted at special education students. However, in the State of Maryland, the Governor's Mental Health Initiative, titled *Maryland Meets the Challenge: The Public-Private Partnership for Mental Health,* allowed for the inclusion of mental health services to be accessible to children in regular education. Based on the CASSP model, funds were provided for a range of community mental health services, such as in-home intervention, therapeutic nurseries, a range of residential options, and day school programs.

There were several concurrent factors that helped pave the way for the development of ESMH services in Maryland. First, during the 1980s there was a shift in educational philosophy toward mainstreaming children in special education into regular schools and classrooms. Although mental health services as provided by school psychologists had been around for some time, they were frequently limited to students in special education. As children in special education became mainstreamed to regular education programs, the philosophy of maintaining continuity of care set a precedent that allowed clinicians to continue their mental health services with these mainstreamed schoolchildren. Furthermore, as the shift in educational policy toward inclusion was taking place, mental health clinicians who worked with children in special education in regular school settings became increasingly aware of students in regular education who were presenting problems that warranted mental health intervention.

The question arises of how a city like Baltimore, with a generally poor revenue base, could become a national leader in the development of ESMH programs. Key players in the development of these programs in the city suggested five factors that were critical in early stages: (1) collaborative partnerships between lead agencies; (2) respectable organizations in leadership roles; (3) working contracts between agencies that ensured control of revenues and expenditures; (4) involvement of well-established institutions; and (5) a high level of political, and to some extent financial, support from the City of Baltimore and the State of Maryland. We discuss each of these stages in more detail in the following:

1. Setting the Stage: Collaborative Partnerships

The initial efforts of Baltimore's Task Force on Mental Health Services for Children and Youth were based on a recognition of the need for significant collaboration between community agencies, and the central importance of the educational institution in improving a system of care for children. Thus the development of a new interagency initiative that would involve the city school system (BCPS) became a top item in the Task Force's agenda. It also wanted to address gaps in communication between the various agencies by proposing that services be rendered in one location.

Recognizing the need for a coordinated approach to child mental health services in the city, the Task Force developed a goal to create a central mechanism for the coordination of mental health services for youth, and for having this mechanism operate in conjunction with the schools. Based on educational and economic data from Baltimore's inner-city schools, Booker T. Washington Middle School was selected as the first demonstration site to receive coordinated mental health and social services from several different agencies. The Health Department, Police Department, Social Services, and Juvenile Services provided services on-site at the school starting in the 1987–88 school year. At the heart of the program at Booker T. Washington was the development of a case management model that ensured the coordination, tracking, and follow-up of services (Task Force, 1987). Thus, while Booker T. Washington was the first school to provide a satellite mental health program, services were rendered through a *case management model* rather than a *primary care clinical model.* Nonetheless, the effectiveness of this interagency partnership is evidenced by the fact that the initiative at Booker T. Washington has become a model program that offers services twelve months a year.

2. Respected Organizations in Leadership Roles

Baltimore City has been nationally recognized for its ability to adopt and implement a primary care mental health program in its schools: that is, on-site clinical services in the form of focused evaluation; individual, group, and family therapies; and referral of youth for more intensive services (e.g., medication) into collaborating CMHCs. It has been noted by several authorities (e.g., Dryfoos, 1994; Fleisch, Knitzer, & Steinberg, 1990) that an important factor in the successful planning and implementation of programs is their link to respected agencies within a given community. In this regard, the Baltimore City Health Department (BCHD) clearly played a leadership role in establishing exemplary models of comprehensive care in the schools.

From the outset, administrative staff from the BCHD were committed to incorporating a strong mental health component in the SBHCs, believing that mental health services were necessary for the health centers to be truly comprehensive. Not only did mental health issues need to be addressed, but it was essential to establish a comprehensive program whereby schoolchildren would receive mental health assessment and treatment services directly in the SBHCs. The BCHD recognized that the mental health needs of its youth were not being adequately addressed, underscoring the need for expansion of mental health services into the schools. Indeed, the Baltimore City commissioner of health, Dr. Peter Beilenson, reported that mental health concerns were involved in many of the health visits during early years of operation of the SBHCs. Information gathered during intakes indicated that 22 percent of visits to these SBHCs were for mental health reasons (BCHD, 1995). These statistics were consistent with findings from Lear et al. (1991), who found mental health concerns were the second most frequent reason for services in a survey of twenty-three SBHCs in eleven states, and with Anglin, Naylor, and Kaplan (1996), who found that 25 percent of students using Denver SBHC services had visits with mental health counselors. These data served to bolster the development of ESMH programs in Baltimore in the 1990s.

3. Working Contract between Agencies for SMH Financing

Regardless of perceived need and institutional respect, funding is obviously what transforms ideas into realities. The BCHD started several initiatives to promote the development of ESMH programs in Baltimore. The first was to engage two community agencies—the Department of Social Services (DSS) and Family and Children Services (FCS)—in the provision of some of their social services for youth in their SBHCs. The Health Department had hoped to bill Medicaid for these mental health services on a fee-for-service basis.

BCHD's second initiative was to secure greater control of their Medicaid revenues and expenditures. Once the city granted the BCHD authority to retain the Medicaid revenues, the BCHD also proposed that their SBHC would be able to carry over funds for use beyond the year they were received, and that the accumulated funds would be used to *expand* rather than replace existing programs. Many leaders in child health in Baltimore and Maryland view this type of supportive climate between the city and state as critical to the expansion of ESMH programs within SBHCs (and eventually promoting the development of "stand-alone" ESMH programs).

4. Involvement of Well-Established Institutions

By the end of the SBHCs' third year of operation in 1988, the Health Department had retained enough revenues ($30,000) to incorporate a mental health program into three of the SBHCs that did not have mental services from block grant dollars. Using these funds, the BCHD contracted with outside agencies for mental health services. In 1989, partnerships were formed with the departments of psychiatry at the University of Maryland, Baltimore (UMB), and Johns Hopkins University (JHU) to develop, supervise, and provide ESMH services in four of the seven existing SBHCs at that time.

These collaborative partnerships proved to be advantageous for both the BCHD and the academic institutions. From the BCHD's perspective, affiliation with respected, well-established academic institutions enhanced the legitimacy and credibility of their school health center programs. Given that these institutions are rich in human and programmatic resources (e.g., clinical postdoctoral programs, ongoing research projects, access to financial grants), BCHD also gained practical benefits from the partnerships.

For their part, the academic institutions benefited from these partnerships by gaining a formal entree to working with a population that has generally been considered difficult to reach. Their value as training institutions was enhanced by their being able to offer their students and postdoctoral fellows the firsthand experience of working "in the trenches." Furthermore, ongoing access to an inner-city population within an institutional setting (i.e., the school system) facilitated the conduct of relevant applied research.

5. Political Support for Developing ESMH Programs in Baltimore

Support in terms of governmental approval, interagency collaboration, and community acceptance can spell success or failure in program development (Weist, 1997). Key players in the implementation process unanimously agreed that there was much enthusiasm and support from both the private and public sectors for the development of a mental health program for the SBHCs in the late 1980s.

Once ESMH services had been established on a preliminary basis, several factors generated support for their further development in the city. First, there was the widespread recognition that inner-city youth had an urgent need for mental health services. Second, a clearly articulated rationale was presented to the effect that providing services early on to youth at high risk for developing mental health problems was more cost-effective than waiting for them to reach the stage of severe psychiatric disorders. Related to this was the recognition that an ESMH program would be a top-rate intervention located in a convenient setting that would provide ease of delivery. Third, the BCHD was able to maintain a low profile when mental health services were added to their SBHCs.

It must be emphasized that the single most critical factor in the successful establishment and growth of ESMH programs in Baltimore was the development of relatively stable financing. The incorporation of the mental health program into preexisting SBHCs was critical here, for it allowed the BCHD to finance the program out of existing funds during the first three years.

To summarize the early development of ESMH programs in Baltimore: While the needs for mental health services among youth became alarmingly self-evident, the social and political climate during the mid-1980s was ripe for turning ideas for alternative types of services into realities. An important factor in the preliminary stages of developing alternative programs, such as ESMH programs, is the collaborative networking of several lead agencies. The key to the success of such a patchwork of interagency linkages in Baltimore City was that all parties concerned shared a common agenda and mission for Baltimore's inner-city youth. There were also economic incentives for these agencies to work with each other: (a) less downtime and a lower no-show rate due to easy access and a broader target population; (b) greater coordination in referrals and ensuring that referrals would actually be followed up; and (c) an increasing proportion of reimbursable services.

Partnerships with medical training institutions had a further legitimizing influence. Moreover, the success of the ESMH programs in Baltimore City was largely due to their initial link with the Health Department. Indeed, research confirms that implementation and management by respected institutions helps facilitate the process of program development (Dryfoos, 1994; Fleisch et al., 1990). The BCHD played a pivotal role in the endorsement and establishment of these ESMH programs through its two earlier mechanisms—the Task Force, whose major contributions included the documentation and assessment of youth mental health needs, and proposing various types of programs; and the SBHCs, whose major contribution was their commitment to implement a mental health component into their comprehensive health program. Such endorsements helped ease the process to secure funds for the development of ESMH programs.

MIDDLE STAGE: EXPANDING TO "STAND-ALONE" ESMH PROGRAMS

Based on the lessons learned from the implementation of mental health services in SBHCs, ESMH programs began to be developed in Baltimore schools without health centers. These "stand-alone" programs have shown significant growth in the 1990s, and now greatly outnumber programs connected to SBHCs. As mentioned, ESMH programs have grown in Baltimore from the initial three in 1987 to well over eighty in 2001. While all of the ESMH programs developed initially were connected to SBHCs, subsequently more of these programs represent stand-alone arrangements. This is because it is much easier to establish an ESMH program than an SBHC in a school. All that is really required is staff, whereas SBHCs present numerous, more costly needs, such as examination rooms and a pharmacy. This is not to downplay the value of SBHCs; in fact, many believe that an ESMH/SBHC collaboration represents the ideal way to bring integrated health–mental health care to youth where they are (Kubiszyn, 1999; Weist & Schlitt, 1998).

A successful funding mechanism underlies the success of stand-alone ESMH programs in Baltimore. Interagency cooperation, crucial to the development of the programs, has also been associated with a mixed funding pattern. Some funds come directly from fee-for-service (i.e., Medicaid revenues). Less direct sources of funds include grants from the city, state, federal agencies, and training institutions, donations from local foundations, and "seed money" retained from adult-related mental health services. This patchwork of funding streams has helped expand the ESMH programs into their current number and scope. It has also helped to ensure that the programs maintain a continuum of services from preventive to tertiary care. That is, ideally, grant and contract revenues should support more preventive services (i.e., schoolwide mental health education, skill training groups), while fee-for-service revenues should support tertiary care (i.e., evaluation, therapy).

Thus, the middle stage of ESMH programs in Baltimore centered on developing interagency connections and funding mechanisms, which has resulted in increasing diversity in both. Currently there are four major mechanisms for ESMH funding in Baltimore. An historical description of the development of these funding mechanisms, and their influence on ESMH program development and service delivery, is provided in the following section.

1. Third-Party Billing Project

The Third-Party Billing Project (TPBP), which relies solely on Medicaid for its revenues, has become the dominant method of financing ESMH program development in Baltimore. With the first revenues, there was a small allocation of TPBP revenues to provide mental health services in one middle school that served special education students who were mainstreamed with non–special education students. As the TPBP revenues increased, the allocation for mental health services was expanded to more schools and made available to all youth, including those in regular education. The guiding principle was, and remains, that if children who exhibit acting-out or other troubling behavior patterns are treated early and preventively, there will be fewer referrals predicated on behavioral problems to the expensive special education programs.

A contractual relationship between BCPS and the mental health agency that served the school community was established to provide funding for ESMH services. Through this initiative, more than sixty ESMH programs, representing all of the city's CMHCs, most hospital community psychiatry programs, and one social work agency specializing in children's mental health, are funded (fully or in part) through the TPBP. This project, which is currently funded at $1.6 million, has become the ***primary*** source of funds for ESMH programs in the city. Of the more than sixty programs, five later became the mental health component of school-based health centers.

2. School-Based Health Centers

School-based health centers (SBHCs) are another major mechanism for supporting the expansion and improvement of mental health services in the schools. Currently there are fifteen SBHCs operated by the Health Department, while an additional six are supported by other agencies (e.g., one by a community health center, one by a local hospital, three by a health maintenance organization (HMO), one by a community task force, and one by the state's School Readiness Initiative). The development of mental health services in SBHCs has been discussed in detail (see Flaherty et al., 1996; Weist, 1997).

3. State Community Mental Health Funds

As an outgrowth of recommendations in the 1987 report by the Task Force on Mental Health Services for Children and Youth, three schools with school-based health centers, two high schools and one middle school, developed full-time mental health services. The policy, implemented by Maryland's Mental Hygiene Administration, allocated three mental health block grant positions for services in three school-based health centers. In addition, the Johns Hopkins University community psychiatry program allocated one of its state block grant positions to a high school–based health center in its catchment area.

Notably, the Department of Psychiatry at the University of Maryland, Baltimore (Lead Agency for South and Southwest Baltimore), recently allocated surplus community mental health funds received from adult services for the initiation of ESMH services in South Baltimore in the Cherry Hill neighborhood, known for high levels of poverty, crime, and drug abuse. The UMB Department of Psychiatry's development of ESMH services at an elementary and a middle school in Cherry Hill in 1995–96 has been very well received, with positive evaluations provided by community members, families, students, and by the two school principals. In fact, based on positive perceptions of the program, the two principals have agreed to a matching-fund arrangement (i.e., the schools pay half and the department pays half for the program). This led to expansion of the program to a full-time staff member at both schools in 1996–97.

4. Futures Program

The Futures Program represents the fourth major mechanism to fund ESMH services in Baltimore. Futures is a statewide prevention program designed for youth at high risk for dropping out of school. In the eighth grade, youth at risk for dropping out are identified and recruited for participation in the program. Consenting youth then receive a summer-long orientation prior to their ninth-grade year, and subsequently receive mental health and case management services throughout high school, combined with an incentive program for grades and attendance. Maryland's Tomorrow receives its support from mental health block grant funds as well as grant and legislative funds supporting the Futures Program. Because of this funding arrangement, this program is less dependent on third-party reimbursements (Webb, 1994). Currently there are six schools in the Futures Program, primarily located in high schools and in some middle schools in the city.

Managing Children's Mental Health Services

Given the complexity in the patchwork of funding sources and the number of interagency partnerships, it became necessary for the City of Baltimore to delegate an institution responsible for developing and managing the system of mental health services for children and youth. However, a more crucial point was a state mandate that required the establishment of such a "managerial" agency. Thus, in July 1993, Baltimore Mental Health Systems, Inc. (BMHS) was chosen to oversee the activities of the seven lead agencies in the city. With regard to ESMH programs, the director of Child and Adolescent Services for BMHS defined its role as an ombudsman, serving as a collaborative partner between the Health Department and the BCPS. In practice, BMHS facilitates the institutionalization of ESMH programs, troubleshoots problems in the system, and helps standardize services and outcomes. The director described BMHS's most important role as one of managing funds coming from the state DHMH and allocating the monies to the seven lead agencies. BMHS has been instrumental in creating and sustaining the policy and values that guide a comprehensive and responsive system of mental health care for children and adolescents.

CURRENT STAGE: STRUGGLING TO MAINTAIN

With dramatic budget cuts in Medicaid (the main funding stream), the future operation of ESMH programs in Baltimore is indeed more challenging. New funding strategies need to be developed in order to ensure the continued existence and effectiveness of these programs. Managed care's monopoly on health insurance policies, especially for the working classes and the poor, is having a tremendous impact on the funding of ESMH programs (see Weist, 1997). An additional threat to the future of ESMH programs is active recruitment by managed care companies to enroll Medicaid-eligible youth in their ranks (School Health Policy Initiative [SHPI], 1993). A majority of these companies have been unwilling to authorize ESMH services, as the precedent has not yet been set to include them in benefit packages. As more and more families are "required" to enroll in these companies, there is the threat that ESMH programs will not represent services covered by the state.

There are several strategies currently in process to address these problems. First, SHPI and other groups have suggested that school health administrators form relationships with managed care companies. There are in fact already a number of instances of managed care companies agreeing to fund SBHCs (Rosenthal & Hinman, 1995). A second strategy is to develop state financial support systems to fund ESMH programs through excise taxes (Schlitt, Rickett, Montgomery, & Lear, 1994). A third strategy is to tap into local dollars associated with the education budget. Another source is surplus funds from adult-focused mental health services, as reviewed earlier.

Trends appear to be moving in the direction of: (a) the federal government putting a "cap" on the amount of Medicaid money given to the states; (b) federal policy giving the states greater discretionary power in the form of block grants; (c) increasing the number of Medicaid recipients in managed care organizations; and (d) welfare reform. Related to these trends, efforts to ensure the survival of ESMH programs will likely be associated with restrictions on the amount of care provided for youth with less severe problems. In this new environment, one could speculate that if educators perceive mental health care as a dwindling resource, their current tendency to disproportionately refer disruptive youth would be greatly reinforced. An unfortunate consequence of this scenario would be that the needs of seriously withdrawn or depressed children might go undetected or unserved in schools. Another way service delivery may be impacted by the above financing trends is that SBHCs would be pressured to downsize their staffs. Such downsizing will have a drastic impact on the ability of SBHC and ESMH programs to deliver appropriate and high-quality services, as these health centers are already operating with no more than one to five full-time staff members housed in densely populated schools. It has become increasingly clear that the health and mental health needs of youth in schools outstrip the abilities of SBHCs to meet them (Dryfoos, 1994; Weist, 1997); staff cuts will only exacerbate an already tenuous scenario.

CONCLUDING COMMENTS

The development of inclusive mental health services in schools was part of a broader movement to establish a package of social services in the schools. In response to a growing need, particularly in urban areas, ESMH programs, which augment assessment and administrative services for youth in special education by offering evaluative and treatment services to all youth in schools, including those in regular education, have progressively developed in schools throughout the United States.

This chapter presented an historical overview of the development of ESMH programs nationally and within Baltimore City. Outlined below is a summary of key elements discussed in this chapter. Five factors were critical in the early stages of the development of ESMH programs: collaborative partnerships, leadership by respected organizations, interagency financing, the involvement of well-established institutions, and political support. A successful funding mechanism underlies the success of stand-alone ESMH programs, and possible mechanisms for ESMH funding include third-party billing, school-based health centers, state community mental health funds, and statewide prevention programs. While the establishment of a managerial agency was instrumental in creating a comprehensive and responsive system of mental health care for children, new funding strategies need to be developed in order to ensure the continued existence and effectiveness of ESMH programs.

Amid the growing disparities between the rich and the poor, ever deeper budget cuts, and shrinking social service networks, the successful development of the Baltimore ESMH programs suggests that administrative improvisation and the rational pooling of resources can create avenues of successful adaptation both for public agencies and academic institutions involved in the mental health field. Modifying the framework of existing programs and maximizing the utility of current resources can yield surprising advances in the provision of care to an underserved population. Yet it is necessary to end on a note of caution and concern. The general public and government officials alike must be informed that as ever greater financial and discretionary constraints are imposed upon mental health services, even low-budget services that piggyback on existing health programs will be threatened, both in the quality and quantity of their services. If management of the mental health profession becomes dominated by a short-term need for cost-cutting, the grievous emotional and behavioral problems that afflict so many inner-city youth will be left unattended—and society at large will ultimately pay a very high price indeed for measures that seemed to save money in the short run.

ACKNOWLEDGMENT: We extend appreciation to Peter Beilenson, Marcia Glass-Siegel, Tom Merrick, and Bonnie Peet for the valuable information shared during the preparation of this article.

Supported in part by project #MCJ24SH02-01-0 from the Maternal and Child Health Bureau (Title V, Social Security Act), Health Resources and Services Administration, Department of Health and Human Services.

References

Anglin, T. M., Naylor, K. E., & Kaplan, D. W. (1996). Comprehensive school-based health care: High school students' use of medical, mental health, and substance abuse services. *Pediatrics, 97,* 318–330.

Baltimore City Children and Youth Task Force. (1987). *Report on the Health and Mental Health of Baltimore City Children and Adolescents.* Baltimore, MD: Baltimore City Health Department.

Baltimore City Health Department (1995, July). *Comprehensive school health services program.* Unpublished manuscript. Author.

Caplan, G. (1964). *Principles of preventive psychiatry.* New York: Basic Books.

Dryfoos, J. G. (1994). *Full-service schools: A revolution in health and social services for children, youth, and families.* San Francisco: Jossey-Bass.

Feigelman, S., Stanton, B. F., & Ricardo, I. (1993). Perceptions of drug selling and drug use among urban youths. *Journal of Early Adolescence, 13,* 267–284.

Flaherty, L. T., Weist, M. D., & Warner, B. S. (1996). School-based mental health centers in the United States: History, current models and needs. *Community Mental Health Journal, 32*(4), 341–352.

Fleisch, B., Knitzer, J., & Steinberg, Z. (1990). *At the schoolhouse door: An examination of programs and policies for children with behavioral and emotional problems.* New York: Bank Street College of Education.

Gallagher, J. J. (1996). Policy development and implementation for children with disabilities. In E. Zigler, S. Kagan, & N. Wall (Eds.), *Children, families, and government: Preparing for the twenty-first century* (pp. 171–187). Cambridge: Cambridge University Press.

Juszczak, L., Fisher, M., Lear, J. G., & Friedman, S. B. (1995). Back to school: Training opportunities in school-based health centers. *Journal of Developmental and Behavioral Pediatrics, 16,* 101–104.

Knitzer, J. (1982). *Unclaimed children: The failure of public responsibility to children and adolescents in need of mental health services.* Washington, DC: Children's Defense Fund.

Kubiszyn, T. (1999). Integrating health and mental health services in schools: Psychologists collaborating with primary care providers. *Clinical Psychology Review, 19*(2), 179–198.

Lear, J. G., & Schlitt, J. (1998, September). Late-breaking findings on school-based health centers in the United States. Paper presented at the meeting of the Center for School Mental Health Assistance, Virginia Beach.

Lear, J. G., Gleicher, H. B., St. Germaine, A., & Porter, P. J. (1991). Reorganizing health care for adolescents: The experience of the school-based health care program. *Journal of Adolescent Health, 12,* 450–458.

Levine, M., & Levine, A. (1992). *A social history of helping services: Clinic, court, school, and community* (2nd ed.). New York: Appleton-Century-Crofts.

National Assembly on School-Based Health Care. (1998). *Status of school-based health centers.* Washington, DC: Author.

Office of Technology Assessment (1991). *Adolescent health.* Congress of the United States, Washington, DC: U.S. Government Printing Office.

Rosenthal, B., & Hinman, E. (1995, June). Negotiating relationships between managed care and SBHCs. Paper presented at the meeting of the National Assembly on School-Based Health Care, Washington, DC.

Schlitt, J. J., Rickett, K. D., Montgomery, L. L., & Lear, J. G. (1994). *State initiative to support school-based health centers.* Washington, DC: George Washington University, Making the Grade.

School Health Policy Initiative (1993). *Ingredients for success: Comprehensive school-based health centers.* Bronx, NY: Author.

Sedlak, M. W. (1997). The uneasy alliance of mental health services and the schools: An historical perspective. *American Journal of Orthopsychiatry, 67*(3), 349–362.

Stroul B. A., & Friedman, R. M. (1986). *A system of care for severely emotionally disturbed children and youth.* Washington, DC: Georgetown University Child Development Center, CAASP.

Warner, B. S., & Weist, M. D. (1996). Urban youth as witnesses to violence: Beginning assessment and treatment efforts. *Journal of Youth and Adolescence, 25,* 361–377.

Webb, M. B. (1994, September). *School-based mental health services in Baltimore City.* Baltimore, MD: Baltimore Mental Health Systems, Inc.

Weist, M. D. (1997). Expanded school mental health services: A national movement in progress. In T. H. Ollendick & R. J. Prinz (Eds.), *Advances in clinical child psychology* (Vol. 19, pp. 319–352). New York: Plenum.

Weist, M. D., & Schlitt, J. J. (1998). Alliances and school-based health care. *Journal of School Health, 68,* 401–403.

CHAPTER TWO

An Elementary School Mental Health Program Serving Immigrant and Minority Children

Jennifer Oppenheim, Psy.D., and
Robert J. Evert, M. A., M.S.W.

INTRODUCTION

The 1990s witnessed an explosion in the movement to bring enhanced health, mental health, and social services into schools. Yet while there is an increasingly impressive body of literature documenting the growth of the school-based health care movement, there are some areas that remain unexplored. For example, only recently has the literature begun to address issues related to school-based health centers in elementary schools. Until a few years ago, most attention was focused on programs for adolescents, beginning with the first national school-based health initiative funded by the Robert Wood Johnson Foundation in the mid-1980s. Secondly, while early efforts were primarily concerned with providing physical health care to underserved youth, increasingly there has been recognition of the need to integrate a range of mental health services into school-based programs.

In this chapter, we share our experiences developing and implementing a mental health program in an elementary school in Montgomery County, Maryland. Experiences in five years of implementing this project have underscored the advantages of school-based as compared to traditional approaches to mental health care with youth. Our prior experiences, as mental health clinicians/administrators in a range of treatment settings (including outpatient mental health clinics, inpatient psychiatric units, and special education classrooms), have led us to see more clearly some of the unique opportunities that school-based mental health programs provide. In this chapter we discuss some of these advantages, and describe factors that might contribute to the successful delivery of school-based mental health services. We will also touch upon some of the challenges that practitioners are likely to encounter, and issues that remain to be explored in this relatively new and exciting field.

WHY PROVIDE MENTAL HEALTH SERVICES?

It is widely held that only a small percentage of children with emotional problems actually receive the care they need. Although estimates vary, the number of youth who receive appropriate mental health treatment is generally believed to be somewhere in the range of 20 to 40 percent of those who need it (Chabra et al., 1999; Kaplan et al., 1998). While in some instances a dearth of available services may lead to this disparity, Flaherty, Weist, and Warner (1996) noted that "children's mental health needs continue to be largely unmet, even when community services are provided" (p. 341).

Increasingly, policy makers and service providers are attending to the barriers to care that lead to underutilization of services by children and families. Some of these barriers include the failure to recognize the need for treatment, stigma related to receiving mental health services, lack of transportation, lack of child care, lack of insurance, lack of knowledge of available services, language barriers, intimidation, and fear (Kaplan et al., 1999; Adelman et al., 1993; Gold, 1992).

It has been suggested that the numbers of untreated children may be even higher among minority populations. Many observers have noted the increased risk factors for minority youth, such as poverty, poor housing, immigration, and discrimination (e.g., Kaplan et al., 1998; Gold, 1992). Recent research further suggests that minority youth may be even more likely to underutilize available mental health services than Whites. For example, Chabra et al. (1999), in a retrospective analysis of the records of almost 5,000 youth hospitalized for inpatient psychiatric services, found that elementary school–aged Hispanic and Asian children were less likely to use inpatient mental health services than Whites. They concluded that it is possible but unlikely that this discrepancy is attributable to lower prevalence rates, while factors related to "real or perceived institutional, cultural, language, or economic barriers" (p. 32) may be significantly related to lower rates of care.

In light of this large number of undertreated youth, recent findings on improved access to care through school-based programs are particularly encouraging. Kaplan et al. (1998, 1999) reported that providing services in schools improves access for both adolescents and elementary school–aged students. In a review of studies on the utilization of mental health services in schools, Evans (1999) concluded that "youth utilize school-based mental health services at a rate higher than traditional clinic- and hospital-based services" (p. 168).

WHY ELEMENTARY SCHOOLS?

Recent literature on school-based programs has also underscored the lack of attention to the elementary school–aged population. Perhaps because of the initial focus on adolescent health services, there have been relatively fewer school-based programs located in elementary schools than in middle or high schools. In a 1998–99 survey of 839 school-based health centers, conducted by the National Assembly on School-Based Health Care (NASBHC, 1999, unpublished preliminary findings), only 14 percent of centers surveyed were in elementary schools (pre-K through grade 6), with an additional 4 percent in K–12 schools. While Kaplan et al. (1998) report a somewhat higher estimate of school-based health centers in elementary settings (32 percent of 914 programs in 1996–97), they nevertheless conclude that "SBHCs serving elementary-aged students are not adequately represented in the literature" (p. 1).

This point is echoed by others who note that little has been written about the mental health needs of elementary school children, or about the availability and types of services provided to this population (Goodwin, Goodwin, & Cantrill, 1988; Heneghan & Malakoff, 1997). McClowry et al. (1996) also underscored the lack of research documenting the effectiveness of elementary school–based programs in improving long-range health and educational objectives.

In this chapter, we offer our experiences in part to add to the knowledge base about services for the elementary school population. We include findings from our program evaluation showing positive changes in behavioral and educational outcomes for students who participated in the program. A brief review of the program, its evaluation, and findings is presented in the following.

THE LINKAGES TO LEARNING PROGRAM

The Linkages to Learning model for school-based services was developed in Montgomery County, Maryland, in the early 1990s in response to concerns about the unmet social, health, and mental health needs of children and families in the county. The initiative involves collaboration between schools and community agencies to provide a range of prevention and early intervention services in schools. The model was originally piloted in two elementary school sites. In 1995, a United States Department of Education grant to the University of Maryland, College Park, provided for the replication of this model at a third elementary school (the one we are describing in this chapter), as well as funding for a longitudinal evaluation of the program's effectiveness. One year into the project, funding from the Robert Wood Johnson Foundation (Making the Grade Initiative) enabled this Linkages to Learning site to expand into a full-fledged school-based health center.

The Linkages to Learning site described here serves an elementary school and neighborhood located in the southeastern part of Montgomery County, Maryland, just north of Washington, D.C. This community is among the most demographically diverse, poor, and mobile within the county. Of the school's 525 students (kindergarten through fifth grade), 99 percent are minorities. The majority of students are Latino (63 percent), while 20 percent are African-American/African, 16 percent are Asian (mostly Vietnamese), and 1 percent are White. Ninety-seven percent of students at the school receive Free and Reduced Meals (FARMS), a well-accepted indicator of family poverty. Results of a community survey conducted in 1996, just prior to the initiation of the school-based program, indicated that 66 percent of children at the school lacked health insurance. It is estimated that 75 percent of families in the school community are recent immigrants, many of whom have experienced war, political strife, separation from family members, severe hunger, and poverty.

Program services were initiated in the spring of 1996. During the course of the 1998–99 school year, 99 percent of students in the school were enrolled in the school-based health center. Of these enrolled students, 75 percent used some program service(s) during the year. There were a total of 3,894 visits to the school-based health center from July 1998 to June 1999. The range of services offered to students and families includes mental health assessments; individual and family counseling; psychoeducational and therapy groups for children and parents; primary medical care; immunizations; laboratory services; medication administration; health counseling and education; English and conversation classes for non–native speakers; computer classes; job training; assistance obtaining employment, legal help, housing, health insurance, food, and clothing; and educational support (e.g., tutoring, SAT preparation).

The study conducted by the University of Maryland was an evaluation of the impact of the Linkages to Learning program on the social, emotional, and academic functioning of children and their families. It involved the collection of data at both the Linkages to Learning school site and at a matched comparison school, also in Montgomery County. Data were collected each spring for four years, beginning just prior to the initiation of the program. A total of 119 children and 69 parents comprised the longitudinal sample.

Evaluation findings suggested that the Linkages to Learning program is positively impacting on the social and academic well-being of students. For example, parents at the Linkages to Learning school site reported significant decreases in behavior problems among their children over the course of three years. These decreases were not found at the control school site. Furthermore, while control school students demonstrated increases in teacher-reported negative behaviors and self-reported emotional distress symptoms over three years, children at the Linkages to Learning school site showed no such increases. We hypothesize that the program is serving some protective function in preventing the escalation of both behavioral and emotional problems among students who participate in it. In addition, some promising academic findings were reported. These included gains in math achievement among students who participated in program educational services, which surpassed improvements among both nonprogram participants at the same school, and control school students.

While this research is hardly conclusive on its own, it does suggest that the presence of a school-based program in an elementary school may lead to improvements in behavioral and even academic functioning among students. In the following, we highlight some of the assets of school-based programs that may help to account for these positive findings.

INCREASED ACCESS FOR CHILDREN AND FAMILIES

As noted earlier, many in the school-based health movement have cited increased access to care as one of the greatest advantages of this model of service delivery (e.g., Flaherty et al., 1996). Our own experiences providing services to children and families in an elementary school community are consistent with these findings.

One of the clear advantages of providing services in school-based settings is convenience. Rather than being in a city or county office building that is located far from families, school-based services are in places that children, and sometimes parents, visit every day. Elementary schools, in particular, are likely to serve children from neighborhoods within a small geographical range. In the case of our program, 95 percent of all students in the school live within walking distance, and basically surround the school in a group of low-cost housing developments. This proximity virtually eliminates transportation problems that are frequently issues for poor families trying to get to clinics in traditional outpatient settings. In our program, parents can not only walk to the center, but they can also take advantage of natural opportunities to come in for services when they drop their children off at school in the morning or when they pick them up at the end of the day.

Comprehensive school-based programs also reduce the likelihood that parents will have to go to multiple sites, and negotiate several bureaucracies, in trying to access services. School-based programs can offer parents a range of services under one roof, while holistically addressing the health, mental health, and social service needs of the child and family. An interdisciplinary team works together to coordinate care and avoid duplications and gaps in service. For those services that are not available on-site, the team can play an important role in helping families to learn about other resources or programs, overcome barriers such as transportation or language problems, and develop the skills to effectively meet their own needs.

Comprehensive school-based programs also reduce barriers to mental health care through offering multiple points of entry. Particularly for individuals from cultures in which mental health services are highly stigmatized, mental health needs frequently emerge only after a family has engaged in other program activities, such as computer classes, English classes, or social service assistance (e.g., help obtaining health insurance, translations, or help completing job applications). As Gold (1992) noted with regard to the Vietnamese population, "in helping refugees deal with physical and concrete matters . . . treatment staff can establish the trusting relations that are essential for addressing submerged psychological issues" (p. 293).

We have often witnessed this phenomenon in our own work in the Linkages to Learning program. Frequently, in the course of attending program activities or getting help with concrete services, parents will begin to talk about other issues with which they are struggling. For example, we have had several situations in which mothers seeking help with social service issues began to discuss marital problems, including spousal abuse. Because our program includes mental health, health, and social service components, it is easy to address these new issues as they emerge by involving additional members of the treatment team.

As others have noted in the literature, mental health issues often initially present as somatic health concerns as well. Gold (1992) described how Vietnamese immigrants, who feel extreme shame about mental health problems, often "indicate their symptoms by referring to physical problems" (p. 293). In a comprehensive school-based program, psychological issues can be addressed through a seamless transition between health and mental health staff. Once an initial relationship has been established with the health practitioner, for example, this staff member can literally walk down the hall with a child and/or parent and introduce a member of the social service or mental health team. This can allow for a transfer of trust that will help to build a new working relationship. This is a very different scenario from a pediatrician giving a parent a referral for a mental health professional (usually a name and phone number) in an outpatient setting. Even if the doctor is trusted by the family, there are myriad barriers to that referral actually being followed through. The parent has to take the initiative to contact, find, and get to know this new person, not to mention the special issues of immigrant parents who may not speak English, and who are reluctant to seek mental health treatment anyway.

In addition to offering multiple entry points, school-based programs reduce barriers to access by becoming known and trusted in the school. In this way, the programs can reduce many of the "personal barriers" to care that Kaplan et al. (1999) described, including fear, intimidation, and distrust. In our program, getting to know parents and teachers are major objectives for all program staff. We use a variety of informal and formal mechanisms to develop these relationships. Early in the school year, program staff participate in schoolwide events that introduce them to the teachers and parents and help to get the word out to the community about our program. These events include kindergarten orientation, Back-to-School Night, and the school book fair. Program staff also look for informal opportunities to get to know parents, including greeting parents as they walk their children to school in the morning, and attending Parent-Teacher Association meetings and other parent events. We have even found that setting up a table on the sidewalk outside our office with a VCR showing a parenting video provides a way to casually interact with parents, share information about our program, and garner interest for our parent support groups.

This kind of outreach is particularly important when working with a large immigrant population. Hall (1976) and others have articulated the differences among cultures in terms of the norms for building relationships. Among other things, he noted that for individuals from "high context cultures" (such as those in Latin America and Asia) the development of a personal relationship needs to precede, and not parallel, the formation of a working relationship. We know that for members of this community, in order to feel comfortable and be willing to seek services, they must first feel that they know, and are known by, members of our staff.

In part as a means of establishing this connection, we try to create an atmosphere in our office that is welcoming and inviting. For example, we have computers in our waiting room with software on learning the English language and tutorials for learning word-processing skills that are available for any parent to use at any time. We also have an area with clothes, furniture, and household items that parents are free to take when they need them. Because we are aware that so many of our parents have negative experiences with social service agencies, we also try to offer a warm and personal environment. When parents enter our waiting room, they are surrounded by children's artwork, books and toys for children, and (perhaps most importantly) quick and easy access to our staff. Offices open right onto the waiting room (there is no receptionist behind a glass window), and the staff make it a high priority to come out and greet parents when they enter. There is the recognition that taking the time to talk to parents, to try to ease their anxiety, or to locate the staff person they are waiting to see, are small gestures that will go a long way toward helping build trust and comfort.

We have also learned, and cannot underscore enough, the importance of having bilingual and culturally competent staff. Parents have repeatedly told us how important it has been to them to be able to talk to someone "like me." We have also seen how not having some ethnic groups adequately represented on our staff has made it harder to establish relationships with parents of that ethnicity in our community.

Other ways to reduce barriers to care include being both flexible and responsive. This includes holding events when it is convenient for parents, providing child care, and including parents in decision making about program activities. Recognizing that parents are more likely to walk in when they have a problem than they are to make appointments, we make every effort to see them (at least briefly) when they come to our office. School-based programs can often operate more flexibly than outpatient clinics since the staff are engaged in a range of activities and do not fill their schedules with back-to-back client sessions. This flexibility enables us to engage parents immediately, rather than making appointments for a later date that may not happen.

The fluidity and flexibility of roles also allows school-based programs to respond quickly to individual, school, and community-wide problems. For example, when the parent of a child in the school was shot and killed, our team of program and school staff worked together to offer counseling and support to the family, as well as longer-term social service assistance (e.g., financial, legal). The school counselor and our mental health therapist intervened immediately by visiting classrooms to discuss the widely publicized event, helping children to process this crisis in their community. Because they knew our program, the family felt comfortable seeking help right away. Perhaps most importantly, unlike a situation in which an outside team is called in to deal with a crisis, we were still available and connected to the family after the initial rush of assistance and support had subsided. Having built an initial alliance, we could then work with the mother and children to help them mourn the loss and rebuild their lives.

EFFECTIVENESS

School-based mental health programs have the potential to deliver highly effective treatment, with several advantages over traditional service delivery models. Among those discussed here are the opportunity to conduct thorough and holistic assessments, the capacity to intervene in multiple settings using an ecological approach, and opportunities for increased effectiveness through reinforcing the generalization of new behaviors.

A. Holistic Assessments

A thorough and accurate mental health assessment should lead to more efficient and more effective treatment. School-based mental health programs have the opportunity to conduct extremely thorough assessments by collecting data from multiple sources in multiple spheres of a child's life. When a child is referred to our program for mental health treatment, our assessment team begins by meeting with the child and his/her parents, as would be the case in most mental health settings. In addition, we meet with the child's teacher (and other school personnel who work intensively with the child) to understand how he/she is functioning in school. We may also observe the child in the classroom, in the lunchroom, or at recess. Sometimes we will meet with the child and his/her family at home (either because family members can't get to the center, or in order to gather additional valuable information about family functioning). With appropriate consent we also review medical and school records, which can be extremely helpful in understanding the role of learning disabilities or medical issues. As needed, we contact other providers who have been involved with the child or family. If there are current health care concerns, the child can be seen by the nurse practitioner or pediatrician.

The value of having easy access to all of these various types of data cannot be emphasized enough, nor do we want to overlook how difficult it can be to obtain these data in traditional outpatient settings. For a therapist in a clinic, for example, just reaching the child's teacher in order to get his/her input can take many rounds of phone calls and hours of precious time. And generally, there is no previous relationship established between these two individuals that would help the clinician to understand the context of the teacher's comments, or a level of trust that might lead the teacher to be open and frank. It is also highly unlikely that the clinician will have the opportunity to see firsthand how the child functions in school, at home, or among peers. Finally, the therapist is often working alone, even if he/she is able to gather information from a range of other providers familiar with the family, such as the child's doctor or his school counselor.

In our program, the assessment process is enhanced by our team approach, involving individuals from the health staff, the mental health staff, the case manager, and school personnel. Working as a team, we can share knowledge and interdisciplinary perspectives in order to best understand the developmental, educational, emotional, medical, social, and family factors that may be contributing to a child's distress. We can also work collectively to identify the strengths that the child, family, school, and community can offer to help bring about resolution of the presenting problems. We work as a team not only in the process of case conceptualization, but also throughout the implementation of the treatment plan. Over time, we continue to meet regularly to review progress and to modify our approach in order to maximize the effectiveness of our interventions.

B. Ecological Approaches to Treatment

Comer and Woodruff (1998) discussed the shortcomings of traditional approaches of mental health professionals in schools who focus exclusively on individual students or groups of students. They advocate that instead, mental health professionals should conceptualize the difficulties children experience "as coming from complex interactions of social environmental forces in and outside the school" (p. 499). They stress that programs need to focus on the interaction between the child and the school, family, community, and society rather than on the child alone.

We share this belief that a child's emotions, behaviors, and physical well-being need to be understood in the context of his/her interactions with the world around him/her, and we feel that as a school-based program, we have unique opportunities to know and understand these environments in which the child lives. This may be particularly true at the elementary school level, when a child's world is more circumscribed, than in the case of the older youth or adolescent who has more independence and increased opportunities to interact with a wide range of individuals and institutions.

Having access to the many spheres of a child's life not only helps us to understand the interactive relationships the child has with different individuals in each of these environments, but also enables us to develop interventions that can specifically address each of these contexts. In the case of a child who presented with severe learning problems and angry outbursts, for example, we worked with the classroom teacher to develop new strategies to reinforce and reward anger control, with the parents to understand the child's needs for support and discipline, with the school system to advocate for more academic services, and with an outside agency to locate a tutor. In addition, we offered the child individual therapy to help him develop anger management skills, and group therapy to address social skills deficits.

We also recognize, as Comer and Woodruff (1998) point out, that behavior is a product of the interaction of the child and his/her environment. When a child is taken for therapy in an outpatient clinic he/she, de facto, becomes the identified patient, and the intervention almost invariably focuses on changing his/her behavior. The clinician is often quite limited in his/her ability to change environments or situations outside the therapy room. While most clinicians recognize the interactive nature of behavior, the traditional therapeutic setting virtually necessitates that the point of intervention be the child. In school-based programs, not only do we have the opportunity to assess the role that intrapsychic issues, family dynamics, the classroom environment, and even neighborhood factors are playing in a child's situation, but we also often have access to these environments in developing our interventions. Thus we can choose to intervene in the way, and in the place, that will maximize the benefit to the child.

As an example, during the second year of our program we received a number of referrals over a span of months that either came from the health staff (children presenting with somatic complaints) or from parents whose children were experiencing symptoms of anxiety. We eventually realized that all of these children were being referred from the same classroom. Observations in the classroom and discussions with the school counselor led us to see that there were some key aspects of the environment in that room that were contributing to these problems. We were then able to make recommendations, and to work with the school principal to help this teacher develop new behavior management techniques. Needless to say, this is a very different "diagnosis" of the problem than would have been achieved by a therapist working with a child in an outpatient clinic. It also highlights how issues that are really environmental can be ascribed to children, leading to inappropriate negative labeling of them.

In another example, one of the things we noticed early on in our work with this community was the large number of parents who showed signs of acculturation stress. Garza-Guerrero (1974) described this stress as deriving in part from difficulties in psychologically adapting to the realities of immigration: leaving behind one's family, culture, and country (in essence, losing one's identity), and having to create an entirely new life in a foreign land. Research suggests that individuals struggling with these issues may be more likely to experience depression or addiction problems, and that the children of these individuals may be more likely to experience depression themselves (Hovey & King, 1996; Sack et al., 1995; Szapocznik et al., 1986).

As our program evolved, we became increasingly convinced that not only were many recently immigrated parents experiencing acculturation stress, but their American-born children were also manifesting symptoms of anxiety, depression, and aggression that were, at least in part, related to the immigration experience. These children were often placed in the position of having to negotiate between two sometimes conflicting cultures: the native culture that dominates at home, and the host (American) culture in the social world around them. They also frequently become caught in anxiety-provoking "role reversals," situations in which they were required to intervene in communications between their parents and other adults (e.g., answering the phone in English, or translating for their parents with teachers or agency representatives).

In thinking about how to address these issues, our program staff felt that the most effective approach would be to work with parents directly to help them resolve their conflicts and struggles related to acculturation. We believed not only that this approach would help parents to become healthier and happier individuals, but also that it would result in less stressful family environments for children. We developed a multifaceted acculturation program that included support groups, English conversation groups, job training, and recreational activities. While still addressing symptoms that children presented individually, we were simultaneously able to adapt our program to develop services that addressed community-wide needs. During the first year of this initiative, we have had close to 100 parents participating in acculturation activities.

C. Increased Generalizability

As Harris (1995) and others have noted, historically one of the greatest challenges for mental health clinicians has been to help clients generalize behaviors learned in the treatment context to other environments. As Evans (1999) points out, many of the conditions necessary for generalization to occur can be created much more easily in school-based settings than in outpatient clinics.

For example, we have already noted the ease with which clinicians can observe children in a range of environments, and not only watch their behaviors, but also learn which contingencies in the environment are serving to reinforce these behaviors or, conversely, to undermine them. The therapist can then make use of this information in several ways. He/she can strategize with the child in the context of therapy about new ways to handle problems. They can then practice new behaviors, and can role-play situations that are very similar to those that the child experiences in other realms. Subsequently, the child can test out these new behaviors and can report back to the therapist. Or the therapist can observe the child at a later time in these natural environments (e.g., the classroom, the playground) and accurately assess the child's behaviors, as well as those of the people around him.

Sometimes our therapists will sit with a child in the lunchroom and serve as a "coach," helping the child to try out a new behavior in his/her interactions with peers. Occasionally these opportunities arise spontaneously as well. Recently one of our therapists was walking down the hall in school and saw one of her clients (with whom she was working on anger management skills) with his class. When she saw this child interacting negatively with a classmate, she was able to pull him aside, encourage him to choose an alternative behavior, and watch him implement the strategy. They were then able to reflect on this interaction together in their next therapy session.

Equally importantly, the therapist can work with important individuals in the child's school, home, and even neighborhood to bring about changes in key environments. Parents can be helped to reinforce new behaviors learned by the child, as can teachers. Often there are also important figures from the church or synagogue, after-school program, or even Boy or Girl Scout troop who are willing to work as members of our team and assist in helping a child to achieve his/her treatment goals.

CONTINUITY OF CARE

School-based mental health programs have a unique opportunity to offer a continuum of care, from prevention all the way to intensive intervention services. Schools offer ideal settings for providing prevention services, since they reach the vast majority of children in our society. In addition, school-based programs in communities like ours reach many children who experience multiple risk factors such as poverty, abuse, exposure to drugs/alcohol, and violence. Outpatient clinics rarely have the opportunity to intervene with a child or family before problems develop, especially when payment is contingent on providing a DSM-IV diagnosis. Health and mental health practitioners in school-based programs can develop activities that build competencies and increase protective risk factors, as well as intervening when more intensive treatment is needed.

Prevention programs offered through our center have included everything from classroom-based skill building groups, to teacher training (e.g., how to recognize warning signs), to parent education workshops. Classroom-based groups, which are co-led by teachers and therapists, focus on developing age-appropriate problem-solving skills. We also frequently focus prevention activities on transition periods, when children may be particularly vulnerable. Each spring we co-lead classroom-based discussions to help prepare fifth graders for the transition to middle school. For those children who are particularly anxious about this transition, we offer a small follow-up group that meets to discuss concerns, develop coping strategies, and offer additional support through the beginning of the next school year.

As a school-based program we also have unique opportunities to reach out to children who are traditionally underserved. For example, children with internalizing problems such as depression, anxiety, and social withdrawal are frequently overlooked (particularly in classrooms) since they do not interfere with teaching and do not necessarily display readily observable behavioral problems (Flaherty et al., 1996). In our program, we run psychoeducational groups specifically targeting children whom teachers have identified as shy or withdrawn. These groups provide the children with a safe environment in which to learn and practice new social skills, including problem-solving, feelings identification, and decision-making skills. In addition, the groups provide an excellent mechanism for us to identify children who may need some additional services. Our experience has been that roughly one in five of these children will at some point be referred for mental health treatment. Either the child is referred to us later (at which point we are already familiar to them, and vice versa), or we initiate a mental health assessment at the conclusion of the group in order to explore whether additional intervention might be helpful.

This ability to move fluidly from less to more (or more to less) intensive interventions is another asset of school-based programs. Over time, the level of intensity of involvement with a child can change, dependent on his/her needs. Yet the connection, and the opportunity to respond quickly to changing events, remains constant. The opportunity to maintain this continuity over time is especially possible in elementary school settings, since children spend more years in elementary school than they do at either the middle or high school level.

Three years ago we began working with a male, Vietnamese fourth-grade student. He and his mother originally came to our center because they needed to get to a doctor's appointment and did not have a car. In the course of taking them to the appointment, our case manager learned that this child had a degenerative eye condition, and that he was quite fearful that he might lose his sight. The case manager also learned that the mother, who spoke only Vietnamese, was having great financial difficulty.

Because the family had no phone, the case manager paid a follow-up visit to the home the next week. Over the course of several meetings, the case manager and the mother strategized about ways that she could increase her economic independence. The case manager helped her to complete an application for health insurance for her son, and helped with the logistics of treatment for his eye condition. Over several months, the case manager also helped the mother to develop a successful business selling handmade crafts. In addition, the mother provided consent for her son to be seen by a therapist to address some of his concerns about his eyes. Consultation with the school staff revealed that this child was experiencing difficulties with peer relations and was manifesting symptoms of anxiety as well.

Individual therapy with the child was conducted over the course of one year. At the end of this period teachers reported fewer peer problems and better academic performance. During the following year, therapy sessions dropped to every other week. In the spring, when the child was preparing to graduate and transition to middle school, he became highly anxious and his functioning decompensated to the point of requiring psychiatric hospitalization. During this extremely stressful period, the program staff worked closely to support both the mother and child. The therapist and case manager worked intensively to help the mother understand what was happening with her son, and to translate for her with hospital staff. (The program staff noted that the child's mother frequently came to our office during this time, and seemed to find some comfort in simply being in this place that felt safe and familiar). The child's therapist also worked with the inpatient treatment team to maintain the continuity of her relationship with her child, and to support the inpatient treatment. She also helped deliver schoolwork, and the program provided money for clothing and transportation for the mother during the hospitalization.

During the summer following the hospitalization, intensive outpatient treatment resumed with the child. This included visits to the middle school, and work with the middle school staff to prepare for a successful transition in the fall. An educational plan was developed with input from our mental health team. The child began the school year in a small special education classroom, and continued weekly therapy sessions through our program. At the end of three months he had been completely academically mainstreamed. At the end of the year he was receiving A's and B's on his report card.

Meanwhile, the child's mother, who had previously told the program staff that her goal in life was to be a parent "and then go back to Vietnam to die," gradually began to get more involved in program activities. Through encouragement from the case manager she began attending an acculturation group with other Vietnamese parents. For the first time since coming to the United States, she acquired telephone service and began a relationship with a male companion. Her son is currently seen for therapy every other week and maintains frequent contact with the program by coming in to use the computer to do his homework on a regular basis. This New Year, both mother and son made a trip to Vietnam together for the first time.

We hope that this case illustrates the flexibility and ease with which treatment intensity can increase or diminish over time in order to be responsive to the needs of the child and family. The comprehensive school-based program also offers the opportunity to engage the child and family in a range of prevention, treatment, and empowerment activities that meet their needs as these evolve naturally.

CHALLENGES THAT LIE AHEAD

Our work over the last several years has affirmed the value of providing school-based mental health services, particularly in an elementary school community. We find this work exciting, rewarding, and ripe with opportunities for creativity and growth. Yet our work, and the work of our colleagues, has also brought a number of challenges and unanswered questions to the fore. For example, it is our view that school-based programs require highly trained and experienced mental health therapists, including licensed social workers and licensed clinical psychologists. Unfortunately, mental health agencies are sometimes reluctant (or unable) to hire more experienced clinicians when they can get unlicensed or new therapists for less money. Sometimes they are limited by contracts with funding to support only entry-level clinicians. However, the challenges of school-based practice will be difficult for many new therapists to handle.

For example, school-based programs seem to work best when staff are not constrained by traditional role definitions, but instead are able to stretch these roles in new ways. This includes mental health practitioners who are willing to make home visits, engage in outreach activities, and can collaborate with individuals from other disciplines. In order to successfully make these role adjustments, clinicians must have very clear and well-defined boundaries, and must be aware of their own clinical strengths and weaknesses. Issues related to confidentiality, consent, and cross-cultural work represent other tricky areas in school-based health care that may be especially difficult for novice clinicians to successfully navigate.

Another obvious challenge in the area of school-based health care is financing. Other observers have documented the difficulties of relying on third-party payments to keep school-based programs afloat (e.g., Armbruster et al., 1999; Dryfoos, 1994), especially when many of the services that make these programs uniquely successful are not recognized by third-party payers as reimbursable. Yet for these programs to work, there needs to be stable and consistent funding over time. Without this long-term investment communities will be reluctant to engage in such programs, and time spent developing collaborative relationships will be wasted. Funding will likely follow if research can demonstrate both the cost-effectiveness of school-based programs, and long-term positive gains. Our challenge is to continue to conduct research that captures the unique value of this service delivery model and demonstrates its true potential to help children and families succeed.

References

Adelman, H. S., Barker, L. A., & Nelson, P. (1993). A study of a school-based clinic: Who uses it and who doesn't? *Journal of Clinical Child Psychology, 22,* 52–59.

Armbruster, P., Andrews, E., Couenhoven, J., & Blau, G. (1999). Collision or collaboration? School-based health services meet managed care. *Clinical Psychology Review, 19*(2), 221–237.

Chabra, A., Chavez, G. F., & Harris, E. S. (1999). Mental illness in elementary school–aged children. *Western Journal of Medicine, 170*(1), 28–34.

Comer, J. P., & Woodruff, D. W. (1998). Mental health in schools. *Child and Adolescent Psychiatric Clinics of North America, 7*(3), 499–513.

Dryfoos, J. G. (1994). *Full-service schools: A revolution in health and social services for children, youth, and families.* San Francisco: Jossey-Bass.

Evans, S. W. (1999). Mental health services in schools: Utilization, effectiveness, and consent. *Clinical Psychological Review, 19,* 165–178.

Flaherty, L. T., Weist, M. D., & Warner, B. S. (1996). School-based mental health services in the United States: History, current models and needs. *Community Mental Health Journal, 32*(4), 341–352.

Fox, N., Leone, P., Rubin, K., Oppenheim, J., Miller, M., & Friedman, K. (1999). *Final report on the Linkages to Learning Program and Evaluation at Broad Acres Elementary School.* Unpublished report, University of Maryland, College Park, MD.

Garza-Guerrero, C. (1974). Culture shock: Its mourning and the vicissitudes of identity. *Journal of the American Psychoanalytic Association, 22,* 408–429.

Gold, S. J. (1992). Mental health and illness in Vietnamese refugees. *Western Journal of Medicine, 157*(3), 290–294.

Goodwin L. D., Goodwin, W. L., & Cantrill, J. L. (1988). The mental health needs of elementary school children. *Journal of School Health, 58*(7), 282–287.

Hall, E. T. (1976). *Beyond Culture*. New York: Bantam Doubleday Dell.

Harris, J. R. (1995). Where is the child's environment? A group socialization theory of development. *Psychological Review, 102*(3), 458–489.

Heneghan, A. M., & Malakoff, M. E. (1997). Availability of school health services for young children. *Journal of School Health, 67*(8), 327–332.

Hovey, J. D., & King, C. A. (1996). Acculturative stress, depression, and suicidal ideation among immigrant and second-generation Latino adolescents. *Journal of the American Academy of Child and Adolescent Psychiatry, 35*(9), 1183–1192.

Kaplan, D. W., Brindis, C., Naylor, K. E., Phibbs, S. L., Ahlstrand, K. R., & Melinkovich, P. (1998). Elementary school–based health center use. *Pediatrics, 101*(6), E12.

Kaplan, D. W., Brindis, C. D., Phibbs, S. L., Melinkovich, P., Naylor, K., & Ahlstrand, K. (1999). A comparison study of an elementary school–based health center: Effects on health care access and use. *Archives of Pediatric Adolescent Medicine, 153*(3), 235–243.

McClowry, S. G., Galehouse, P., Hartnagle, W., Kaufman, H., Just, B., Moed, R., & Patterson-Dehn, C. (1996). A comprehensive school-based clinic: University and Community partnership. *JSPN, 1*(1), 19–26.

National Assembly on School-Based Health Care. (1999, June). *1998/1999 school-based health center survey, preliminary findings*. Preliminary data presented at the annual meeting of the National Assembly on School-Based Health Care, Washington, DC.

Sack, W. H., Clarke, G. N., & Seeley, J. (1995). Post-traumatic stress disorder across two generations of Cambodian refugees. *Journal of the American Academy of Child and Adolescent Psychiatry, 34*(9), 1160–1166.

Szapocznik, J., Rio, A., Vidal, A., Kurtines, W., Hervis, O., & Santisteban, D. (1986). Bicultural effectiveness training (BET): An experimental test of an intervention modality for families experiencing intergenerational/intercultural conflict. *Hispanic Journal of Behavioral Sciences, 8*, 303–331.

CHAPTER THREE

Establishing Successful School Mental Health Programs: Guidelines and Recommendations

Olga M. Acosta, Ph.D., Nancy A. Tashman, Ph.D., Christine Prodente, Ph.D., and Eric Proescher, Psy.D.

Expanded school mental health (ESMH) programs grew out of the realization that children's mental health needs were not being met effectively by traditional community-based programs. There are a host of barriers that have prevented children from accessing services in community mental health centers, including long waiting lists, financial obstacles, transportation problems, and a lack of knowledge about mental health services (e.g., when mental health services are needed, what services are available, how services can be accessed) (Weist, 1997). ESMH programs provide comprehensive mental health services to youth and their families within the school setting. Services can include assessment, treatment, prevention, case management, and staff consultation. Advantages of ESMH programs include reduced stigma, increased accessibility, improved outreach to youth with internalizing problems, and increased opportunities to collaborate with school staff (Evans, 1999; Weist, 1997). Research suggests that ESMH programs are indeed reaching youth who might not otherwise have access to services (Weist, Myers, Hastings, Ghuman, & Han, 1999), and are effective in achieving desired outcomes (Armbruster & Lichtman, 1999; Evans, 1999).

Their pragmatic appeal, programmatic advantages, and positive outcomes have contributed to the progressive growth of ESMH programs over the last ten years. They are entering new school districts every day. Currently there are over 1,200 school-based health centers in the United States (Lear, Eichner, & Koppelman, 1999). While the individual programs vary, together the experiences of different ones can combine to help suggest some best practices for program design and delivery (Adelman et al., 1999). The work of ESMH pioneers has helped to set the stage for future programs. For the movement to continue to expand and to offer quality services, it is important to establish a blueprint that can guide the development and implementation of new programs.

The goal within this chapter is to offer practical suggestions for developing, implementing, and maintaining a successful school mental health program. The chapter will be divided into six sections: (1) funding; (2) collaboration; (3) needs assessment and resource mapping; (4) program structure; (5) staffing, education, and training; and (6) quality assurance and evaluation. This chapter offers a program development outline and is intended as a general guide. The actual application of the guidelines may vary depending on the unique needs of the individual school and community.

FUNDING

Historically many school-based mental health programs were funded through federal, state, and local grants and funding provided through private foundations, hospitals, and local health departments (Koppelman & Lear, 1998). With budget cuts leading to decreases in funding from state and federal grants, other sources of funding have been increasingly necessary. Securing funding has become one of the most serious problems facing the expanded school mental health movement. Some programs that had relied on private foundation funding have found that to continue to survive they needed to turn to local, state, and federal funding (Advocates for Youth, 1993). There has been a growing expectation that programs need to figure out how to become self-sustaining.

In the past five years, two main funding trends have occurred. First, there has been a move toward third-party revenue models (Brellochs, Zimmerman, Zink, & English, 1996; Koppelman & Lear, 1998). Increasingly, programs have depended on funds generated through fee-for-service in order to support their staff. As a means of maintaining and expanding services, school-based health centers have been reaching out to and trying to partner with managed care organizations (MCOs) (Armbruster, Andrews, Couenhoven, & Blau, 1999; Making the Grade, 1998). MCOs may require that providers be licensed, meet their credentialing and reporting standards, and receive preauthorization for all services. As a way of addressing these requirements, school and community mental health/hospital programs have partnered to expedite the readiness for reimbursement and to expand available resources for school-based programs (e.g., staff, funding). Collaborative endeavors can be cost-effective in that they are less likely to duplicate services and more likely to meet service needs (Flaherty et al., 1998). In addition to helping address the practical issues inherent in implementing a school-based program, a willingness to collaborate with various community agencies may increase the likelihood that a program is awarded funding in the future. Many grantmakers want evidence of community support for and willingness to collaborate with a given program before they will offer funding.

While some programs have had great success in using the fee-for-service model, it is rare that a program could recover all of its costs through third-party revenues (School Health Resources Services, 1997). The fee-for-service model seems well fitted for higher-end cases that involve insurance and a diagnosis. This leads us to the second trend regarding funding school-based mental health programs: blended funding. That is, instead of depending on one source for funding, programs are reaching out to secure several funding sources, both private and public (Center for School Mental Health Assistance, 1997; Making the Grade, 1998). Funding sources can include the school district's revenues from the Individuals with Disabilities Education Act (IDEA), private insurance, block grant funding from federal, state, and local awards, funding from hospitals and community mental health centers, fee-for-service or capitation reimbursement, and private foundation money.

In trying to locate funding available within a state or region, several databases exist that can help program administrators figure out what sources may be available. In particular, three databases are recommended, each of which are easily accessed by the Internet. The first is a database created by the Centers for Disease Control in collaboration with the Office of the Assistant Secretary for Planning and Evaluation.[1] This provides information on federal, state, and foundation funding sources related to the development of school health programs. The second recommended database is one created by the National Conference of State Legislatures.[2] Their School Health Finance Project is divided into two main sections: block grants and state revenue. The database provides information about and the procedures needed to apply for funding for school health programs.

1. Centers for Disease Control Web site (http://www.cdc.gov/nccdphp/dash/funding.htm).

2. National Conference of State Legislators Web site (http://www.ncsl.org/programs/health/pp/schlfund.htm).

The third database is maintained by Making the Grade, a national program of the Robert Wood Johnson Foundation.[3] Making the Grade maintains an extensive online resource center, including information about funding. It includes contact information for state partners, state fact sheets, and state resources.

Once funding is obtained for the startup of a program, it is important to assess funding strengths and weaknesses. An analysis should be conducted that considers the relative contributions of each of the funding resources in view of the time, energy, and clinical hours that are invested. Overall, the cost in terms of time, effort, and money should be viewed as reasonable when compared to the results. Monitoring the status of each source of funding is also important. Unfortunately, even though there are several sources that can fund school mental health programs, many of these are not stable from year to year. For example, with health care reform, any change in policy could drastically impact funding provided through Medicaid. Programs need to be aware of legislative changes in funding that may occur and need to have contingency plans in place in case funding sources fall short. Given that funding is an emerging area of focus within the school mental health field, it is imperative that programs combine their knowledge and experience to try to develop some best practices for funding.

COLLABORATION

Developing partnerships. Considering the tremendous needs of today's youth, it is not surprising that any single agency or organization would feel ill equipped to cope with the rising demand for services. ESMH programs typically represent a partnership between schools and hospitals, or schools and community agencies. In combining the skills and resources of each of the partners in this joint endeavor, access to mental health care and the breadth of services available to a community can be increased.

ESMH programs are, by their very nature, collaborative endeavors. Social workers, psychologists, nurses, psychiatrists, parents, students, teachers, and school administrators work together to address the emotional and behavioral difficulties that hinder learning, and to optimize overall student health and well-being. Children and their families are afforded access to a broader range of professional expertise and can benefit from utilization of a wide range of services. Furthermore, the interdisciplinary alliance among ESMH professionals provides the opportunity for an integrated

---

3. Making the Grade Web site (http://www.gwu.edu/~mtg).

programmatic treatment approach rather than a reliance on piecemeal interventions (Rosenblum, DiCecco, Taylor, & Adelman, 1995). Additional potential benefits for ESMH providers include an enhanced support network, opportunities for shared decision making, and improved communication and negotiation skills (Flaherty et al., 1998). Although the advantages of interdisciplinary collaboration seem obvious, establishing school-community partnerships and coordinating school support services can be, at best, challenging and, at worst, a significant hurdle to the development of ESMH programs. For this reason, the focus of this section will be on establishing and maintaining community partnerships and collaborative relationships.

Planning committee. In the initial development phase of an ESMH program, it is recommended that the school district and the collaborating community mental health agency establish an ESMH planning committee. Included on the committee should be representatives of the school administration, leaders of school-employed mental health professionals (e.g., school psychologists, guidance counselors), teachers, and coordinators of the collaborating community mental health program (Waxman, Weist, & Benson, 1999). This committee will serve to guide the early development of the ESMH program. The joint planning of the ESMH program by school-hired and community agency staff affords the opportunity to establish explicit expectations about program structure; professional roles and responsibilities; organizational policies; and legal/ethical mandates. Clarifying these issues at the outset will enhance collaborative relationships and increase program acceptance once established.

The planning committee's initial meetings are crucial in that they will set the tone for the ongoing interaction. The goal is for the different stakeholder groups on the committee to agree to actively work together. As with any interdisciplinary team, differences among committee members may lead to misunderstandings and increased tensions. The professional language used by clinicians and educators, for example, can serve as a barrier to effective communication. Whereas school administrators and teachers typically talk about maximizing academic achievement, clinicians tend to refer to the child's emotional problem or diagnosis. In light of this, school personnel may perceive a conflict between the school's mission and that of the proposed ESMH program and may resist the idea of excusing students from classes to attend therapy appointments. One method for facilitating collaborative communication is for clinicians to frame their goal as the treatment of mental health problems that serve as "barriers to learning" (Adelman & Taylor, 1997). Educators may then view this goal as compatible with their primary mission and may be more comfortable talking in these terms.

Stakeholder involvement. The collaborative effort of school administrators and mental health professionals, while essential, is not sufficient to ensure the continued success of an ESMH program. One of the primary tasks of the planning committee is to establish relationships with those community groups that might benefit from and/or contribute to the program. These stakeholder groups include youth, parents, clergy, community leaders, administrators of health/mental health programs, and funders. Meaningfully involving key stakeholders in the planning phase increases the likelihood that community members will feel some responsibility for and commitment toward the emerging ESMH program. It also ensures that the program's mission is consistent with stakeholder goals and that the program addresses prevailing community needs (Nabors, Weist, Tashman, & Myers, 1999).

Once a school, schools, or school district has been targeted, it is important for the planning committee to begin building relationships with school board members, school staff, and community leaders. Additionally, the planning committee will want to outline the benefits of ESMH programs and clarify the viability of implementing an ESMH program in a specific school. Successful meetings with the school board can solidify a partnership that will maximize school and community buy-in. Program developers should also meet with the principals of each school in which an ESMH program will be implemented. In this meeting, the rationale for the program can be outlined using the barriers-to-learning framework and the potential benefits to the school can be highlighted (Adelman & Taylor, 1997).

Building relationships with some other stakeholder groups can be even more challenging, since these groups may not realize that they share a common interest with the ESMH program. Taking the time to identify common goals or interests can be helpful in soliciting support from these stakeholders. A medical insurance company, for example, may need to be informed about the potential cost benefits associated with ESMH. Colleges or local businesses might find that they could provide mentoring and job training programs.

Learning what motivates various stakeholder groups to support a project will also help program developers establish collaborative relationships. Social marketing research is one method that can be used to gather information regarding key stakeholder groups and determine what would make them want to support an ESMH program. For example, one aspect of a social marketing agenda might involve surveying potential stakeholders to assess the community's perception and understanding of the professional language used by mental health providers. From the perspective of students and parents, it could be that the term "school mental health clinic" is not as effective as "school health center" in reducing the stigma associated with seeking mental health services. Thus, the labels used can strongly influence whether stakeholders will be willing to support the program. For more information about social marketing, refer to the National Association of State Boards of Education resource *Building Support for School Health Programs: An Action Guide* (1999).

Identifying and responding to the needs and concerns of stakeholders is another method of increasing their involvement. Families, for example, constitute an important ESMH stakeholder group, and parental involvement is a critical aspect of delivering mental health services to children. Parents can facilitate positive ESMH outcomes by providing background information concerning their child's social, emotional, and intellectual development; instituting recommended changes in the home environment; and monitoring the effectiveness of therapeutic interventions (Bickham, Pizarro, Warner, Rosenthal, & Weist, 1998). Yet concerns about maintaining family privacy, misconceptions about ESMH, worries about potential harm to the student, concerns about being criticized or blamed by mental health providers, or limited resources (e.g., time) may contribute to parental reservations about ESMH programs. Parental support can be enhanced by incorporating family input and eliciting family involvement as partners on ESMH committees; providing resources for families; assessing the needs of the families served by the program; and establishing quality assurance procedures to inform and improve the process of involving families.

Advisory board. One practical and effective strategy for maintaining stakeholder involvement once the ESMH program is operational is to develop a program advisory board that includes representatives from each stakeholder group. The advisory board can assist the ESMH program in continuing to assess community needs and resources, further developing its vision and mission, forming specific programs, developing quality assurance and evaluation procedures, and obtaining additional funding. Thus, the board can provide ongoing guidance about improvements or refinements needed within the ESMH program. The varied experiences that each advisory board member brings to the group will provide a broad representation of local needs and viable resources from which a planning committee can draw.

NEEDS ASSESSMENT AND RESOURCE MAPPING

Selecting a School. Building relationships with school and community leaders will help in many phases of program development, from choosing a school site to successfully implementing a program. When deciding where to establish an ESMH program, state and city health leaders can be consulted about regions that are in need of mental health programs and schools that would benefit from expanded services. Representatives from state departments of education and health are acquainted with the types of assistance that are available to youth and their families throughout the state and can recommend jurisdictions where ESMH might be needed. Statistics can be obtained from school districts, health departments, police stations, and hospitals on the incidence of juvenile crime, poverty and community violence, dropout rates, teenage pregnancy, numbers of suspensions and expulsions, rates of psychiatric hospitalization, emergency room visits, and other related risk factors. Additionally, data on the number of agencies, social service providers, and general resources within a community should be added to this equation when choosing locales in which to establish ESMH programs. Furthermore, knowing whether schools have school-based health centers would be another important variable to consider. Providing a structured environment on school grounds where mental health and health needs are simultaneously addressed would constitute an ideal arrangement for youth who struggle with concurrent health and mental health issues. This information taken together will allow program planners to identify and prioritize schools where ESMH may be most needed.

Evaluating needs. Once relationships have been built with key stakeholders and a school site has been selected, a needs assessment should be conducted to illuminate the specific services that would benefit the particular school environment. Individual schools vary greatly in needs, concrete problems faced, day-to-day operational styles, and availability of resources. ESMH programs should be developed based on a careful analysis of the needs of youth and the resources that are available (Weist, Myers, Danforth, McNeil, Ollendick, & Hawkins, 2000).

The needs assessment, regardless of method employed, should ask each stakeholder group for their perspective on: (1) the most significant life stressors encountered by youth in the community; (2) the most common emotional and behavioral problems presented by youth in elementary, middle, and high schools; (3) social, health, mental health, and other programs (e.g., recreational) available to youth in the community as well as their adequacy; and (4) whether, and in what form, mental health services should be delivered in the school(s). Results from needs assessments not only help illuminate gaps in services for youth, but also may outline barriers that prevent youth and their families from accessing mental health care (Acosta, Weist, Lopez, Shafer, & Pizarro, 1999).

Resource mapping. In addition to outlining the needs of youth in a local community, ESMH programs should conduct an analysis of the resources already available and utilized in a community or school. Each clinician assigned to a school should learn what resources are available within the school and the community and be open to making referrals (Adelman & Taylor, 1997; Tashman, Waxman, Nabors, & Weist, 1998).

Resource mapping is another important contribution that stakeholders can make to ESMH programs. Stakeholders may be more knowledgeable about the types of services already utilized within a community than mental health clinicians (Nabors et al., 1999). The planning committee should be aware of the key service providers in a school and the surrounding community, what kinds of services they provide, and the number and types of students they typically see, in order to know how best to integrate with existing services once the ESMH program is implemented. Furthermore, obtaining information about health, mental health, recreational, and other social activities in the community is essential to establishing an ESMH program that will avoid duplicating services already in existence and operating effectively. Needs assessment and resource mapping will enable programs to find out what is available to youth and their families and what services are still needed.

A thorough evaluation, although imperative to the development of a program, should not be utilized only at the beginning stage of program implementation. Continued needs assessments or a program evaluation can provide information on how well the program is functioning, whether it is meeting program goals and standards, and can help identify strengths and weaknesses within a program. The advisory board, as a representative of key stakeholder groups, helps determine the success of the program through its involvement in continued needs assessment and can, therefore, provide recommendations for areas in need of improvement. The advisory board can not only provide guidance about the content of an ESMH program, but can also be used to problem-solve about improving program structure and training.

DEVELOPING PROGRAM STRUCTURE

Structural concerns. Once funding has been secured, a school site has been selected, an extensive needs assessment has been conducted, and the initial plan has been developed, the structural concerns of the ESMH program need to be addressed. Traditionally, school-related resistance to ESMH has stemmed from concerns over limited resources, unclear referral mechanisms, and general "turf" issues (Center for School Mental Health Assistance, 1999). Grossly inferior office space, a lack of privacy, an inability to secure phone lines, and concerns over the security of clinical records may seriously hinder efforts provided by outside agencies. Alternatively, school-hired mental health professionals may perceive ESMH clinicians as a potential threat to their jobs and may view modifications in resource allocations as an unwelcome change. The principal and the ESMH program coordinator, in an initial meeting about program development and structure, can work out the logistical issues necessary for housing an ESMH program within a school. Concerns over office space, telephone service, and a secure area for clinical records should be negotiated prior to the delivery of services and recorded in a contract. This should be done with input from school-hired personnel, particularly if the option of shared resources is the most feasible. Meeting with pupil personnel service staff (e.g., school counselor, school psychologist, school-hired social worker), as well as other school administrators, early in the program initiation phase will allow the program developer to fully explain the ESMH program and to stress the intention of becoming a partner with programs already in the school. This provides another opportunity to clarify the community agency clinician's role as unique, yet complementary, to the school-hired mental health provider.

Establishing a logical and clear referral process will also help eliminate concerns over the duplication of services and dispel fears over "turf." Bringing together individuals in the school who provide mental health or support services provides a forum where referrals can be discussed and triaged appropriately. One strategy might be to ask to become a part of the student support team. An ESMH clinician might also suggest the creation of a "mental health team" where information sharing, problem solving, and team building can take place. Within these teams, all of the mental health providers for the school (both outside agencies and school-hired professionals) can develop a referral process that will best suit their needs. Some programs may have school-hired mental health professionals serve the students in special education while providers from collaborating agencies serve students in regular education. Other support or mental health teams may decide to assign referrals based on provider expertise, student grade, or on a case-by-case basis. Any of these referral procedures can work as long as there is joint planning with explicit expectations about the roles of the various team members. Agreements should be established early about which individual is responsible for what services. Furthermore, this is an important time to help define or refine the role of the ESMH clinician and to set limits on the functions that he or she will perform within the school.

Administrative and organizational requirements that will apply to ESMH clinicians should also be discussed in advance with the principal and the other mental health providers. School administrators should be consulted about school procedures for reporting emergencies, as well as the legal and ethical issues that will arise when outside services are brought into the school to provide services. For example, the limits of confidentiality and concerns over information sharing should be discussed early in the development of a program. This is especially important if an ESMH clinician will be a part of a mental health team where referrals are made within a group format. Having a mutual understanding of what can be shared will help eliminate miscommunication and/or possible ethical violations. Therefore, taking the time to meet with school administrators and school-hired mental health providers to outline the structure for how the program will function is a critical step in the eventual success of the program.

Crisis planning and management. One topic that needs to be addressed before a clinician is placed within a school concerns crisis planning and management. Unlike providing therapy off-site, where crises are typically reported retrospectively, school mental health clinicians are frequently asked to intervene directly in crisis situations. This requires clinicians to develop some comfort in dealing with emergencies (Tashman et al., 1998). Two types of crises typically occur within the school: those focused on individual students (e.g., suicidal or homicidal ideation and behavior, and physical or sexual abuse), and those occurring schoolwide (e.g., exposure to violence, death due to suicide, accident, natural disasters). With regard to the first type of crisis, clinicians need to be educated about how to explain the limits of confidentiality to students and families at the start of any formal treatment. Students need to be aware that a clinician cannot legally keep suicidal or homicidal intent or information about abuse or neglect confidential. If warranted, the clinician must contact protective services and give them an account of what has occurred. With regard to suicidal and homicidal ideation, student safety is a priority, so students cannot be left alone. The parent or guardian should be contacted and informed of what is occurring and what action is recommended. Additionally, some agreement should be reached about how and when school officials should be notified in instances where clinicians are concerned about a student being a danger to themself or others.

The second type of emergency affects the larger school community. It is recommended that schools form crisis teams before a crisis actually occurs (Warner & Weist, 1997). The crisis team should be comprised of key stakeholders from both the school and the larger community. Collision et al. (1987) recommend that several roles be assigned within this team: team coordinator, communications, medical provider, family liaison, information gatherer, security staff, resource staff, trainers, counselors, and school administrative staff. They recommend that the core group of the committee consist of the team coordinator, a lead counselor, a family liaison, and a designated school administrator. If a crisis were to occur, this core group would meet to discuss an initial plan and would then call on the larger team as appropriate. Once a crisis is identified, the team needs to assess the extent and breadth of the incident and determine if there are still safety concerns and who is in need of assistance. Following such assessment, interventions should be outlined and implemented. In addition to general debriefing, individual, group, and general supportive counseling should be made available to the school community. After the initial intervention, progress in the recovery process should be monitored and referrals should be made for those in need of additional services.

Introducing the program. The manner in which a program is introduced has important implications for how well received it is by the school community. School administrators can provide invaluable guidance on how to best introduce the program to students, staff, and families, and how to integrate the ESMH clinician into other programs or groups already in existence within the school. A letter of introduction given to staff and sent to parents is usually an effective way of introducing a new program to the community. New clinicians can also offer to make presentations during faculty meetings or homeroom periods to orient the students and staff about what the mental health program offers and how to make appropriate referrals. In addition, educational/media campaigns can be held within the school to help reduce the stigma related to mental health treatment. Misconceptions about mental health services can be addressed in these campaigns. ESMH clinicians are advised to form alliances within the school and make themselves available at convenient times to answer questions or address concerns from staff and families. Attending parent-teacher meetings, becoming a part of new student orientation, and assisting with schoolwide assemblies may provide additional opportunities for exposure of the ESMH program. More informally, the clinician can become a part of the school by attending school sporting events and other competitions, school performances, and school dances. Becoming involved in these more casual events can help students and staff feel comfortable with the clinician outside of the formal mental health role. All of these strategies will increase the visibility of the program and help market the expanded services available to staff, students, and families.

STAFFING, EDUCATION, AND TRAINING

Hiring. For ESMH programs to be successful, careful consideration needs be given to the hiring process. It is recommended that sufficient time be taken in the interview process to get a sense of each applicant's level of experience and general personality characteristics. Working in ESMH can be quite isolating and requires an ability to navigate through the politics of a school, handle crises calmly and effectively, and manage a large and clinically complex caseload. Beyond just solid clinical skills, a successful applicant is one who is energetic, flexible, independent, committed to helping youth, and able to establish rapport with children, families, and school staff. Consideration should also be given to overall program diversity. In order that the staff learn from one another, it can be helpful to have individuals representing several mental health professions, diverse ethnic and cultural backgrounds, and varied training and prior work experience. Another issue that may need to be considered when hiring staff concerns whether an applicant is licensable and meets the credentialing standards that may be required by MCOs. If a program is depending on a fee-for-service model for sustainability, the applicant may need to be licensed in order for any billing to occur.

Orientation. Once staff are hired, it is important for them to receive some orientation and training before they enter the school setting. Recommended orientation topics include: a history of the overall program, a history of each school in which a trainee is placed, necessary supplies, supervision, collaboration and integration into the school, expectations and roles, paperwork and billing, legal and ethical issues, reporting abuse, and crisis management. These topics need to be discussed before the clinician is placed within the school. Further, to help the clinician adjust to the school environment and be able to recognize some of the unique benefits of being in a school setting, new staff can be invited to shadow clinicians already in the ESMH program. This affords the new staff the opportunity to get a sense of how clinicians may structure their work and can also help them establish relationships with other clinical staff. Having the support of fellow clinicians and being able to seek advice from them is a crucial aspect of training. In addition, it is recommended that each new staff member be taken to his/her school, introduced to key staff, and given a tour by either a clinician placed in the same school or an administrator of the ESMH program who is familiar with the dynamics of the school. Orientation can also include exposure to different therapeutic techniques and tools that have worked well in the school setting.

Supervision. In addition to completing an orientation, each clinician should be assigned a clinical supervisor. Ideally, supervisors should be licensed providers with several years of experience in school mental health. They can be matched with clinicians such that they have expertise in the primary age group within the school. Supervisors serve not only in a managerial role, but also as mentors who assist clinicians in outlining career goals.

Not only should supervisors have strong clinical skills, but they should also be able to help the clinician navigate the system challenges offered within a school. Supervisors can help the clinician define his or her role as one that is separate and unique from other school staff. They can also suggest ways in which to collaborate with and create solid partnerships with key stakeholders within the school. Helping clinicians find a balance between the needs of the students and the needs of the school is a challenge that must be revisited throughout supervision.

Continuing education. Training and education continue to be important even after the orientation period ends. Education can occur on two levels: The first level concerns the professional development of clinicians, and the second level involves the educational development of the school community (Tashman et al., 1998). Clinicians can expand their training both informally and formally. Informally, clinicians can form peer support networks to discuss cases and review children's mental health books and studies, and can co-lead groups with other school staff. Forming these networks is not only educational, but can also help reduce the sense of isolation clinicians may experience in the school. More formal training experiences can include attending professional conferences and training workshops, taking graduate courses, and collaborating on grant writing and research projects. Training should be included as part of regularly scheduled program meetings and can also be a focus of program retreats.

In addition to expanding their own education, clinicians need to educate the school community at large (e.g., students, teachers, administrative staff, parents, community leaders) about what is meant by school mental health and why these services are being offered in the school. On a formal level, clinicians can attend and present staff development workshops at the school and provide information about when and what symptoms to look for in deciding whether to refer students to the ESMH program. Perhaps the best education about mental health will come from the students themselves. Students who have received help from clinicians often begin to refer their own friends and may set the tone for changing attitudes in their community. The extent of staff training and education is one component of an ESMH program that can be evaluated to provide a measure of the quality of clinical care being provided in the school.

QUALITY ASSURANCE AND EVALUATION

Systems of quality assurance and evaluation have an important place in an ESMH program. The quality assurance and evaluation component of an ESMH program gauges whether it is accomplishing its goals. It offers a built-in feedback mechanism that can provide critical information and guidance about needed areas of program improvement and development. Quality assurance programs typically utilize several strategies for assessing whether a program is effective. Common assessment strategies include the use of peer review teams, focus groups, standardized questionnaires, and interviews. Quality assurance programs strive to get input from all stakeholders, including clinicians, families, school staff, and students. Data collection is an ongoing process beginning in the ESMH program planning stage.

Mental health programs, more than ever before, are feeling the pressure from funding agencies to demonstrate that they are effective and are addressing the emotional, behavioral, and social needs of youth. In order to maintain and expand funding sources, it will be important for school-based programs to document the utilization and effectiveness of their programs. Programs that can demonstrate their impact may increase the likelihood of obtaining ongoing funding. Once evaluated, findings need to be readily available in a brief, easy-to-read format.

Planning for the evaluation of a program should occur in the early stages of development. A program may want to measure how counseling correlates with attendance, grades, disciplinary removals, and psychosocial functioning. Outcome measures need to be chosen carefully to reflect the types of changes that stakeholders deem important and that will highlight meaningful clinical changes in students' behavior. Consideration should be given to the reliability of assessment tools used, the applicability of each measure to the population of students being served, and the amount of time it will take stakeholders to complete the questionnaires. ESMH programs should not rely solely on self-report measures in their evaluation process but should also employ collateral information (e.g., from teachers and parents) to provide a variety of data that will highlight the positive impacts of a program. Further, program planners may determine, with the help of their advisory board, that certain indices of academic performance or behavior are important to include in their program evaluation. Ideally ESMH programs should document that stakeholders are satisfied with their services, that programs are doing what they are intended to do, and that there is measurable clinical improvement with students seen in the program.

CONCLUSION

Within this chapter a blueprint that can guide the development and implementation of ESMH programs has been offered. The actual application of these guidelines will vary depending on the structure and goals of individual programs and schools. The guidelines offer recommendations about activities that should occur before, during, and after programs are implemented into a school setting. With limited funding and resources available to many programs, it is important that programs learn from and share information with each other.

School mental health is a relatively new field. There are few documented standards of best practice available as a reference for new program planners. Core components of effective ESMH programs still need to be identified and distributed among programs and individuals interested in child mental health issues. Future empirical studies can help determine the types of programs that work best under particular circumstances (e.g., depending on the student population, school setting, level of community involvement, or presenting issues) and should inform program planners of the critical services that are essential to include in the development of an effective ESMH program. The recommendations outlined above speak more to the procedures and processes involved in developing ESMH programs than to the clinical services necessary for any school-based mental health program to succeed.

In addition to the development of standards of practice, program planners should mobilize communities to lobby and advocate for federal and state support of ESMH programs. This organized effort can help ensure that the school mental health movement continues to receive national recognition as a viable service delivery model for children and adolescents in need of mental health services. Establishing guidelines about the types of activities necessary for the successful implementation and sustainability of an ESMH program constitutes the first step in standardizing this process and provides some guidance about factors that support or undermine the expansion of ESMH in this country and worldwide.

ACKNOWLEDGMENT: Supported by project #MCJ24SH02-01-0 from the Office of Adolescent Health, Maternal and Child Health Bureau (Title V, Social Security Act), Health Resources and Services Administration, U.S. Department of Health and Human Services.

References

Acosta, O. M., Weist, M. D., Lopez, F. A., Shafer, M. E., & Pizarro, L. J. (1999). *Assessing the mental health and academic needs of Latino youth.* Unpublished manuscript.

Adelman, H. S., & Taylor, L. S. (1997). Addressing barriers to learning: Beyond school-linked services and full-service schools. *American Journal of Orthopsychiatry, 67,* 408–421.

Adelman, H. S., Taylor, L., Weist, M. D., Adelsheim, S., Freeman, B., Kapp, L., Lahti, M., & Mawn, D. (1999). Mental health in schools: A federal initiative. *Children's Services: Social Policy, Research, and Practice, 2*(2), 99–119.

Advocates for Youth. (1993). *A guide to school-based and school-linked health cen-*

ters, Volume III: Potential sources of federal support for school-based and school-linked health services. Washington, DC: Author.

Armbruster, P., Andrews, E., Couenhoven, J., & Blau, G. (1999). Collision or collaboration? School-based health services meet managed care. *Clinical Psychology Review, 19*(2), 221–237.

Armbruster, P., & Lichtman, J. (1999). Are school-based mental health services effective? Evidence from 36 inner-city schools. *Community Mental Health Journal, 35*(6), 493–504.

Bickham, N., Pizarro, L., Warner, B., Rosenthal, B., & Weist, M. (1998). Family involvement in expanded school mental health. *Journal of School Health, 68*(10), 425–428.

Brellochs, C., Zimmerman, D., Zink, T., & English, A. (1996). School-based primary care in a managed care environment: Options and issues. *Adolescent Medicine: State of the Art Reviews, 7*(2), 197–206

Center for School Mental Health Assistance (1997). *Funding: Managed care and school-based mental health.* Baltimore, MD: Author.

Center for School Mental Health Assistance. (1999). *Addressing resistance to expanded school mental health.* Baltimore, MD: Author.

Collision, B. B., Bowden, S., Patterson, M., Snyder, J., Sandall, S., & Wellman, P. (1987). After the shooting stops. *Journal of Counseling and Development, 65,* 389–390.

Evans, S. W. (1999). Mental health services in schools: Utilization, effectiveness and consent. *Clinical Psychology Review, 19,* 165–178.

Flaherty, L., Garrison, E., Waxman, R., Uris, P., Keys, S., Glass-Siegel, M. & Weist, M. (1998). Optimizing the roles of school mental health professionals. *Journal of School Health, 68*(10), 420–424.

Koppelman, J., & Lear, J. G. (1998). *The new child health insurance expansions: How will school-based health centers fit in?* Washington, DC: Making the Grade, George Washington University.

Lear, J. G., Eichner, N., & Koppelman, J. (1999). The growth of school-based health centers and the role of state policies. *Archives of Pediatrics & Adolescent Medicine, 153,* 1177–1180.

Making the Grade. (1998, spring). *Local funding for SBHCs: How did they do that?* Washington, DC: Author.

Nabors, L. A., Weist, M. D., Tashman, N. A., & Myers, C. P. (1999). Quality assurance and school-based mental health services. *Psychology in the Schools, 36,* 485–493.

National Association of State Boards of Education. (1999). *Building support for school health programs: An action guide.* Washington, DC: Author.

Rosenblum, L., DiCecco, M. B., Taylor, L., & Adelman, H. S. (1995). Upgrading school support programs through collaboration: Resource coordinating teams. *Social Work Education, 17,* 117–124.

School Health Resources Services. (1997). *School-based mental health programs: Funding strategies.* Denver, CO: University of Colorado Health Sciences Center.

Tashman, N. A., Waxman, R. P., Nabors, L., & Weist, M. D. (1998). The PREPARE approach to training clinicians in school mental health programs. *Journal of School Health, 68*(4), 162–164.

Warner, B. S., & Weist, M. D. (1997). *A crisis intervention plan for schools.* Unpublished manuscript.

Waxman, R., Weist, M., & Benson, D. (1999). Toward collaboration in the growing education–mental health interface. *Clinical Psychology Review, 19,* 239–253.

Weist, M. D. (1997). Expanded school mental health services: A national movement in progress. *Advances in Clinical Psychology, 19,* 319–352.

Weist, M. D., Myers, C. P., Danforth, J., McNeil, D. W., Ollendick, T. H., & Hawkins, R. (2000). Expanded school mental health services: Assessing needs related to school level and geography. *Community Mental Health Journal, 36,* 395–412.

Weist, M. D., Myers, C. P., Hastings, E., Ghuman, H., & Han, Y. L. (1999). Psychosocial functioning of youth receiving mental health services in the schools vs. community mental health centers. *Community Mental Health Journal, 35*(1), 69–91.

CHAPTER FOUR

Practical Issues in School Mental Health: Referral Procedures, Negotiating Special Education, and Confidentiality

Steven W. Evans, Ph.D., Jennifer L. Sapia, M.A., Jennifer Axelrod Lowie, Ph.D., and Nancy K. Glomb, M.A.

Theories and ideas regarding the development and implementation of school-based mental health services sound reasonable in their conceptualization, but often can be very daunting to implement. Practical issues related to referral procedures, special education regulations, and confidentiality can interfere with our ideas and plans. This chapter focuses on some of these practical issues that can impede a successful school mental health partnership and illustrates their importance through a description of the development and implementation of a school-based treatment program for students with attention-deficit/hyperactivity disorder (ADHD). Direct conversation and mutual agreement on referral procedures, the handling of special education issues, and confidentiality procedures should occur prior to the implementation of these collaborative projects. Each of these issues will be reviewed, followed by a description of how one school-based mental health program has addressed them.

REFERRAL PROCEDURES

Regardless of the types of services that a provider offers to children at a school, there needs to be some mechanism for referring and accepting those children into the program. Many schools have referral systems whereby teachers refer children who are demonstrating learning or behavior problems to a child study team. These teams are frequently composed of guidance counselors, school psychologists, administrators, and teachers who attempt to work with the referring teacher to assist him/her in helping the child. This assistance may include suggesting new teaching strategies, modifying behavior management plans, or developing ways that the teacher and the student's parents may effectively work together. Sometimes the child study team may recommend a referral for community health or mental health services, special education, or other internal or external evaluation or intervention services. Optimally, school-based mental health services should be one of the alternatives that the team has available for assisting teachers in addressing children's needs.

If the child study team believes school-based mental health services are appropriate, a member of the team or the referred child's teacher should make the initial contact with the parents to inform them of this recommendation. Sometimes school personnel prefer to give information about the child to the school-based mental health staff and let them contact the family. In spite of the possible convenience afforded by this option, it places the school-based mental health provider in the undesirable position of calling the parents to offer a service for their child that they may not know they need. In addition, parents may not have signed a release-of-information form to allow the school to talk about their child with the mental health provider. Therefore, it is important that school personnel complete the initial contact with the parents to inform them of the problems they believe the child is exhibiting and their recommendations regarding potential intervention services. After explaining the problems and recommendations to the parents, it is important that the school provide parents with a variety of options for obtaining assistance. School districts should avoid exclusively referring to one provider, since this practice could have implications for unethical business practices and potential liability by the district for any mistakes made by the mental health provider.

Once a parent contacts a school-based mental health provider about obtaining services, the provider usually begins the intake process by asking parents to complete forms and evaluation procedures. The forms are an important but sometimes cumbersome portion of this process, as they are time-consuming. The completion of consent-for-treatment and release-of-information forms does help demonstrate to the parents that the provider is a separate entity from the school. In addition, it provides a forum for careful discussion of issues such as payment, confidentiality, the storage of clinical records, and the differences between children's and parents' legal rights in the mental health system as compared to the education system. Clarifying these issues at the beginning of treatment is standard practice in the mental health field; however, the provision of services at a school can lead to inaccurate expectations by parents that need to be clarified before the initiation of services.

The range of services provided at a school is frequently less than what is offered at a clinic. Therefore, students will be referred whose needs exceed the services that can be provided at a school. A careful evaluation is an important step in determining which students' needs can be met by the school-based services. It is vital to avoid the temptation to assume that an available service is necessarily an appropriate service. Some of the most frequently delivered school-based interventions, such as social skills training, are clearly ineffective and insufficient for many children. An evaluation to identify those children for whom these interventions are not appropriate is crucial. Once the evaluation is completed, the provider can supply the parents with valuable information about the nature of their child's problems and specific recommendations about appropriate services. Furthermore, an evaluation that takes advantage of the vast amount of data available in the school through observations, functional assessments, interviews, and historical records will probably be far more accurate and informative than one completed based solely on interaction and conversation at a clinic.

SPECIAL EDUCATION REGULATIONS

Children who receive both special education and school-based mental health services can be a challenge to administrators. For example, one difficult administrative issue is deciding whether services provided by school-based mental health services should be listed on a child's Individualized Education Plan (IEP). If the services are listed on the IEP, then school districts are required to provide them and pay for them. This means that third-party payers may decline payment. In addition, if the school-based mental health partnership is discontinued, the district is still required to obtain and provide these services. Since school-based mental health services frequently target many of the problems that lead to children's qualifying for special education, many parents have successfully argued that they be listed on the IEP. These issues have led some administrators to be very cautious about what services are placed on an IEP and have resulted in concerns about the provision of school-based mental health services. Before addressing these specific issues, a review of special education laws and procedures is presented.

When students who are receiving school-based mental health services are also receiving special education services through the Individuals with

Disabilities Education Act (IDEA), the coordination of services can be greatly enhanced. However, while some special education classifications are similar to those included in the fourth edition of the Diagnostic and Statistical Manual (DSM-IV), the eligibility criteria for special education services can differ from DSM-IV diagnostic criteria. The development of collaborative partnerships between educators and mental health professionals can facilitate a clear articulation of these differences as well as the parameters and limitations of each service. An overview of special education legislation and procedures is very useful when attempting to establish and maintain these partnerships.

PUBLIC LAW 105-17: THE INDIVIDUALS WITH DISABILITIES EDUCATION ACT AMENDMENTS OF 1997

The Individuals with Disabilities Education Act Amendments of 1997, commonly referred to as IDEA '97, is the current federal legislation that guarantees appropriate educational services to all school-aged children with disabilities. According to this legislation, students with disabilities include those with specific learning disabilities, mental retardation, emotional disturbance, hearing impairments, speech or language impairments, visual impairments, orthopedic impairments, autism, traumatic brain injury, or other health impairments. The specific eligibility criteria for these classifications can be accessed through each state's department of education. Table 4.1 includes a summary of the provisions of IDEA '97 and other key federal legislation impacting school-aged children with disabilities. Additional information regarding IDEA '97 can be found at www.ed.gov/offices/OSERS/IDEA.

Special education services under IDEA '97 are designed to provide accommodations for students whose disability adversely affects their educational performance. The goal of special education is to ensure that students with disabilities have the same access to a free, appropriate, and beneficial educational experience as their nondisabled peers. In essence, special education "levels the playing field." To determine whether special accommodations are necessary, the child study team monitors the steps in the special education process as defined by IDEA '97.

The first step in this process is to identify students who may be in need of educational accommodations. Referrals may come from classroom teachers, parents, school counselors, school psychologists, social welfare agencies, community mental health agencies, and physicians. If the referred student is receiving educational services in a general education classroom at the time of the referral, many states require that classroom teach-

TABLE 4.1. Key Federal Legislation Impacting School-Aged Children with Disabilities

Section 504 of the Vocational Rehabilitation Act of 1973

Provides that:

- "no otherwise qualified handicapped individual in the United States . . . shall, solely by reason of his handicap, be excluded from the participation in, be denied the benefits of, or be subjected to discrimination under any program or activity receiving federal financial assistance."
- all school-age children with disabilities are entitled to a free and appropriate education, but does not include funding provisions.

Public Law 94-142: The Education for All Handicapped Children Act of 1975

Provides that:

- all students with disabilities are guaranteed a free, appropriate public education.
- the assessment procedures used to evaluate students with disabilities must be nondiscriminatory with respect to race, ethnicity, language, culture, or disability.
- students with disabilities must have an Individualized Education Plan (IEP).
- to the greatest extent possible, students with disabilities must be educated in the "least restrictive environment" with their non-disabled peers.
- parents have the right to participate in planning and monitoring their child's educational program.
- students with disabilities and their parents have the right to due process.
- federal funding is available to support the education of students with disabilities.

Public Law 101-476: The Individuals with Disabilities Education Act (IDEA)

Amended PL 94-142 to include:

- eligibility criteria for autism and traumatic brain injury as specific disability classifications.
- rehabilitation counseling and social work to the list of appropriate related services.
- community-based instruction for students with disabilities.
- the requirement that transition services be included in a student's IEP by age 16.

Public Law 105-17: The Individuals with Disabilities Education Act Amendments of 1997

Provides that:

- children between the ages of 3 and 10 may be considered for eligibility for special education services under the classification "developmentally delayed."
- students with disabilities receive the necessary accommodations to participate in state- and district-wide assessments whenever possible.

(*Continued*)

TABLE 4.1. Key Federal Legislation Impacting School-Aged Children with Disabilities, Continued

- the IEP include a statement about the extent of the student's involvement in the general education curriculum.
- the IEP team must include general education teachers if the student will be involved in general education activities.
- schools articulate specific procedures for disciplining students with disabilities for drugs, alcohol, weapons, and injury to self or others.
- charter schools must serve students with disabilities.

ers attempt to address the student's difficulty by implementing and documenting "pre-referral interventions" before the process of formally referring a student for assessment can begin.

The next step in the special education process is to evaluate the student's educational needs and determine whether special accommodations are necessary. Parents should be collaborative members of the team, and must provide written and informed consent for their child to be evaluated. If the student is found to be eligible for special education services according to IDEA, the team is responsible for designing an Individualized Education Plan (IEP). An IEP includes (1) the student's current levels of performance; (2) a statement of measurable short-term objectives and annual goals; (3) a statement of the special educational and related services required to meet the student's needs; (4) a statement regarding the extent to which the student will participate in the regular classroom; (5) modifications to state and school division assessments; (6) the projected date for the beginning of services; (7) a statement of transition services; and (8) evaluation procedures.

Some students may not be eligible for special education services according to the criteria established in IDEA '97 but may qualify for services under Section 504 of the Rehabilitation Act of 1973 (see Table 4.1). Services for children who have been diagnosed according to the DSM-IV criteria as having attention-deficit/hyperactivity disorder (ADHD) are often articulated in a 504 Plan, a written document that includes recommended modifications for ensuring that a student is not treated differentially as a function of his or her disability. It is not as extensive as an IEP and is not mandated. Examples of recommended modifications for students with ADHD that might appear on a 504 Plan are supplementing verbal instructions with visual instructions and modifying instructional materials to reduce distractions (U.S. Department of Education, 1991). ADHD is not included in the current version of IDEA as an educational disability, although some students with ADHD do receive special education services because they meet criteria for a learning disability, emotional disturbance, or other health impairments.

When school-based mental health services are part of the mix of services for a child in special education, it is important for special educators and mental health professionals to clearly articulate the parameters of each type of service. Special education services, as mandated by law, provide educational accommodations to students with disabilities that adversely impact educational performance; however, this has come to be interpreted as including medical and mental health services that are deemed necessary to allow a child access to a free and appropriate public education. Therefore, until there is greater clarification on the extent of our schools' responsibility for the provision of mental health care, there are risks associated with any decision in this area. Some administrators have feared that by having school-based mental health services available in their school, they increase the risk for litigation in this area.

Our typical strategy has been to not list the school-based mental health services on the IEP. The rationale for this omission has been that mental health services provided at a community-based clinic are typically not listed on students' IEPs and similar logic should apply to services located in a school. This argument has not been tested in the courts and is not a legal opinion; however, it is an arrangement that has been accepted by many school districts that we have worked with and has been used by other programs across the country. The value of resolving this issue is that students in special education are often those most likely to get referred for school-based mental health services. In addition, by being in special education, these students have a special education teacher whose orientation and role is often similar to that of school-based mental health providers. This frequently results in tremendous opportunities for collaboration that can result in substantial benefits to the referred student.

LIMITS OF CONFIDENTIALITY

There are large differences between practices pertaining to confidentiality in the mental health and education fields. Confidentiality procedures tend to be much less conservative in a school than they are in a mental health practice. While both may be very appropriate for their own purposes, the provision of school-based mental health services may result in these differences leading to problematic and/or awkward situations. Problems can be minimized if the mental health provider and school personnel discuss these differences prior to initiating services and establish specific confidentiality procedures.

Neither the mental health provider nor the school can realistically be expected to completely conform to the standard of the other. There is considerable temptation for the mental health provider to loosen its confidentiality standards to accommodate to the school. Furthermore, educators may be offended if they have embraced the mental health provider's overtures for collaboration and partnership only to learn that records and other information pertaining to each child will not be available to them. The main tenets of mental health procedures, which involve active consent for all procedures and the revealing of information only on a need-to-know basis and only in conjunction with appropriate releases, still apply. In fact, the importance of these procedures has been recently documented by reports that one of the reasons that students and parents avoid school-based mental health services is a perception that confidentiality will not be maintained (Adelman et al., 1993; Evans, 1999).

Implementing appropriate confidentiality procedures from the beginning, including the off-site storage of charts and the use of releases, are important parts of starting a program. In addition, clinicians will need to limit their discussions with teachers and other school personnel to only that information which is necessary for their role with the student. Beginning with these procedures in place is important for the development of appropriate expectations.

Working in a school setting has a "fishbowl" quality to it. Mistakes can quickly become apparent to many people. For example, problems can arise when parents come to meet with a school-based provider and it is clear from the conversation that the clinician has more information about the child than what the parent provided during the initial phone call. This confusion may be further exacerbated when the clinician asks the parent to sign a release to allow communication between educators and the clinician when it is obvious that this communication has already occurred. In addition to the ethical violations inherent in this example, the situation will result in a lack of trust between the parents and the clinician.

Strict adherence to these confidentiality guidelines will sometimes be awkward. Most breaches of these procedures are the result of well-intentioned behavior and frequently go unnoticed. Nevertheless, adherence to these standards is a necessary ingredient to establishing trust, which is the core element of clinical relationships and reputation. While some infractions may go unnoticed, it only takes one violation for the clinical relationships and reputation of a school mental health partnership to be destroyed. When appropriate expectations are established at the beginning of a school mental health relationship, these procedures become automatic, the awkwardness dissipates, and many risks for a failed project are diminished.

Referral procedures, special education issues, and confidentiality procedures are critical elements in the initial arrangements of school-based mental health services. While discussion of these issues can temper the initial enthusiasm for school-based services, it is important to avoid the temptation to neglect these topics. Following is a description of the development of a school-based mental health program. This account of its evolution describes how its developers addressed some of these issues. In addition, some of the other specific programmatic information is provided to broaden the focus of practical issues addressed.

A Case Example—The Challenging Horizons Program

The Challenging Horizons Program (CHP) is a school-based mental health program that provides treatment for middle school students with attention-deficit/hyperactivity disorder (ADHD). It operates out of the Human Development Center at James Madison University and is a collaborative project with the Rockingham County Schools. The services are provided at Montevideo Middle School outside of Harrisonburg, Virginia. The program utilizes techniques developed in the adolescent version of the Summer Treatment Program (Pelham & Hinshaw, 1992) when it operated at Western Psychiatric Institute and Clinic (WPIC) in Pittsburgh (e.g., Evans, Pelham, & Grudberg, 1995). These techniques were combined with the school-based mental health methodology developed in the Bridges for Education program also operated at WPIC and gleaned from the work of numerous other individuals working in the field and sharing their work in text, at conferences, and in person. The synthesis of these techniques is an after-school treatment program that operates three days per week during the school year. Family therapy and school consultation, observations, and generalization plans operate outside the hours of the program. The program began on November 15, 1999, and this section of the chapter chronicles its development as an example of many of the points described in the beginning of this chapter.

The first step in developing the CHP was to form working partnerships between the Human Development Center and a local school district. In an effort to establish ties in the community and find a willing school participant, the director of the CHP began by talking to educators, mental health providers, and pediatricians in the community to gather recommendations for a school that would be an ideal place to start this program. Following the lead of these recommendations, discussions were initiated with the principal of Montevideo Middle School. At this time, it was useful to have a preliminary brochure and written description of the program available. Meeting with the school principal was crucial, as his enthusiastic support was necessary not only for program implementation, but also that he might serve as a guide through the administrative process. The presentations to both the principal and school officials focused on the key issues of service access and the likely increase in treatment effectiveness. A useful strategy in these initial discussions was to keep the focus of the conversation on what was going to be the most beneficial for children. This principle should guide decision making and hopefully reflect the priorities of the program. The community recommendations for a starting point were quite valuable in this situation, as the priorities, energy, and organization of this school were ideally suited to developing a partnership and program such as the CHP.

The organizational discussions with the principal and school administrators resulted in some changes to the design of the services being proposed. These modifications were the result of compromises, cost issues, and suggestions for improvements. The final product was enhanced as a result of this collaborative planning. Specific issues such as starting dates, selection of space, teacher involvement, and student recruitment were some of the final details arranged. In the case of the CHP, it was necessary to articulate that only a limited number of students (ten to twelve children) would be able to participate at any one time, due to constraints of staffing and the desire to provide a comprehensive service. In addition, the rationale for restricting the program to youth with ADHD was also discussed. This was because the program was developed for youth with that disorder, and to ensure the integrity of its implementation and effectiveness, youth with other emotional/behavioral disorders were not included. The CHP has a very focused mission in that it provides long-term intensive services to a fairly small number of youth.

Once the principal, school administration, and program leadership agreed upon the global plans for the program, the next task was to present this information to the teaching staff and solicit their input on specific practices and procedures. This task was accomplished through attending staff meetings, child study team meetings, and informal encounters with teachers to answer individual questions and to gather feedback about possible referrals and obstacles to program implementation. Again, programmatic and procedural changes were made as a result of these presentations and discussions.

After the principal, school administrators, and teachers had worked with the program leadership to develop the program, the next step was to present the information to parents. This was accomplished through multiple methods. Presentations to the PTA were made, outlining the program as well as providing general information about ADHD and its impact on middle school–aged children. The director of the CHP also met with a smaller group of parents who were actively involved in school leadership. As with the other steps of this process, parents were invited to have input into the program design and procedures.

Throughout these series of discussions with administrators, teachers, and parents, referral procedures, implications for special education, and confidentiality limits were discussed. Applications of the principles outlined in the first part of this chapter were individualized to this school setting and the CHP. From the beginning, we established the rationale for the procedures discussed and the expectations for practices pertaining to these issues. By doing so, we created a foundation that has resulted in our experiencing no problems in these areas up to this point. While the proactive work described in this chapter does not guarantee the absence of problems, it reduces the risks. Furthermore, if problems do arise, lines of communication have already been established on these issues that should help to manage the difficulty.

As we began to implement the program we distributed brochures to teachers before parent-teacher conferences so that they could provide information to the parents of children who appeared to be eligible and who would benefit from the intensive intervention that the CHP offered. Teachers and counselors began distributing the brochures, and parents decided whether to contact the CHP for additional information. This practice protected parents' confidentiality and ensured that they were invested, since they had to contact the program directly rather than be contacted.

When parents called the CHP, treatment services and the referral process were explained and they were sent an application packet and assessment measures. This step served a dual purpose. First, parents had to be invested in the program to complete the measures. Second, the assessment measures provided information for an initial screening to ensure that enrollment in the CHP was appropriate. Initial screening measures were selected for their usefulness in identifying children with ADHD and the type and severity of impairment. They included a broad-based standardized measure of behavior to be completed by parents and two teachers. In addition, both parents and teachers completed an ADHD rating scale and a measure of functional impairment. Cross-situational ratings were sought in accordance with the DSM-IV criteria that the problems must occur in multiple settings. Parents also completed a data form detailing previous interventions, diagnoses, special education classifications, and general information (e.g., parents' educational levels and marital status, siblings' ages and names, and contact information). In order to protect parent confidentiality, parents were asked to deliver teacher packets to the school and to have the school send the information to the program. At this stage, the program did not have permission to exchange information with the school and therefore could not contact teachers directly. These initial screening instruments were crucial for determining the appropriate placement of students in the program. Once the screening instruments were returned to the program staff, they were scored and the case was reviewed. If there was a strong indication that the child met formal diagnostic criteria for ADHD and was experiencing significant impairment at home, at school, and with friends, the child was admitted to the program and a comprehensive evaluation began. If the screening data were less than convincing, then after obtaining signed consents and releases a comprehensive evaluation was completed prior to the child's being admitted. The comprehensive evaluation included the administration of the WISC-III, WIAT, and DISC-IV. Following this, a counselor in the CHP met with the parents to explain the assessment results. If the evaluation indicated that the child did meet the criteria for ADHD (with or without other comorbid conditions) then the child was admitted to the program. On the contrary, if the results of the evaluation indicated that the child's problems were not related to ADHD, then the child was referred elsewhere for services. For example, one child's parents contacted the program, and after the initial measures were completed it appeared that his presenting problems were not likely to be addressed in the program and a diagnosis of ADHD did not appear to be warranted. Program staff completed evaluation procedures and it was determined that the child's problems were primarily related to depressive symptomatology and unrelated to ADHD. This child was referred for individual treatment to appropriately address the presenting problems.

Once a child has been accepted into the CHP, the child and his/her parents attend an introductory meeting with the CHP director and a staff member to explain the details of the program, expectations, and procedural issues (e.g., meeting days, times, agenda, evaluation procedures), and to complete additional forms including emergency contacts and medication history. This meeting provides an individualized forum to begin establishing a good working relationship with parents, and to clarify any issues regarding treatment, expectations, and misconceptions about the program. This meeting also affords the opportunity for program staff and the child to discuss any apprehension the child may have about attending the first day.

If the child has not been evaluated prior to admission, he or she receives the assessment battery described above after beginning the program. A review of the child's academic records provides educational history regarding grades, attendance, previous assessments, and/or special education classifications and IEP. Since the evaluation procedures can be cumbersome to parents, clinicians make every effort to work with the school to try and arrange mutually convenient times to assess the child during the regular school day. This limits the onus on parents to take time off from work to transport the child to the clinic site for assessments. In addition to the initial assessments, there are ongoing assessments completed throughout the academic year. Every six weeks, corresponding to the end of the grading period, the primary counselors update each child's academic data form (e.g., grades, attendance, and disciplinary actions for that grading period). In addition, a medication assessment update is completed with parents to record any medication changes. At the end of each semester, parents and the same two teachers who initially completed the assessment instruments complete them again to assess progress.

Intervention strategies are individually developed for each child based on the assessment information. The first step in the development of an intervention is to identify a deficient skill or inappropriate behavior (e.g., inability to take effective notes). This skill is then taught to the student in isolation (notetaking practice at the program) or the behaviors are modified. Following the child's development of competencies in this area, gradual programming for the generalization of these skills is implemented. The CHP is designed to enhance the development and generalization of skills, since children need to be trained in the requisite skills in the program in order to set up behavioral contingencies in the classroom. First, a set of prompts is established with the child that s/he is comfortable with and assessment procedures to be used in the child's natural setting (e.g., classroom, home, school bus) are designed. Therapist presence in the classroom is an example of a salient prompt for generalization, allowing the therapist to directly assess implementation of the skill by the child and the related functional contingencies. However, the therapist is rarely present in the classroom environment and hence must rely on teachers to assist with the prompts and assessment procedures. This is where collaborative working relationships with teachers are essential. Teachers may complete rating scales, provide daily or weekly report cards, furnish descriptive accounts, and complete other monitoring techniques that provide data that can be used to track progress and for the establishment of home or program contingencies. As with most behavioral interventions, this process of initial assessment, implementation, assessment, and revision is continued until the goals have been achieved.

PROGRAM ROUTINE

At the end of the school day, the participating children come to the school cafeteria for the program services. The initial activity is a snack and informal conversation between the students and counselors. Following this period, daily announcements are made and then each child meets with his/her primary counselor. The goals of these meetings are to establish a therapeutic relationship with the child, to identify and prioritize goals, to negotiate and implement interventions, and to monitor progress on goals. The establishment of an individual therapeutic relationship with each child is essential, as it functions as the conduit through which all interventions are implemented.

The counselors begin by developing two to three specific goals with their students. The process leading to these goals stems from discussions related to the child's self-image and reputation, family relations, academic standing, and social status. The child's perspective is often adopted in these initial goals. For example, a teacher's complaints of disruptive behavior are often described from the student's viewpoint as a desire to "have the teacher quit picking on me." The debating of perceptions is avoided at this point by adopting the student's perspective and developing strategies for what the student can do so that the teacher "quits picking on him." Primary counselors work with their supervisors, the child's parents and teachers, and the treatment team to develop goals, methods, and measurement techniques for two to three goals for each child. These are reviewed weekly in the primary meetings, and the student and his/her primary counselor graph progress every Thursday. The primary meetings are the forum for establishing, modifying, and measuring progress on goals in the context of a one-on-one therapeutic relationship.

GROUP THERAPY AND SKILLS TRAINING

Following the primary meeting, the students attend a group intervention. Groups are selected and tailored to meet the needs of each child. Three specific groups that are in operation in the program are for interpersonal skills, cognitive-behavioral therapy, and handwriting. Students experiencing significant conflict and communication difficulties with their parents and/or peers are placed in the interpersonal skills group, which focuses on helping children develop effective methods of communicating with parents, coping with their anger during conflicts, and creating appropriate strategies for getting their needs met. Students are assigned homework to help them understand and practice these goals outside of the group setting. Assigned practice is reviewed at the group meetings and serves as the context for continued work in this area. Students with low self-esteem and other mood disorder symptoms participate in the cognitive-behavioral therapy (CBT) group. While the efficacy of this treatment with youth with ADHD has been questioned (Abikoff, 1991), it has never been evaluated with adolescents with ADHD and is one of the most supported treatments for youth with depressive symptoms. The CBT group addresses students' beliefs and cognitions and provides strategies for changing irrational beliefs and thoughts related to depressive symptoms. This intervention does not target any of the three core symptoms of ADHD. Students are taught a CBT program that includes homework to increase generalization. Homework assignments are completed in primary meetings, in classrooms, and at home. The third group focuses on the remediation of handwriting deficits. A considerable number of the youth referred to this program have significant problems with the legibility of their writing, and the handwriting group has evolved out of that need. The group starts with very elementary concepts of cursive letter formation and then progresses to requiring students to use these skills during other program activities and then on school assignments.

RECREATION TIME

Recreation time is an essential part of the program, not only as a fun, social time but also as a forum to begin to practice some of the individual goals in a controlled setting. Many children have goals related to interpersonal skills and learning how to be a contributing member of a group. Goals and practice can be integrated into this recreation time. For example, one of the students in the program had difficulty sharing the ball and including other players in the game, resulting in peers becoming increasingly frustrated with her. Her counselor established and operationalized a goal focused on involving other players. This was measured by the number of times the child passed the ball in basketball, made appropriate comments to other children, and appropriately managed her frustration/anger (i.e., did not quit or push another player). These behaviors were counted during games and she was rewarded for reaching preestablished levels of these skills (i.e., passing more times than she shot the ball). This was a real problem for this student since she was participating in a recreation league basketball team and was receiving criticism from coaches and rejection from her peers for these behaviors.

At the beginning of some of the recreational periods a certain interpersonal skill is presented and students discuss methods of exhibiting it and practicing it during the activity. Following a period of recreational activity, the group reconvenes to review and discuss their success in exhibiting the skills. The activity is then resumed with a similar follow-up session at the end. Another variation on the recreation theme involves the counselors withdrawing from the activity. For example, the counselors may throw a basketball out onto the floor and instruct the students to get a game started. After a few minutes, the counselors pull the group together and discuss their relative success with this activity. This "less-supervised" version of the recreation time usually results in a number of arguments and some pushing and shoving. These are exactly the emotionally charged situations we strive for in our controlled practice training, since they present a wonderful opportunity to target skill deficits and implement generalization plans. Furthermore, this practice simulates real situations that these students face when attempting to participate in social and recreational situations with their peers.

EDUCATION TIME

The activities during the first half-hour of the education period shift their focus every other week. One week the activities focus on notetaking and study skills, and the next week on written language. These areas of emphasis continue to alternate and are based on interventions and findings in the literature pertaining to adolescents with ADHD (Evans et al., 1995; Evans et al., 1999).

During the notetaking and study skills weeks, activities are designed to parallel classroom experience, but the time frame is shortened to allow for the repeated practice of skills. Specifically, each Monday the students are presented with a lecture and/or group discussion about a topic from one of the school's science or social studies texts. In the context of this lecture, students are taught notetaking and questioning skills relevant to a classroom presentation of information. During the lecture the group leader stops to discuss and help students determine what information should be recorded in their notes. This process is repeated every other Monday, and gradually the group leader fades the prompts used to solicit the notes, resulting in the notetaking responsibility being transferred to the students.

On Tuesdays these notes are used to study for a quiz that occurs on Thursdays. One of the study skills taught in the program is summarizing. Verbal and written summaries involve having the students either write or tell a counselor about the lecture, including enough information that s/he could succeed on the quiz. The students are instructed to pretend that the counselors are approximately two to three years younger than them and did not hear the lecture. These assumptions force the students to explain the information instead of just reading their notes. Counselors are trained to encourage students to be specific and to question vague statements. Once a student has gained some competency in these techniques, the primary counselor adds goals pertaining to the generalization of these skills. The family counselors help to facilitate the use of these techniques at home.

During the weeks that focus on written language the activities begin with writing a rough draft of a document on Monday. This document may be fiction or nonfiction and may take the form of a story, report, letter, or whatever seems appropriate. The students spend the entire time writing, although prewriting exercises (e.g., outlining) are sometimes included in this day's activities. On Tuesdays the students focus on revising and editing the document. On Thursdays these stories are rewritten into a final draft form or further revising and editing occurs. The counselors integrate these skills into their treatment goals and develop generalization plans accordingly.

During the final fifteen minutes of education time the primary counselors meet with the student and review his/her assignment notebook to ensure that everything is accurately recorded and the student has all of the requisite books and materials to take home to complete the assignments. Sometimes this time is used to clean out lockers or book bags. In addition, when time permits a student may start some of his or her homework.

OTHER INTERVENTIONS

In addition to the treatment activities that occur during program hours, the CHP also provides family therapy, in-school observation, assessment, and consultation with teachers. When a student enters the CHP s/he is assigned a family therapist. This individual works with the family using procedures similar to those described by Robin and Foster (1989). One of the first tasks of the family therapist is to assess existing homework management strategies and help the family manage homework. The family therapist assesses and prioritizes problems for the family and then proceeds with strategies to help facilitate the parent-adolescent relationship through improved communication, problem-solving, and behavior management techniques.

In addition to family therapy, the CHP counselors maintain consistent communication with the students' teachers to monitor academic progress and behaviors. They complete initial observations of the majority of each student's classes to familiarize themselves with the contexts and expectations of those classes. The counselors also complete functional assessments of the target behaviors to identify those contingencies that are maintaining the disruptive behaviors and to determine what contingencies are available that may help reinforce new behaviors. When goals for target behaviors have been achieved in the program, the counselor then works with the teachers to develop generalization plans to transfer the behaviors to the classroom settings. Similarly, these plans may be established with lunch monitors, parents, or other adults. Usually the counselor goes to the classroom or other setting as the first step in the generalization plan in order to observe the student's attempts at the new behavior, monitor his/her progress, and identify potential obstacles to his/her success. The counselor's presence is then replaced with different prompts and measures such as daily report cards and other mechanisms.

SUMMARY

The CHP is unique in some respects and typical in others. Its procedures are documented in a program manual and it targets middle school youth with a specific diagnosis. Doctoral interns, graduate students, and undergraduate students staff the program. While students are less expensive than typical employees, their rotation through the experience places heavy demands on the training component of the program. This demand is facilitated by the use of a treatment manual and training procedures that are not only useful to the functioning of the current program, but also help to make it transportable.

The organizational challenges of confidentiality policies, referral procedures, and special education regulations impact the CHP as they would most any program. Similarly, the procedures for initially developing and implementing the CHP were similar to most school-based mental health programs. As stated at the beginning of this chapter, theories and ideas regarding program development sound reasonable in their conceptualization, but often can be very daunting to implement. Nevertheless, accepting the challenge to develop these services can be the most rewarding professional experience available and is greatly needed to advance our field.

References

Abikoff, H. (1991). Cognitive training in ADHD children: Less to it than meets the eye. *Journal of Learning Disabilities, 24,* 205–209.

Adelman, H. S., Barker, L. A., & Nelson, P. (1993). A study of a school-based clinic: Who uses it and who doesn't? *Journal of Clinical Psychology, 22,* 52–59.

Evans, S. W. (1999). Mental health services in schools: Utilization, effectiveness, and consent. *Clinical Psychology Review, 19,* 165–178.

Evans, S. W., Axelrod, J. L., & Sapia, J. L. (2000). Effective school-based interventions: The development of a social skills training paradigm. *Journal of School Health, 70,* 191–195.

Evans, S. W., Pelham, W. E., Gnagy, E., Smith, B., & Molina, B. (1999). Behavioral and educational interventions to improve academic performance in youth with ADHD. In S. Evans (Chair), *Effective strategies for behavior therapists in schools.* Symposium conducted at the annual meeting of the Association for the Advancement of Behavioral Therapy, Toronto, Canada.

Evans, S. W., Pelham, W., & Grudberg, M. V. (1995). The efficacy of notetaking to improve behavior and comprehension of adolescents with attention deficit hyperactivity disorder. *Exceptionality, 5,* 1–17.

Gresham, F. M. (1998). Social skills training: Should we raze, remodel, or rebuild. *Behavioral Disorders, 24,* 19–25.

Pelham, W. E., & Hinshaw, S. P. (1992). Behavioral intervention for ADHD. In S. M. Turner, K. S. Calhoun, & H. E. Adams (Eds.) *Handbook of clinical behavior therapy* (pp.259–283). New York: John Wiley & Sons.

Robin, A. L., & Foster, S. L. (1989). *Negotiating parent adolescent conflict: A behavioral–family systems approach.* New York: Guilford Press.

Stokes, T. F., & Osnes, P. G. (1989). An operant pursuit of generalization. *Behavior Therapy, 20,* 337–355.

United States Department of Education. (1991). *Memorandum: Clarification of policy to address the needs of children with attention deficit disorders within general education and/or special education.* Office of Special Education and Rehabilitative Services.

C H A P T E R   F I V E

Evaluation and Quality Improvement in School Mental Health

Melissa Grady Ambrose, L.C.S.W.C., Mark D. Weist, Ph.D., Cindy Schaeffer, M.A., Laura A. Nabors, Ph.D., and Susan Hill, M.A.

INTRODUCTION

Mental health programs are under increasing pressure to demonstrate accountability, which refers to the obligations of these programs to assure that high-quality services related to positive outcomes are being provided (Hoagwood, Jensen, Petti, & Burns, 1996; Mattson, 1984). In fact, the press for accountability in health care has become a national theme (President's Advisory Commission on Consumer Protection and Quality in the Health Care Industry, 1998). Material presented in this chapter provides school-based mental health programs with important information about acquiring accountability data with which to document the quality and effectiveness of their services.

Literature reviewing ways to improve the quality of mental health services for children (Hoagwood et al., 1996; Kutash, Duchnowski, & Sondheimer, 1994) underscores the importance of integrating quality assurance and improvement ideas in programs for youth. This research is moving the field toward a standard in which children's mental health programs have well-developed and evolving plans for ensuring that goals and services are consistent with those of stakeholders (e.g., youth, families, school staff, community leaders), and that mechanisms are in place to ensure program efficiency, cost-effectiveness, consumer satisfaction, and impacts on desired outcomes. Guidelines for developing quality improvement programs are available from the National Committee for Quality Assurance (NCQA) (1995), a branch of the Office of Health Maintenance Organizations, and the Agency for Health Care Policy and Research (AHCPR, 1990; Raskin & Maklan, 1991). A continuous quality improvement evaluation consists of activities evaluating (1) the impact of treatment (outcomes); (2) the building blocks of effective programs, such as training and supervision, quality assurance, wraparound service planning, and collaboration; (3) the process of treatment — or what occurs during therapy sessions; and (4) the satisfaction of children, families, and mental health clinicians with the treatment that was provided (Nabors, Weist, Holden, & Tashman, 1999).

In 1998, a national conference was sponsored by the Association for Health Services Research (AHSR) to develop a research agenda for children's health services. At this conference seven workgroups developed research priorities in a document entitled *Improving Quality of Health Care for Children: An Agenda for Research*. Priorities included monitoring the health of children, assessing the quality of health care provided to children, improving the quality of health care within health systems, and assessing the performance of community systems for children and adolescents. The research priorities were broadly stated to cover: (1) implementing measures of the quality of care in program evaluations on a routine basis; (2) investigating the impact of prevention activities; (3) conducting cost, outcome, and efficiency studies; and (4) incorporating stakeholder perceptions (e.g., satisfaction surveys and needs assessment) into program development. This type of research agenda fits with the mission statement and standards for many expanded school mental health (ESMH) programs, which provide an array of mental health care (assessment, treatment, prevention, case management) to youth in general and special education (Weist, 1997; Flaherty & Weist, 1999).

Although it may be difficult to implement quality improvement and program evaluation activities in ESMH programs due to fiscal and time constraints, these activities are critically important for several reasons. First, evaluating the effectiveness of services will provide accountability data that may help to ensure program sustainability. Second, information from these activities can be used to inform clinical practice efforts. Relatedly, quality improvement and evaluation represent the nexus between research and practice, providing a forum whereby research informs practice and vice versa. Third, while ESMH programs are growing rapidly in the United States, evaluation of them has not kept pace. It is imperative for this emerging field to be able to document that the increasing resources going into

ESMH programs are matched by positive outcomes for the youth served by them.

PROGRAM EVALUATION

Expanded school mental health programs are being developed in many communities in the U.S. (e.g., Albuquerque, Baltimore, Cincinnati, Dallas, Memphis, Philadelphia, Pittsburgh, Memphis), and mission statements for these programs reflect the goal of providing state-of-the-art mental health care to youth. Formal quality improvement and evaluation programs are central to meeting the goals of these mission statements (Armbruster, Gerstein, & Fallon, 1997; Kutash, Duchnowski, Johnson, & Rugs, 1993; Weist, Nabors, Myers, & Armbruster, 2000). Relevant background to quality improvement and evaluation in school mental health is presented in the following section.

Process Evaluation

Process evaluations focus on how program components work and interact. Examples of process indicators for ESMH programs include: (1) the training and supervision of staff; (2) the effectiveness and productivity of clinicians; (3) the percentage of referred youth who are actually seen; (4) the latency between referral and first contact with a clinician; and (5) the ongoing involvement of stakeholders (e.g., youth, families, school and community leaders) in the program. These indicators are monitored on an ongoing basis, and enable corrections in service delivery to address problems when they are identified (e.g., a long latency between referrals and initial meetings).

Outcome Evaluation

Outcome evaluations are used to determine whether the program has affected factors that are identified to be important by stakeholders for the population served: for example, improved grades, attendance, and behavioral functioning of students; increased satisfaction by school staff. After goals are developed, it is important to create a realistic evaluation plan; that is, one that can be accomplished realistically by the program. Clinical staff and stakeholders served by the program (e.g., through an advisory board that includes all relevant stakeholders) should review the evaluation plan annually, for both processes and outcomes identified. Findings can then be used to improve the program and the evaluation plan for the next year, consistent with a priority for continuous quality improvement. Thus, program evaluation should not be viewed as an endpoint, but instead as the end of one program phase and the beginning of the next. In the following, we provide a step-by-step review of evaluation in school mental health.

Steps in Doing ESMH Program Evaluations

Targeting program services and the evaluation. Ideally, ESMH programs will have a considerable focus on enhancing empirically supported factors among youth (see Weist, Ollendick, & Finney, 1991). This "empirical validation" process involves identifying factors that have been shown in previous work to be associated with positive adjustment for youth in the situation of interest. Targets may be generally important, such as the "resilience" factors of social skills, problem solving, family support, and spirituality (Garmezy, 1987; Weist, Ginsburg, & Shafer, 1999), or may be specifically important in a particular situation. The important point is for ESMH programs to strive, whenever possible, to focus interventions and the evaluation of them on behaviors and factors that are in fact important for the youth they serve.

In choosing outcome indicators for evaluation, quantitative (e.g., changes in self-reported behavioral problems, grades) and qualitative (e.g., themes identified in focus groups) measures should be considered. Optimally, outcome measures should be obtained from multiple individuals related to the program (e.g., youth, clinicians, parents, teachers, school administrators, community leaders). We have learned that school-based programs should always target indicators that relate to the academic success of students, such as grades, attendance, and classroom behavior. Mental health staff may assume that a worthwhile goal is to reduce negative symptoms, such as depression and anxiety, for students in the program. However, school administrators may not value such reductions, if no changes in academic functioning occur. Adelman and Taylor (1993) review the effective strategy of engaging the support of schools for an ESMH program by framing interventions as "addressing barriers to learning." Using this frame, reducing anxiety symptoms in a child could be justified by a school if such symptom reduction served to "enable" child learning.

When using checklists or rating scales, established measures should be used that have an adequate normative base and good psychometric properties. Programs should resist the common tendency to make measures up, as these often reflect a "reinvention of the wheel" or cause problems down the road when data are being analyzed and interpreted (see Ollendick & Herson, 1993; Weist et al., 2000).

Assuring cultural competence. A very important function of the program evaluation is to document that provided services are appropriate for the age range and cultural/ethnic background of the youth and families who receive them (Yule, 1993). Pumariega (1996) underscored the need for an intensive and ongoing focus on cultural competence in *every* aspect of program evaluation; one way to accomplish this is by having stakeholders who represent the various cultural/ethnic groups of the community involved in all phases of the program design and evaluation.

Assessing multiple domains of youth environment and functioning. A straightforward organizing schema for mental health efforts with youth involves four major factors: (1) life stressors and risk factors, or variables that increase the likelihood of problems among youth; (2) protective or resilience factors, or variables that decrease the likelihood of problems, while increasing the likelihood of positive functioning; (3) emotional and behavioral problems; and (4) indices of life functioning, such as school performance, and peer and family relations (Weist & Baker-Sinclair, 1997; Weist, Ginsburg, & Shafer, 1999). The most effective program will directly target variables in each of these realms—reducing stress, increasing protective factors, reducing behavioral problems, and providing skill training and other assistance to promote positive functioning. Ideally, the evaluation plan also enables the assessment of changes for youth in each of these categories.

Specific measurement strategies. There are a number of approaches to the evaluation of school mental health programs. For example, self- and other reports of life stress, emotional and behavioral problems, and resilience factors can be collected from students, their parents, and teachers, before and after intervention. Similarly, clinicians can provide ratings of student functioning at regular intervals, such as before treatment, after three months, and after six months. When using self- and other report measures, issues related to who completes them will need to be addressed. For example, self-reports are relatively easy to obtain, but the validity of these can be in question, particularly for younger students. Clinician ratings are also relatively easy to obtain but tend to be positively biased (i.e., clinicians expect to see positive change, and therefore find it). Combining these measures with measures from parents and teachers, and with assessment of changes in student academic functioning, is the best strategy. Excellent reviews of issues related to mental health evaluation and youth are presented by Piancentini (1993) and Reynolds (1993).

University of Maryland School Mental Health Program Evaluation

In our own expanded school mental health program at the University of Maryland School of Medicine, we have an ongoing commitment to program evaluation and quality improvement. This section reviews three aspects of our program evaluation: assessing staff productivity, evaluating functional improvement among students seen in therapy, and conducting formal treatment outcome studies.

Assessing staff productivity. Our School Mental Health Program (SMHP) provides ESMH services to youth in 21 Baltimore schools. In the 1998–99 school year the program (employing the equivalent of 13 full-time clinicians) provided services to a total of 1,717 students at 18 schools (elementary, middle, and high). Contact with students occurred primarily through individual (6,328) and group (6,714) sessions. Clinicians saw an average of 10 students a day; elementary school clinicians saw 8–10 students per day, while middle and high school clinicians typically saw 9–15 students a day. These figures are well above the "show rate" of most community mental health centers. Statistics for the program in 1998–99 are presented in Table 5.1.

In addition, clinicians worked with family members on over 1,000 occasions and conducted almost 3,000 consultations with teachers. When these contacts with key adults in children's lives are summed with the number of times children were seen in individual sessions or group sessions, the total number of contacts made by clinicians during the school year was 17,187 (as shown in Table 5.1), roughly the same as the number of youth who were seen the previous two school years.

Evaluating student functional improvement. Of special interest to all stakeholders involved in school mental health programs are indicators of how successful students are in meeting goals related to school success. This includes documenting attendance, discipline encounters, grades, and referrals for special education for students who were seen at least four times for therapy sessions. For example, the mean grade point average of elementary students who were seen four or more times in the 1998–99 school year increased from 1.8 to 2.11 from before to after intervention. These data lend support for the effectiveness of clinical services, as well as providing accountability to the school system to justify contractual funds awarded to our program.

Conducting treatment outcome studies. Youth served by the SMHP face challenges associated with living in economically disadvantaged urban areas, including poverty, un- and under-employment, high crime, limited school and community resources, and exposure to violence. These factors in turn affect their ability to respond to the challenges of school. Thus evaluation should measure other factors that could be affected by school

TABLE 5.1.

				1998–99 School Year					
Schools	FTE	New Refs	Tot. Std.	Ind. Sess.	Grp. Sess.	Grp. Cont.	Fam. Cont.	Tch. Cont.	Tot. Cont.
Elementary (7)	4.2	299	314	1428	335	1259	415	1073	4175
Average/school		37	45	204	48	180	59	179	597
Elemen.-Middle(2)	2.0	156	185	934	280	926	326	506	2692
Average/school		78	92	467	140	463	163	253	1346
Middle (4)	3.4	487	528	1602	412	1887	321	1113	4923
Average/school		122	132	401	103	472	80	278	1231
High (3)	2.4	458	487	1725	317	974	86	211	2996
Average/school		153	162	575	106	325	29	70	999
Futures Prog. (2)	0.8	120	203	639	550	1668	29	65	2401
Average/School		60	102	320	275	834	15	33	1201
Total:	13	1520	1717	6328	1894	6714	1177	2968	17187

FTE = full-time equivalency in days; New Refs = new referrals; Tot. Std. = total number of students in the program; Ind. Sess. = individual session; Grp. Sess. = group session; Grp. Cont. = number of students seen in groups; Fam. Cont. = number of students seen in family meetings; Tch. Cont. = number of consultation and/or information-gathering meetings held with teachers; Tot. Cont. = total number of all contacts. Future Prog. = a special program to prevent high school youth from dropping out.

mental health services, such as emotional, behavioral, and family functioning, as well as stakeholder satisfaction. Since the early years of our program, we have sought to document impacts in these realms. A pilot outcome study conducted during the 1992–93 school year found some initial support for the effectiveness of program services in one of our high schools. Participants were thirty-nine high school students who received four to twelve sessions of ESMH services for a variety of presenting problems (treatment group), and thirty-four students enrolled in the school's health center, who received physical health but not mental health services (comparison group). Participants completed a brief self-report instrument prior to their first appointment with the mental health or health practitioner and again at the end of their course of treatment. From pre- to post-intervention, the treatment group showed significant decreases in depression and improvements in self-esteem when compared to the comparison group (Weist, Paskewitz, Warner, & Flaherty, 1996).

Since this pilot study, we have enhanced our focus on evaluating outcomes. We are in the middle of a formal treatment outcome study for middle and high school students whose parents/guardians provide permission for them to participate. In this study, clinicians, students, parents, and teachers complete ratings of student emotional and behavioral functioning at intake, and at several intervals post-intake. In particular, clinicians complete the Child and Adolescent Functional Assessment Scale (CAFAS) (Hodges, 1990), a measure of life functioning in various domains (e.g., school, home, behavioral); students aged eleven and older complete the Youth Self-Report (YSR) (Achenbach, 1991), a broad band measure of emotional and behavioral functioning; and parents complete the Child Behavior Checklist (CBCL), a parent-report version of the YSR. In addition, students, parents, and teachers complete surveys on youth resilience, and to indicate their satisfaction with mental health services provided.

Preliminary findings from the 1998–99 school year demonstrated promising results, with mean positive change in emotional and behavioral functioning shown in a sample of 181 middle and high school students who had received therapy in our program (Nabors & Reynolds, 2000). Significant changes in clinician ratings of student functioning using the CAFAS were shown from intake to three-month follow-up. Clinicians reported fewer behavior problems, less self-injurious behavior, and more positive functioning in the home environment for youth who had received therapy services. Students also reported significant change in behavioral and emotional functioning, with average scores on the YSR decreasing by three points from intake to the six-month follow-up (Nabors, 2000). Please note that this change was statistically significant, but not clinically significant according to guidelines for the YSR (Achenbach, 1991).

This section of the chapter has focused on program evaluation along the dimensions of staff productivity, functional change in students, and formal treatment outcome assessment. We now turn to a discussion of quality improvement activities in school mental health.

QUALITY IMPROVEMENT AND EXPANDED SCHOOL MENTAL HEALTH

A major element of program evaluation, and overall program monitoring and enhancement, is quality improvement (QI). Quality improvement is a term used to refer to activities designed to assure or improve the quality of services received by consumers of services. Measuring quality of care involves learning whether service delivery was well executed, beneficial, and resulted in improved functioning for those who received services (Wyszewianski, 1988).

Nabors, Weist, Tashman, and Myers (1999) identified four phases for QI programs in ESMH. The first phase consists of developing a mission statement and standards, which involves specifying program goals and assessing the needs of youth and the mental health resources available to them. The second phase involves appraising the program's structure, which includes staff training activities, the supervision of trainees, the physical aspects of office space, and the resources available to staff. The third phase involves evaluating assessment, treatment, and supportive processes, such as therapy, supervision, interdisciplinary collaboration of staff, and the coordination of school- and community-based services. The fourth and final phase involves assessing program outcomes.

In many ways, quality improvement activities cut across all four of these phases. Central to the functioning of any QI process is the active involvement of stakeholders, including youth (both those receiving and not receiving mental health services), parents, teachers, administrators, clinicians, community leaders, and clergy. Stakeholder involvement in QI activities helps to ensure that programs are working to address pressing school and community concerns, and are meeting community goals for youth. Feedback from stakeholders can be used to guide program development and improve service delivery. This section reviews four important QI activities for ESMH programs that have provided significant contributions to the quality of care in our School Mental Health Program: (a) the implementation of an advisory board; (b) the use of focus groups; (c) the use of satisfaction surveys to access consumer perceptions of care; and (d) a peer review program to assess therapy processes. All four of these activities involve significant stakeholder participation.

Developing an Advisory Board

Advisory bodies are supportive structures, referred to as advisory boards, councils, or committees. In general, they do not control hiring, firing, or budgetary decisions, thus distinguishing them from governing boards. Rather, their role is to advise, inform, and make recommendations to the programs they serve. We use the term "advisory board" for our program and will employ it here on out. A primary purpose of an advisory board is to identify and evaluate services that already exist in the community, and to guide the program in coordinating and integrating its services to better meet the needs of the community. The board should also be involved in developing plans for program evaluation, in reviewing them, and in making recommendations for program improvement.

An important task in forming an advisory board is to ensure adequate representation of relevant community stakeholders (as above). In addition to community stakeholders, Duca (1996) underscored the need to have at least one member from the staff participate on the board to serve as a liaison. The liaison can serve many functions, but most importantly, he or she helps to ensure that the board is operating within the scope of the organization's mission.

Presently, our advisory board consists of nineteen enthusiastic members who convene four times a year. Each of the previously mentioned stakeholder groups is represented, as well as media and corporate representatives. The board has identified four specific areas of interest that they feel will enrich our program: outreach, resources, mentoring, and peer counseling. Members are working in subcommittees to develop recommendations for program development that are reflective of the needs of the community.

Focus Groups

Because focus groups provide an opportunity to yield a great deal of information about service delivery and are inexpensive to conduct, they are an ideal QI activity for ESMH programs. Focus groups have been defined as informal discussion groups about specific topics (Vaughn, Shay-Schumm, & Sinagub, 1996). Having the researcher present is an important advantage of using focus groups, because he or she is in a position to clarify and understand responses made by the participants. In addition, participants may contribute new information or perspectives after hearing from others (Nabors, Weist, & Tashman, 1999). Focus groups may be conducted with a variety of stakeholder groups, including youth, parents, community leaders, school administrators, and clinicians. Such groups can be of particular value in the area of cultural competence, because they can be used to assess the values and beliefs of the children and families in the surrounding communities.

In our expanded school mental health program, focus groups have been conducted with adolescents in therapy, adolescents not in therapy, clinicians, administrators, health center staff, and parents. Findings from these group meetings have emphasized the positive impact of our program. Across each of these groups, participants expressed that the program is effective in improving student functioning, family relationships, and academic performance. Along with this positive feedback, participants were able to provide us with several ideas for enhancing our program. These included working to reduce the stigma related to mental health, better integrating clinicians into the school and neighborhood, improving methods to reach students in need, refining and improving evaluation strategies, and reducing disruptions during student therapy sessions (Nabors, Reynolds, & Weist, 2000).

Satisfaction Surveys

Satisfaction is an indicator of the client's overall positive or negative evaluation of services (Sheppard, 1993). Satisfaction with mental health services is one method for examining consumer perceptions of treatment effectiveness and quality. Client perceptions of effectiveness of service and service delivery are arguably important indices of treatment quality (Nabors, Weist, Reynolds, Tashman, & Jackson, 1999). However, consumer satisfaction as a component of program evaluation activities has received scant attention in children's mental health services literature (Byalin, 1993). The majority of reports in the literature have focused on parents' perceptions of the effectiveness and quality of treatment. Although parents' satisfaction with their children's mental health services may be related to children's satisfaction, it should not be considered identical (Shapiro, Welker, & Jacobson, 1997). Children's perceptions of the quality of treatment may differ substantially from adult perceptions. For those who question children's and adolescents' capability of providing such important input, recent research has demonstrated that they are in fact capable of evaluating and conveying their perceptions of the health services they receive (Garland & Besinger, 1996).

In our program evaluation, we are collecting parent, teacher, and student satisfaction data. Results have shown that parents, teachers, and students were highly satisfied with the school-based mental health services they received (Nabors, Weist, Reynolds, Tashman, & Jackson, 1999). Students reported that they counted on the relationship with their therapist as a buffer against stress in their daily lives and that they benefited from the skills they learned during therapy sessions. These reports were consistent with those made by other adolescents in previous studies (Garland & Besinger, 1996; Shapiro et al., 1997).

Peer Review

Peer review is a useful QI activity that provides important accountability data for improving service planning and delivery. Conducting a peer review team provided us with an opportunity to learn about interventions being used by our clinicians and their expected impact on functioning for youth receiving treatment. The purpose of the review was to learn about therapy processes in a nonthreatening environment. Eight clinicians participated in the random selection of eleven cases. Each review consisted of a two-hour meeting that was divided into three activities: case presentation by clinicians, mutual problem solving and the development of recommendations by clinicians and reviewers, and feedback to clinicians by reviewers. Clinicians reported that the meetings were a supportive venue for intensively reviewing cases, generating new ideas for approaching them (especially approaches that focused on enhancing youth strengths and resilience factors), and receiving peer support. Negative aspects included the significant amount of time and energy the process required, and having difficulty following through on the numerous recommendations made by the reviewers (Nabors, Acosta, Tashman, Higgins, & Weist, 1999).

POTENTIAL BARRIERS TO IMPLEMENTATION OF QI AND PROGRAM EVALUATION ACTIVITIES

Although the implementation of program evaluation and QI activities in ESMH programs ultimately represents best practice, several challenges or barriers to implementing them need to be overcome. One commonly encountered obstacle is that, because ESMH programs operate in a host setting, it is sometimes difficult to obtain permission from school administrators to conduct these activities, since they may not seem immediately relevant to academic performance of students. Furthermore, gaining permission from institutional review boards (IRBs) that govern such research is often an arduous task. Another frequently encountered barrier is resistance on the part of clinicians, who may be against participating in such activities for a variety of reasons, including time constraints and demanding caseloads. Other stakeholders, such as parents, teachers, and children, also may be hesitant to invest time and energy into activities that can be viewed as "research." Financial constraints are another barrier; in fact, many of the activities reviewed in the above are very difficult to carry out without explicit funding to do so. The unfortunate reality is that most children's mental health programs, including school-based programs, receive minimal if any funding to conduct evaluation and QI activities.

Measuring the outcomes of mental health treatment is not a precise science. Although symptom reduction is an evaluative criteria often used by mental health professionals, many argue that symptom reduction or changes in psychosocial functioning may be hard to detect. Nonetheless, evaluating the quality of care provides useful data for documenting treatment effectiveness, which is an important task in this era of accountability in health care. Further, incorporating QI programs into service delivery is a standard of care for clinicians providing services in schools (School Health Policy Initiative, 1996), and is an important avenue for informing policy makers, funders, clinicians, and researchers of the value of these programs.

The previously described evaluation efforts, in combination with our advisory board, focus groups, and peer review activities, are providing our program with a rich data set that accomplishes many purposes. These include: (1) the furnishing of important accountability data on the number of youth seen, the productivity of our clinicians, and the outcomes of their efforts; (2) the opportunity for stakeholders to be actively involved in providing ideas to improve the program and in evaluating it; and (3) the opportunity for clinical staff to receive information that helps them improve and modify therapeutic efforts with individual students. We hope that the background and examples provided in this chapter provide encouragement to efforts that seek to improve the quality and document the impact of mental health services delivered in schools.

ACKNOWLEDGMENTS: Supported by project #MCJ24SH02-01-0 from the Maternal and Child Health Bureau (Title V, Social Security Act), Health Resources and Services Administration, U.S. Department of Health and Human Services. Also supported by grant #R03 HS09542 from the Agency for Healthcare Research and Quality (AHRQ).

References

Achenbach, T. M. (1991). *Manual for the youth self-report and 1991 profile.* Burlington, VT: University of Vermont Department of Psychology.

Adelman, H. S., & Taylor, L. (1993). School-based mental health: Toward a comprehensive approach. *Journal of Mental Health Administration, 20,* 32–45.

Agency for Health Care Policy and Research (AHCPR) (1990, March). *Medical treatment effectiveness research.* Program Note, U.S. Department of Health and Human Services, Rockville, MD.

Armbruster, P., Gerstein, S. H., & Fallon, T. (1997). Bridging the gap between service need and service utilization: A school-based mental health program. *Community Mental Health Journal, 33,* 199–211.

Association for Health Services Research. (AHSR) (1998, January). *Improving quality of health care for children: An agenda for research* (Executive Summary). Washington, DC: Author.

Byalin, K. (1993). Assessing parental satisfaction with children's mental health services: A pilot study. *Evaluation and Program Planning, 16,* 69–72.

Duca, D. J. (1996). *Nonprofit boards.* New York: John Wiley & Sons.

Garland, A. F., & Besinger, B. A. (1996). Adolescents' perceptions of outpatient mental health services. *Journal of Child and Family Studies, 5*(3), 355–375.

Garmezy, N. (1987). Stress, competence, and development: Continuities in the study of schizophrenic adults, children vulnerable to psychopathology, and the search for stress-resistant children. *American Journal of Orthopsychiatry, 57,* 159–174.

Hoagwood, K., Jensen, P. S., Petti, T., & Burns, B. J. (1996). Outcomes of mental health care for children and adolescents: A comprehensive conceptual model. *Journal of the American Academy of Child and Adolescent Psychiatry, 35,* 1055–1063.

Hodges, K. (1995). *Child and Adolescent Functional Assessment Scale (CAFAS; Version 2.15.96).* Ann Arbor, MI: University Publishing.

Kutash, K., Duchnowski, A., Johnson, M., & Rugs, D. (1993). Multi-stage evaluation for a community mental health system for children. *Administration and Policy in Mental Health, 20,* 311–322.

Mattson, M. R. (1984). Quality assurance: A literature review of a changing field. *Hospital and Community Psychiatry, 35,* 605–615.

Nabors, L. (2000). *AHCPR uniform research reporting guideline. School mental health quality assessment and improvement.* Grant/Contract Number: RO3 HSO9542.

Nabors, L. A., Acosta, O. M., Tashman, N. A., Higgins, M., & Weist, M. D. (1999, June). *Implementation of a peer review program in an expanded school mental health program.* Poster presented at the 5th meeting of the National Assembly on School-Based Health Care: Finding Our Voice, Shaping a National Agenda, Washington, DC.

Nabors, L. A., & Reynolds, M. W. (2000). Program evaluation activities: Outcomes related to treatment for adolescents receiving school-based mental health services. *Children's Services: Social Policy, Research, and Practice, 3,* 175–189.

Nabors, L. A., Reynolds, M. W., & Weist, M. D. (2000). Qualitative evaluation of a high school mental health program. *Journal of Youth and Adolescence, 29,* 1–14.

Nabors, L., Weist, M. D., Holden, E. W., & Tashman, N. (1999). Quality service provision in children's mental health care. *Children's Services: Social Policy Research and Practice, 2,* 57–79.

Nabors, L. A., Weist, M. D., & Tashman, N. A. (1999). Focus groups: A valuable tool for assessing male and female adolescent perceptions of school-based mental health services. *Journal of Gender, Culture, and Health, 4*(1), 39–48.

Nabors, L. A., Weist, M. D., Reynolds, M. W., Tashman, N. A., & Jackson, C. (1999). Adolescent satisfaction with school-based mental health services. *Journal of Child and Family Studies, 8*(2), 229–236.

Nabors, L. A., Weist, M. D., Tashman, N. A., & Myers, C. P. (1999). Quality assurance and school-based mental health services. *Psychology in Schools, 36,* 485–493.

National Committee for Quality Assurance (NCQA, 1995). Standards for Accreditation, 1995 Edition. Washington, D.C: Author.

Ollendick, T. H., & Herson, M. (1993). Child and adolescent behavioral assessment. In T. H. Ollendick & M. Herson (Eds.), *Handbook of child and adolescent assessment.* Needham Heights, MA: Allyn and Bacon.

Piacentini, J. (1993). Checklists and rating scales. In T. H. Ollendick & M. Herson (Eds.), *Handbook of child and adolescent assessment.* Needham Heights, MA: Allyn and Bacon.

President's Advisory Commission on Consumer Protection and Quality in the Health Care Industry (1998). *Quality first: Better health care for all Americans. Final report to the President of the United States* (SB No. 017-012-00396-6). Washington, DC: U.S. Government Printing Office.

Pumariega, A. J. (1996). Culturally competent outcome evaluation in systems of care for children's mental health. *Journal of Child and Family Studies, 5,* 389–397.

Raskin, I. E., & Maklan, C. W. (1991). Medical treatment effectiveness research: A view from inside the Agency for Health Care Policy and Research. *Evaluation & the Health Professions, 14,* 161–186.

Reynolds, W. M. (1993). Self-report methodology. In T. H. Ollendick & M. Herson (Eds.), *Handbook of child and adolescent assessment.* Needham Heights, MA: Allyn and Bacon.

School Health Policy Initiative (1996). *A partnership for quality and access: School-based health centers and health plans.* Special Report of the 1995 National Workgroup Meetings. School Health Policy Initiative, Division of Adolescent Medicine, Department of Pediatrics, Montefiore Medical Center, New York. Supported by the Carnegie Corporation of New York and the Ewing Marion Kauffman Foundation.

Shapiro, J. P., Welker, C. J., & Jacobson, B. J. (1997). The youth client satisfaction questionnaire: Development, construct validation, and factor structure. *Journal of Child and Clinical Psychology, 26*(1), 87–98.

Sheppard, M. (1993). Client satisfaction, extended intervention and interpersonal skills in community mental health. *Journal of Advanced Nursing, 18,* 246–259.

Vaughn, S., Shay-Schumm, J., & Sinagub, J. (1996). *Focus group interviews in education and psychology.* Thousand Oaks, CA: Sage.

Weist, M. D. (1997). Expanded school mental health services: A national movement in progress. In T. H. Hollendick & R. J. Prinz (Eds.), *Advances in clinical child psychology* (Vol. 19) (pp. 319–352). New York: Plenum.

Weist, M. D., & Baker-Sinclair, M. E. (1997). Use of structured assessment tools in clinical practice. *Annals of Adolescent Psychiatry, 21,* 349–360.

Weist, M. D., Ginsburg, G., & Shafer, M. E. (1999). Progress in adolescent mental health. *Adolescent Medicine: State of the Reviews, 10,* 165–174.

Weist, M. D., Nabors, L. A., Myers, C. P., & Armbruster, P. (2000). Evaluation of expanded school mental health programs. *Community Mental Health Journal, 36,* 395–412.

Weist, M. D., Ollendick, T. H., & Finney, J. W. (1991). Toward the empirical validation of treatment targets in children. *Clinical Psychology Review, 11,* 515–538.

Weist, M. D., Paskewitz, D. A., Warner, B. S., & Flaherty, L. T. (1996). Treatment outcome of school-based mental health services for urban teenagers. *Community Mental Health Journal, 32,* 149–157.

Wyszewianski, L. (1988). The emphasis on measurement in quality assurance: Reasons and implications. *Inquiry, 25,* 424–436.

Yule, W. (1993). Developmental considerations in child assessment. In T. H. Ollendick & M. Hersen (Eds.), *Handbook of child and adolescent assessment.* Needham Heights, MA: Allyn and Bacon.

PART TWO

Home- and Community-Based Approaches

CHAPTER SIX

Home- and Community-Based Services: Historical Overview, Concepts, and Models

Harinder S. Ghuman, M.D.

INTRODUCTION

Professionals from mental health and social agencies working with youth are frequently confronted regarding the best setting in which youth can be cared for and treated. In general the goal is to keep the youth in their home and community and with their parents and family. Alternative placements are considered only when a youth is in a dangerous situation due to abuse or neglect by the parent or caregiver or the youth's difficulty in controlling dangerous behaviors despite the best efforts by the caregiver. Different approaches in dealing with a disturbed youth and their families due to philosophical differences, training, and orientation do exist, however. For example, social service agencies may not consider medication as an option as a first line of intervention for a disturbed youth and thus may only involve a psychiatrist when everything else fails. Quite the opposite can be true when a youth is involved with a mental health agency with a medical model orientation. In addition, even within a mental health or social agency the approach to treatment and placement may vary depending upon the leadership and orientation of the program. Lastly, the economics and politics of the geographic location of a youth's residence is a major factor. For example, in most inner cities marked with poverty, the threshold for mental health or social agency involvement and intervention is much higher and may also vary in quality, due to meager resources and poorly trained staff, as compared to suburban areas. The politics of location is the least studied and may be one of the important (if not the most important) variables influencing how youth are treated in the community. For example, how well the governor of a state gets along with the mayor of a city can determine how much money is allocated to the city and even to which programs. One other important variable, which is often overlooked, is the influence of the local media in defining issues and championing potential solutions for the community.

HISTORY

The traditions of home-based care for mentally ill adults are long and legendary. Europe and North America have been inspired by humanitarian and compassionate home-based care given in Geel, Belgium, recorded as early as the thirteenth century. Geel is the town where in 500 A.D. a beautiful Irish princess, Dymphna, was decapitated by her father after attempting to escape his incestuous advances. The people of Geel preserved Dymphna's body, and gradually her remains became invested with magical significance for the mentally ill. As the curative powers of Dymphna attracted many pilgrims, the Geeloise responded by taking mentally ill persons into their home (Dumont & Aldrich, 1962). Thus started a tradition of community and family care for the mentally ill. The first family care program in the United States was started in Massachusetts in 1885. It is of interest to note that Doyle (1963), writing about coordinated home care as a part of a total medical care plan, stated, "As a rule, the disabled and ill are happier, get well faster, and their dignity is preserved when at home in familiar surroundings," and "Coordinated home care is a methodology whereby it might be possible to brake the trend of spiraling costs of health insurance."

The modern history of home-based services to youth and their families dates from around the 1950s. Most of the home-based work was done by social agencies with a focus on child protection and child abuse prevention. Various federal, state, and local government authorities largely funded this work. It was only in the 1980s that home-based services became a focus for severely emotionally disturbed youth. This was the result of number of factors, including: (1) increased awareness that a large number of children with serious emotional disturbance were receiving no treatment or inappropriately restrictive care (Knitzer, 1982; Saxe et al., 1986); (2) home-based services can be more effective in a large number of seriously disturbed youth compared to other alternatives; (3) home-based services may be less costly compared to residential or hospital-based treatment; (4) the youth's improvement during hospitalization or residential treatment may not be sustained without intensive home-based services; and (5) home-based services may prevent out-of-home placement or reduce the length of stay of out-of-home placement.

One of the major forces defining, conceptualizing, and integrating systems of home- and community-based services has been the National Institute of Mental Health's Child and Adolescent Service System Program (CASSP), which was created in 1984. The goal of CASSP is to assist states and communities in developing comprehensive, community-based systems of care, and to help in forming coalitions of policy makers, providers, parents, and advocates. The CASSP initiative has focused on severely emotionally disturbed youth requiring long-term interventions of mental health and other agencies. The term "system of care" was defined and promoted as the foundation for CASSP. The program has established two fundamental "core values" for the system of care (SOC) for emotionally disturbed youth and promoted ten guiding principles (Stroul & Friedman, 1986) (see the introduction to this book for more details). Currently a number of states are involved in the CASSP initiative.

The remainder of this chapter is focused on reviewing some of the major concepts and models of home- and community-based treatment.

THE WRAPAROUND

Definition and Historical Background

According to VanDenBerg and Grealish (1996), the wraparound is a philosophy and overall approach that tailors services to the specific needs of all children and families, even when services are delivered as part of a categorical service program. The wraparound process is a specific set of policies, practices, and steps used in the development of individualized services and support for youth with emotional problems and their families. Children and families served by the process are considered to have complex needs, with the children at risk of being removed from their homes.

The wraparound approach is associated with pioneering work by Dennis, VanDenBerg, Burchard, and others. Elements of it were first applied in Canada in the 1960s, in the Kaleidoscope program in Chicago in the 1970s, and later in the Alaska Youth Initiative and Project Wraparound in Vermont. Currently, the wraparound process is implemented in various states.

Essential Elements

In 1992, Dennis, VanDenBerg, and Burchard outlined the following "framing elements" that serve as the philosophical base for the wraparound process: (1) efforts must be community-based; (2) the children and families should receive individualized support and services; (3) the wraparound process should be built on the unique values and strengths of the youth and families, and be culturally competent; (4) parents must be part of every level of development; (5) there must be access to flexible and noncategorized funding; (6) implementation of the wraparound process should be on an interagency basis; (7) services must be unconditional and changeable according to the child's and family's needs; and (8) the outcome of the process must be studied.

Procedures

The first major step of the wraparound procedure is the setting up of a community team composed of key stakeholders from schools, clergy, business leaders, parents, and other community advocacy groups. A community team with a broad base is essential in enlisting the community to own the program. This team sets up subcommittees to oversee the wraparound process. In most communities, the target population includes children who are at risk of out-of-home placement or are already placed in restrictive care. The screening committees use a consensus vote to decide inclusion or exclusion of a child and/or families. The child and family record is sent to a broker agency responsible for hiring resource coordinators, managing cross-agency funds, and providing oversight to the wraparound process.

The resource coordinator identifies key players in child's life, performs strengths assessment, configures child-family teams, assesses training needs, and arranges training for key players. In addition, the resource coordinator conducts child and family team meetings, helps in developing an individualized service and support plan, identifies existing services and their usefulness, creates and arranges services and supports that are not present, and develops crisis plans (Sewell, 1990).

An assessment of the strengths of the child and family is an important aspect of the wraparound process, as individualized services and support plans are based on these strengths. The resource coordinator performs this task by way of a "strength chat" with the child and family, and sometimes includes relatives, friends, or professionals who know the family. The chat focuses on family resources, preferences, values, and family members' view of themselves.

The child and family team meetings often start by reviewing the results of the "strength chat" instead of a traditional reading of the social history, which has often been noted to discourage the family by making them feel blamed and thus alienated. These meetings are often held at a neutral site such as a room in a library or in the family home, and are scheduled at a time convenient for team members. The resource coordinator's role is to arrange team meetings, get input from all the team members, and facilitate these meetings.

The resource coordinator selects team members by soliciting names of potential candidates from the child and family. The team has four to ten members, and at least one-half should be nonprofessional, such as extended family members, friends, and neighbors. This encourages family ownership in the process and ensures cultural competency.

The team evaluates needs for the development of individualized services and support by examining life domain areas such as: (1) residence; (2) family; (3) social; (4) emotional/psychological; (5) educational/vocational; (6) safety; (7) legal; (8) medical; (9) spiritual; (10) cultural; (11) behavioral; and (12) financial. The resource coordinator involves the team in discussion regarding the needs of the child in the community. The team prioritizes the life domain areas in which the child or family is experiencing the most needs by using a voting method. The family is given veto power or more votes to ensure that it has the major voice in decision making. After identifying each major need, the team brainstorms possible solutions and strategies to meet it. The team identifies top solutions by voting and assigns responsibility to each member for each action step within a time frame.

VanDenBerg and Grealish (1996) state that the plan should include the following elements: strengths, needs, the outcome to be produced, strategies, the responsible person, a crisis plan, a budget, funding possibilities, intervention priority levels, and methods of evaluating outcomes. The resource coordinator is responsible for presenting this plan to the community team or to a subcommittee of the community team. The community team reviews the plan and can make suggestions and send the plan back to the child and family team for further consideration, but it is not allowed to second-guess the child and family team and change the ways that needs are met. The resource coordinator is responsible for the implementation of the approved plan and for ensuring that team meetings are held frequently to evaluate progress and revise the plan if necessary. The resource coordinator is responsible for setting up a procedure to measure the outcomes of the wraparound process by collecting quantitative child and family behavioral data such as decreases in substance abuse and aggression, and improvement in school attendance (Burchard & Clarke, 1990). Consumer satisfaction surveys and interviews are also utilized to measure family reaction and service outcome (Burchard & Schaefer, 1992).

HOME-BASED FAMILY-CENTERED SERVICES (HBFCS)

Definition and Historical Background

HBFCS is a method of service delivery to children and families in their homes in order to maintain and strengthen families. These services include traditional and nontraditional child welfare service components such as homemaker service, respite, cash assistance, transportation, child care, vocational counseling, and substance abuse treatment. In the 1970s and 1980s, HBFCS became popular as a result of many state social service agencies' efforts to reduce the number of children in foster care, to return the children home or to placement with adoptive parents, and to prevent the placement of children in foster care.

Several family-centered services approaches have been tried with success, including Multiple Impact Therapy (MacGregor, Ritchie, Serrano, & Schuster, 1964), in which a team of therapists works intensively for several days in a row with a family in crisis, and the Nashville Comprehensive Emergency Services (Burt & Balyeat, 1974), which furnished emergency caretakers and homemakers who provided responsible adult care and supervision to children in crisis. Another well-known and studied approach is the Homebuilders Program, initiated in Pierce County (Tacoma), Washington, in 1974 (Kinney, Madsen, Fleming, & Haapla, 1977). In this program, therapists were on call twenty-four hours a day to come to the homes of families in crisis in order to prevent the removal of one or more family members to an alternative living situation. Each therapist was expected to see twenty families per year or about two per month, allowing them as much time as necessary within a six-week period to facilitate crisis resolution and teach new skills to the family. Another home-based and family-centered program, Maine Model for Home-Based Services, has been described as a cost-effective alternative to residential care (Hinckley & Ellis, 1985). This program employed a team approach, and services were provided for three months.

Theoretical Basis

The HBFCS model is based on an expanded ecological view incorporating family, extended family, friends, and community into the service delivery plan. HBFCS is to support all family members instead of focusing primarily on the child. Parents and other family members are involved in all aspects of planning and evaluating service delivery. The major emphasis in HBFCS is on family support, family empowerment, and reduction of the burden of care, thereby helping the family to live as normally as possible despite the child's difficulties (Hunter & Friesen, 1996).

Essential Elements and Interventions

HBFCS programs share the following features (Pecora et al., 1985): (a) there is a primary worker or case manager who establishes and maintains a supportive and nurturing relationship with the family; (b) services are on a twenty-four-hour-a-day basis to deal with crises; (c) each staff member carries a small caseload and staff availability is essential; (d) the services are provided at home and maximum use is made of immediate and extended family, neighborhood, and the community; (e) the parents are the primary caregivers and are in charge of their family, and (f) programs should be willing to invest at least as much in a child's family to prevent placement as society is willing to pay for placement outside the home.

The clinical interventions are combinations of crisis intervention techniques, family therapy, parent training, and behavior modification. In addition, the staff is involved in advocacy and in linking the family with appropriate community support agencies. In the Homebuilders Program, the first step is to defuse the explosiveness of the situation and to gather data. During this stage, each family member has a chance to talk separately at length with the staff. The staff member uses a procedure called "active listening" to obtain information in a supportive manner. Listening stops only when a family member says, "Yes, I think I've said everything I want to say," and "Yes, I feel like you understand my position." Often this results in a feeling of relief for all family members and everyone agrees to meet the following day. If the family members are calm, the Homebuilders staff member moves the discussion to the next step, the identification of problems, by a group discussion. If family members are still too upset, the alternative is to continue their physical separation and to help them explore their own perceptions individually. Family members are encouraged to arrive at behavioral definitions of the problems, how they will know when there is improvement, and how much improvement is desired.

The next step in the Homebuilders Program is problem resolution, in which the family members are helped in improving their communication by modeling good communication skills, reinforcing family members as their skills improve, and supporting them in communicating with other family members. They are taught how to prevent crisis recurrence by using better communication skills, being assertive instead of aggressive or hostile, and negotiating behavioral contracts. Lastly, staff members, in coordination with case managers, help the family to set up a treatment program to maintain progress and achieve future goals by presenting and linking community resources. The families are usually then ready for referral for outpatient treatment or case management services. Homebuilders staff keep close contact with the family until the family, staff, and follow-up personnel agree that the referral has been satisfactory and the prognosis for the prevention of future crisis is good. Homebuilders staff maintain availability for "booster shot" sessions if the family has difficulty dealing with a crisis (Kinney et al., 1977).

MULTISYSTEMIC TREATMENT (MST) MODEL

Historical Background

MST was developed in the late 1970s by Henggeler and colleagues and was intended to treat juvenile delinquents and their families in a clinic-based setting. However, the home-based model was quickly implemented due to treatment noncompliance by the families of juvenile delinquents. In the 1980s and 1990s, MST has been used and studied in the treatment of various types of juvenile offenders such as violent offenders, sexual offenders, and substance-abusing and -dependent offenders. Although the major focus of MST has been on juvenile offenders in the late 1980s and 1990s there was an increased interest in its use for abusive families (Brunk et al., 1987) and for seriously emotionally disturbed youth presenting psychiatric emergencies (Henggeler, Rowland, et al., 1997). More recently, MST has been used with substance-abusing parents of young children, pregnant adolescents, adolescent parents, and maltreated children in foster care. Most of the original MST programs were in Tennessee, Missouri, and South Carolina, and more recently in Texas, Delaware, and Ontario, Canada.

Theoretical Basis

MST is based on general systems theory (von Bertalanffy, 1968) and social ecology theory (Bronfenbrenner, 1979). Systems theory emphasizes focus on the entire system and the system's transaction with the surrounding ecology, rather than with a single cause or chain of causes resulting in certain kinds of behaviors in the youth and family. The theory of social ecology is similar to systems theory but is broader in scope and focuses on reciprocal interchange between an individual and numerous contextual concentric structures in that individual's life. The youth, caregiver, extended family, peers, neighborhood, school, provider of care, and community at large are considered to interact and play a part in a youth's behavior and thus MST interventions are not just limited to family but involve all the systems.

Essentials of MST

Henggeler et al. (1998) state the following nine MST treatment principles: (1) assessment is primarily geared to understand the fit between the identified problems and their broader systemic context; (2) therapeutic contact is to emphasize the positive features and the use of systemic strengths as levers for change; (3) interventions are to promote responsible behavior and diminish irresponsible behavior among family members; (4) interventions target specific and well-defined problems and are present, here-and-now focused, and action oriented; (5) the targets of intervention are sequences of behavior within and between multiple systems maintaining the identified problems; (6) interventions need to be developmentally appropriate and meet the developmental needs of the youth; (7) interventions require daily or weekly effort by family members; (8) the effectiveness of interventions is evaluated continuously from multiple perspectives and with the provider assuming accountability in overcoming barriers to positive outcome; and (9) interventions are designed to encourage treatment generalization and the maintenance of changes over time by empowering caregivers to address family members' needs across multiple systemic contexts.

Interventions

The initial assessment carefully examines the strengths and needs of the youth, family members, extended family, school personnel, possibly neighbors and family friends, probation officers, and peers, as well as their relationship to the identified problems. The therapist, in collaboration with the treatment team and clinical supervisor, develops testable hypotheses based on the initial assessment, and interventions are implemented and tested on the basis of these hypotheses. Additional hypotheses are developed depending upon the outcome of the initial interventions. There is systemic application of behavioral contingencies to promote responsible behavior in youth. MST therapists and the treatment team develop and maintain a strength focus approach to foster a therapist-family partnership by the use of nonpejorative language in nontechnical terms in all verbal and written communication, the use of positive reinforcement, providing hope to the families, incorporating and maintaining a problem-solving stance, and emphasizing what the family does well.

Family interventions used in MST are based on various problem-focused models of family therapy such as behavioral parent training (Munger, 1993; Patterson, 1979), cognitive behavior therapies (Kendall & Braswell, 1993), behavioral family system approaches (Robin & Foster, 1989), and behavioral family interventions (Sanders, 1996). These interventions are to address ineffective parenting styles, parent-child interaction, and parental marital problems. The first step is to build rapport with the parent by providing support—highlighting any positive aspects of parenting, not focusing on finding the parent at fault, and avoiding confrontation with the parent. The parent is helped to set clearly defined rules for the child's behavior, to develop a set of consequences that are linked to the rules, and to learn how to effectively monitor compliance or noncompliance by the child. In addition, the MST practitioner assesses parental beliefs, parental social support, their level of cognitive functioning and the presence of any psychiatric disorder, and their knowledge regarding child development. Such an assessment helps the clinician in planning strategies and interventions to deal with the child's problems and also to increase parental effectiveness.

A careful assessment is made of the youth's relationship with peers. Peer-directed interventions serve to decrease association with deviant peers and to increase affiliation with prosocial peers. Interventions are focused on parental involvement in monitoring the youth's activities with peers, on helping the parent set firm limits regarding the youth's contact and interaction with deviant peers, and on helping the parent facilitate the youth's participation in prosocial activities related to the youth's interests. Social skills training may be necessary for socially rejected or neglected youth and those with deficit social skills.

School-related interventions are to address academic and social issues. The MST clinician is encouraged to respect the hierarchy and operating procedure of the school and to develop a positive relationship with school staff. The implementation of interventions requires that the clinician work closely with teachers, guidance counselors, and parents. Family-school linkage is considered essential for a successful outcome. Assessment is made regarding a youth's intellectual and academic abilities and emotional/behavioral problems, which may interfere with school success. Interventions are to help parents structure after-school hours, to increase parental involvement in the remediation of the youth's academic and motivational difficulties at home, and to improve parent-teacher communication.

Individual treatment interventions may include systemic desensitization and cognitive processing therapy for anxiety and PTSD (post-traumatic stress disorder) symptoms (Resick & Schnicke, 1992), cognitive therapy for depression (Beck, 1993), multicomponent behavior therapy for substance abuse (Higgins & Budney, 1993), and problem-solving training for aggressive or impulsive behavior (Kendall & Braswell, 1993), and are often implemented when the youth continues to display serious difficulties even after systemic interventions.

MST Staffing and Training

MST staff have a low caseload of three to six families per clinician, and each clinician functions within a team of three to four staff. This team provides coverage twenty-four hours a day, seven days a week. Staff have daily face-to-face or phone contact with families, and appointments are scheduled at the family's convenience. Services are time-limited to three to five months and are provided in the home, school, and neighborhood setting (Henggeler et al., 1998). MST staff receive formal intensive training, including "booster" sessions in addition to ongoing weekly supervision from trained staff.

MST Outcome

MST outcome research has been primarily focused on violent, chronic, or substance-abusing and -dependent juvenile offenders (Henggeler et al., 1986, 1993, 1998; Borduin et al., 1990, 1995). These carefully designed studies document that MST has been effective in reducing arrest and rearrest rates and drug use in juvenile offenders, has improved family and peer relations of the youth, and has been successful in preventing out-of-home placement. MST is currently being studied as an alternative to the hospitalization of youth presenting psychiatric emergencies, in the treatment of substance-abusing parents of young children, and with pregnant adolescents and adolescent parents.

YALE INTENSIVE IN-HOME CHILD AND ADOLESCENT PSYCHIATRY SERVICES MODEL (YICAPS)

Historical Background

The YICAPS model was developed in the 1980s and 1990s through the combined efforts of the Family Support Service at the Yale Child Study Center and the Children's Psychiatric Inpatient Services at Yale–New Haven Hospital (Woolston et al., 1998). Both of these programs highly valued the integrity of the family and placed heavy emphasis on strengthening the family unit. The Family Support Service has been a grants-funded family preservation home-based intervention program to serve multiproblem families. The Children's Psychiatric Inpatient Services focused on enlisting parents, schoolteachers, and outpatient providers to be actively involved during inpatient treatment in order to ensure that inpatient gains could be shifted to the home and school environment. Due to managed care pressure to reduce inpatient length of stays and flexibility with Medicaid funding for alternative approaches, these two programs joined resources to provide more in-home psychiatric services.

Theoretical Basis

The YICAPS model is based on five principles (Woolston et al., 1998): (1) A mental health professional, usually a child and adolescent psychiatrist, has ultimate responsibility for the treatment plan, and the focus of treatment is on defined problems so that progress can be measured objectively. (2) All evaluations and interventions are based on the transactional model. (3) Services are child-centered, home-based, and family-focused. (4) Work is done in an interdisciplinary team. The primary team consists of the child and family, the in-home psychiatric team, and the care coordinator. This primary team becomes the greater team when all the other important people in the child's life, such as teachers, pediatrician, protective social worker, minister, and probation officer are included in teamwork. (5) Interventions are based on concepts from system and brief therapy models.

Essentials of YICAPS and Interventions

There are six basic program elements to YICAPS: (1) A two-person clinical team is involved in home-based evaluation and interventions. Interventions include individual psychotherapy, family therapy, behavior management, parent training, and medication management. (2) The treatment team evaluates assets and risk factors in the child's home and neighborhood that may affect the treatment outcome. (3) Intensive case management is provided by the team by linking and coordinating services and empowering the family. (4) The team and the family develop and implement a treatment plan that is presented to the managed care utilization reviewer for payment. (5) Service is individualized in both intensity and duration. The services are "bundled"—for instance, five hours, eight hours, twelve hours, and twenty hours per week and reviewed every week. (6) The crisis intervention service is provided on a twenty-four-hour, seven-day basis.

The YICAPS model encourages the home-based services to have close ties to various traditional psychiatric services (hospital pediatric emergency room, inpatient, day program, outpatient, respite care) and community settings (schools, social service agencies, health care providers, juvenile justice workers, churches, recreational organizations, parent organizations, and funding agencies).

Staffing and Team Structure

YICAPS organizational structure includes a program director, a medical director, a child psychiatrist, a clinical coordinator, two senior clinician and mental health teams, three to five casual status fee-for-service clinician and counselor teams, and a financial administrative assistant for a caseload of twenty-five patients.

The clinical team meets once a week for a general team meeting or rounds for supervision, ongoing learning, and documentation of cases. There is at least a once-weekly case-specific planning meeting by each individual treatment team. Each full-time clinician-counselor team receives one hour per week of supervision by a child psychiatrist or clinical child psychologist. The necessity for staff continuity during assessment and interventions is considered as an essential element of this model.

CONCLUSION

Over the last decade, there has been an increased interest and emphasis on home- and community-based treatment for severely emotionally disturbed youth and their families. This has resulted in significant growth in the development of new home- and community-based programs, which have been clinically successful and well received by the insurance industry, considering their cost-effectiveness. As with any other business opportunity, however, there is a danger of developing new programs driven by economic forces without careful consideration of what are the clinical needs and/or if the proper model or models of treatment are applied in the program. Of equal concern with such new programs is the need to be vigilant for professionals who are either overzealous and/or undertrained in applying principles of home- and community-based interventions.

The effectiveness of some home- and community-based programs has been studied and shows promising results. Further clarification is needed of the indications for home- and community-based interventions and the documentation of which models are effective in dealing with what kinds of problems, as well as in elucidating the drawbacks and limitations to home- and community-based treatment. Long-term outcome studies and program replication studies are essential.

References

Beck, A. T. (1993). Cognitive therapy: Past, present, and future. *Journal of Consulting and Clinical Psychology, 61,* 194–198.

Borduin, C. M., Henggeler, S. W., Blaske, D. M., & Stein, R. (1990). Multisystemic treatment of adolescent sexual offenders. *International Journal of Offender Therapy and Comparative Criminology, 35,* 105–114.

Borduin, C. M., Mann, B. J., Cone, L. T., Henggeler, S. W., Fucci, B. R., Blaske, D. M., & Williams, R. A. (1995). Multisystemic treatment of serious juvenile offenders: Long-term prevention of criminality and violence. *Journal of Consulting and Clinical Psychology, 63,* 569–578.

Bronfenbrenner, U. (1979). *The ecology of human development.* Cambridge, MA: Harvard University Press.

Brunk, M., Henggeler, S. W., & Whelan, J. P. (1987). A comparison of multisystemic therapy and parent training in the brief treatment of child abuse and neglect. *Journal of Consulting and Clinical Psychology, 55,* 311–318.

Burchard, J. D., & Clark, R. T. (1990). The role of individualized care in a service delivery system for children and adolescents with severely maladjusted behavior. *Journal of Mental Health Administration, 17,* 48–60.

Burchard, J. D., & Shaefer, M. (1992). Improving accountability in a service delivery system in children's mental health. *Clinical Psychology Review, 2,* 867–882.

Burt, M. R., & Balyeat, R. A. (1974). A new system for improving the care of neglected and abused children. *Child Welfare, 53,* 167–179.

Dennis, K., VanDenBerg, J. & Burchard, J. D. (1992). *The wraparound process.* Presented at the First National Wraparound Conference, Pittsburgh, PA.

Doyle, J. C. (1963). Role of the private physician in coordinated home care. *Journal of the American Medical Association, 185,* 146–147.

Dumont, M. P., & Aldrich, C. K. (1962). Family care after a thousand years—a crisis in the tradition of St. Dymphna. *American Journal of Psychiatry, 118,* 116–121.

Henggeler, S. W., Melton, G. B., Smith, L. A., Schoenwald, S. K., & Hanley, J. H. (1993). Family preservation using multisystemic treatment: Long-term follow-up to a clinical trial with serious juvenile offenders. *Journal of Child and Family Studies, 2,* 283–293.

Henggeler, S. W., Rodick, J. D., Borduin, C. M., Hanson, C. L., Watson, S. M., & Urey, J. R. (1986). Multisystemic treatment of juvenile offenders: Effects on adolescent behavior and family interaction. *Developmental Psychology, 22,* 132–141.

Henggeler, S. W., Rowland, M. D., Pickrel, S. G., Miller, S. L., Cunningham, P. B., Santos, A. B., Schoenwald, S. K., Randall, J., & Edwards, J. E. (1997). Investigating family-based alternatives to institution-based mental health services for youth: Lessons learned from the pilot study of a randomized field trial. *Journal of Clinical Child Psychology, 26,* 226–233.

Henggeler, S. W., Schoenwald, S. K., Borduin, C. M., Rowland, M. D., & Cunningham, P. B. (1998). *Multisystemic treatment of antisocial behavior in children and adolescents.* New York: Guilford Press.

Higgins, S. T., & Budney, A. J. (1993). Treatment of cocaine dependence through the principles of behavior analysis and behavioral pharmacology. In L. S. Onken, J. D. Blaine, & J. J. Boren (Eds.), *Behavioral treatments for drug abuse and dependence* (National Institute on Drug Abuse Research Monograph no. 137; NIH Publication No. 93-3684, pp. 97–122). Rockville, MD: National Institute on Drug Abuse.

Hinckley, E. C., & Ellis, W. F. (1985). An effective alternative to residential placement: Home-based services. *Journal of Clinical Child Psycholgy, 14,* 209–213.

Hunter, R. W., & Friesen, B. J. (1996). Family-centered services for children with emotional, behavioral and mental health disorders. In C. A. Heflinger & C. Nixon (Eds.), *Families and mental health services for children and adolescents* (pp. 18–40). Newbury Park, CA: Sage.

Kendall, P. C., & Braswell, L. (1993). *Cognitive-behavioral therapy for impulsive children* (2nd ed.). New York: Guilford Press.

Kinney, J., Madsen, B., Fleming, T., & Haapla, D. (1977). Homebuilders: Keeping families together. *Journal of Consulting and Clinical Psychology, 45,* 667–673.

Knitzer, J. (1982). *Unclaimed children: The failure of public responsibility to children and adolescents in need of mental health services.* Washington, DC: Children's Defense Fund.

MacGregor, R., Ritchie, A. M., Serrano, A. C., & Schuster, F. P., Jr. (1964). *Multiple impact therapy with families.* New York: McGraw-Hill.

Munger, R. L. (1993). *Changing children's behavior quickly.* Lanham, MD: Madison.

Patterson, G. R. (1979). *Living with children.* Champaign, IL: Research Press.

Pecora, P. J., Delewski, C. H., Booth, C., Haapla, D., & Kinney, J. (1985). Home-based, family-centered services: The impact of training on worker attitudes. *Child Welfare, 64,* 529–541.

Resick, P. A., & Schnicke, M. K. (1992). Cognitive processing therapy for sexual assault victims. *Journal of Consulting and Clinical Psychology, 60,* 748–756.

Robin, A. L., & Foster, S. L. (1989). *Negotiating parent-adolescent conflict: A behavioral–family systems approach.* New York: Guilford Press.

Sanders, M. R. (1996). New directions in behavioral family intervention with children. In T. H. & R. J. Prinz (Eds.), *Advances in clinical child psychology* (Vol. 18) (pp. 283–3300. New York: Plenum.

Saxe, L., Cross, T., Silverman, N., Batchelor, W., & Daugherty, D. (1986). *Children's mental health: Problems and services.* Durham, NC: Duke University Press.

Sewell, R. (1990). *What are some principal functions performed by an AYI coordinator?* Juneau, AK: Department of Health & Social Services.

Stroul, B. A., & Friedman, R. M. (1986). *A system of care for severely emotionally disturbed children and youth.* Washington, DC: Georgetown University Child Development Center, CASSP Technical Assistance Center.

VanDenBerg, J. E. & Grealish, E. M. (1996). Individualizing services and supports through the wraparound process: Philosophy and procedures. *Journal of Child Family Study, 5,* 7–22.

von Bertalanffy, L. (1968). *General systems theory.* New York: Braziller.

Woolston, J. L., Berkowitz, S. J., Schaefer, M. C., & Adnopoz, J. A. (1998). Intensive, integrated, in-home psychiatric services. In S. J. Berkowitz & J. A. Adnopoz (Guest Eds.) and M. Lewis (Consulting Ed.), *Child and adolescent psychiatric clinics of North America: The child psychiatrist in the community* (vol. 7) (p. 3). Philadelphia: W. B. Saunders.

CHAPTER SEVEN

Development and Implementation of Mobile Crisis Services for Emotionally Disturbed Youth

Paramjit T. Joshi, M.D., Mark E. Greenberg, L.C.S.W.-B.C.D., and Michelle Leff, M.D.

INTRODUCTION

Children and adolescents experiencing a psychiatric crisis have historically received services primarily at an emergency room of a nearby hospital. This has proven to be an ineffective and in many instances an expensive way of delivering acute psychiatric care. Children in psychiatric crisis who are evaluated in the emergency room are often sent home after a brief psychiatric evaluation, and are typically not connected to needed psychiatric services. As a result, these children return to the emergency room when the next psychiatric crisis arises. Unless the child is hospitalized, there is often no consistent psychiatric treatment or aftercare, resulting in unmet mental health needs. Recent changes in health care, and the advent of managed care, have forced us to rethink the manner in which these services are provided. Many cities around the country are beginning to grapple with this issue, and are exploring ways in which to develop child and adolescent crisis response systems, to serve youth in psychiatric crisis and their families. Governmental agencies responsible for public mental health services as well as third-party private insurers of health care are demanding outcome-based services, cost-effective alternatives to traditional service delivery systems.

REVIEW OF LITERATURE

For many decades now there has been debate about the fragmentation within the mental health service systems for children with severe emotional disturbances. It is believed by many that this fragmentation of service delivery in fact compromises the effectiveness of the interventions offered by service agencies (Behar, 1988; Stroul & Friedman, 1986; Saxe et al., 1987; Beachler, 1990). Friedman and Duchnowski (1990) wrote about improved clinical outcomes if these youngsters were treated in the least restrictive and most normative environments. Ralph Nader in his writings has strongly criticized the absence of community-oriented crisis services for patients needing mental health services (Chu & Trotter, 1974). In the last decade there have been increasing numbers of juveniles in the justice system or homeless and in shelters. Many have serious and chronic mental illnesses, and many either receive very poor and fragmented mental health services or no services at all (Yank et al., 1992). Frank (1989) also pointed out the plight of the mentally ill, who were often lost to the system, and sometimes found their way to the local ER, or more likely were found in jails or on the street.

Hospitals must continue to provide inpatient care to the most seriously ill. However, well-designed and adequate community services should be available to serve those who are often at risk of being discharged from inpatient care to inadequate outpatient care. In fact, such services should also be in place to prevent unnecessary and expensive inpatient care in the first place. There is general agreement that comprehensive, community-based systems of care are needed and that those systems of care should include crisis response systems for youngsters who are severely emotionally disturbed.

The Child and Adolescent Service System Program (CASSP), funded by the National Institute of Mental Health, was designed to identify and describe three types of service approaches: home-based services, crisis services, and therapeutic foster care. Stroul and Goldman (1990) studied community-based services for children and adolescents who were severely emotionally disturbed, and concluded that innovative crisis-oriented and long-term home-based programs have been successful as alternatives to more restrictive placements in crisis situations.

The optimal goals of an ideal crisis response system should be to provide a single point of entry to a full array of short-term, coordinated interventions to assist individuals through a crisis situation, and to link them, as necessary, to longer-term mental health services. Such a system would seek to improve access, proximity, and integration of services and promote the provision of crisis treatment in the least restrictive environment. Consequently, it would be expected that implementation of such a crisis response system would reduce the number of individuals presenting to hospital emergency rooms in psychiatric crisis, divert inpatient admissions whenever possible, and reduce acute-care lengths of stay in those cases where diversion cannot be achieved initially. Ultimately, children and their families would benefit from the delivery of coordinated crisis services in their homes and communities.

The remainder of this chapter describes the development of a psychiatric crisis response system for children, adolescents, and their families in a medium-sized city on the East Coast. In most instances the development of an effective, efficient, and comprehensive crisis system will require a partnership between various providers in a given city. Typically no one organization has the capacity to single-handedly provide the array of services that are necessary for such a crisis response system. When developing partnerships, it is important to consider organizations that have considerable experience in providing mental health services to youth and their families. By doing so, the potential partners capitalize on the combined strengths of these organizations. In addition, the partnership organizations usually have relationships with other existing service providers, and can strengthen the crisis system by cultivating these relationships. This will ensure that the crisis response system provides consumer choice, geographic accessibility, and the integration of crisis and longer-term mental health services.

DESCRIPTION OF PARTNERSHIP ORGANIZATIONS

This crisis system was developed in response to a "Request for Proposals" by the Mental Health Authority of the City of Baltimore, which had already implemented an adult crisis response system. Funding for the crisis response system was provided through a combination of billable services and federal and state grants. No single program or organization in the city provided all of the requisite services to respond to the request for proposals, so a partnership was developed between four organizations with complementary programs. The four partnership organizations in this model program included the following:

a) A community hospital, affiliated with a teaching hospital and university;
b) A religiously based charitable organization that provided a continuum of mental health services;

c) The child and adolescent psychiatry services of an academic university/teaching hospital; and
d) A child care agency that provided residential treatment, respite care, and an array of other services for youth and families.

Each of these organizations had a long history of providing mental health services to children and families in the City of Baltimore. The services provided by these four organizations were complementary, which further strengthened the collaboration and commitment to develop a successful crisis response system for children and adolescents and their families. Each organization made a commitment to reach the following objectives:

- A comprehensive continuum of high-quality services to meet the needs of children and adolescents and their families;
- The care and treatment of youth and their families in the least restrictive environments;
- Culturally competent family-centered practice;
- Easy access and streamlined services;
- Cooperation and coordination with other service providers;
- The development of an integrated network of care;
- Ongoing consumer input and evaluation of the system of care;
- Consumer choice;
- Quality improvement; and
- Evaluation and research.

DESCRIPTION OF INTERVENTIONS

The partnership proposed the following six interventions to meet the needs of youth in psychiatric crisis, divert emergency room usage and hospitalization when appropriate, and reduce lengths of stay for those cases where inpatient diversion could not be achieved initially:

1. Crisis hotline (24/7)
2. Mobile crisis (100 hours per week)
3. Enhanced patient services (24/7)
4. In-home intervention (24/7)
5. Crisis beds—therapeutic foster care
6. Crisis beds—group care

Each of the partnership organizations assumed a specific and defined role in delivering services in the crisis response system. The discussion that follows describes each of these interventions, offers a description of the flow of service in the crisis response system, and concludes by discussing the coordination and management of service delivery among and between the partner organizations.

1. Crisis Hotline

The first point of contact with the crisis response system is the crisis hotline. This twenty-four-hour-a-day, seven-day-a-week call-in service is available to any and all children and adolescents in crisis and/or their families as well as to citywide emergency rooms, care providers, and agencies that interface with children and adolescents (e.g., the Department of Social Services, the public school system, the Department of Juvenile Justice, the Police Department, and the Health Department). The crisis hotline is designed to serve as the single point of entry to the crisis response system. Intake information is entered electronically into an automated record system included in the information management system (IMS) designed for the project.

This service is staffed at all times by individuals trained in crisis response. The role of the crisis hotline is to provide psychiatric triage, by phone, to ascertain if in fact there is an actual crisis and if so to assess what interventions are necessary in order to de-escalate and stabilize the situation. It was estimated that this service would triage approximately 3,000 calls over the course of a year. The disposition of calls to the hotline would usually include one of the following:

a) De-escalation of the situation over the phone with appropriate referrals to local mental health providers;
b) Deployment of the mobile crisis team directly to the crisis location; or
c) Referral to appropriate emergency services with follow-up by the mobile crisis team.

The crisis hotline staff would enter the disposition of each call, and when the assessment determined the need for intervention, the case and the electronic record would be forwarded to the mobile crisis team. In addition, the crisis hotline staff would assist in the collection of client and customer satisfaction data and other data required to track the outcomes of the crisis response intervention.

2. Mobile Crisis

The mobile crisis team would be dispatched to the location of a crisis when referred by the crisis hotline. In addition, the mobile crisis team would provide either on-site or telephone consultation when individuals presented in psychiatric crisis to hospital emergency rooms.

a) Capacity and Composition

Two mobile crisis teams are available seven days per week between the hours of 2:00 P.M. and midnight and also Monday through Friday from 8:00 A.M. to 2:00 P.M. The Baltimore City Mental Health Authority determined that the time limit for this service should be two weeks. The mobile crisis teams are staffed to respond to a maximum of 1,200 individuals per year. An analysis of the hospital utilization data from the prior year, about children referred for psychiatric treatment to the city's ERs and inpatient units, indicated that the system could expect approximately three referrals of individuals and their families a day.

The role of the mobile crisis team is to provide: (i) time-limited, community-based services to youth and their families; (ii) ensure that long-term services, when needed, are in place prior to discharge; (iii) divert unnecessary hospitalizations; and (iv) decrease lengths of stay for individuals who present in acute crisis and require hospitalization.

The staffing pattern for each mobile crisis team is as follows:

- Child and adolescent psychiatrist (.20 Full Time Equivalent)—to provide psychiatric evaluation related treatment for youth and clinical consultation to staff
- Nurse clinical specialist (1.0 Full Time Equivalent)—to serve as team leader and to provide psychiatric assessment, take vital signs, and observe for side effects of medications
- Social worker (1.0 Full Time Equivalent)—to provide crisis-oriented therapy
- Rehabilitation therapist (.5 Full Time Equivalent)—to provide case management services, linkages, case/agency coordination, and resource procurement

b) Response at Location of Crisis

The mobile crisis team members would respond to the crisis hotline's call within one hour and attempt to de-escalate the crisis. The mobile crisis team assesses the mental health needs of the youth and his/her family and determines the appropriate level of care. If the services of the crisis response system are indicated, the mobile crisis team develops an initial treatment plan. When the mobile crisis team determines that more intensive services are required to maintain the child/adolescent in the community, the following interventions are made available through the crisis response system:

- One-to-one supervision (enhanced patient supervision);
- Intensive in-home intervention;
- A therapeutic foster care crisis placement;
- A group care residential crisis placement;
- Any combination of the above.

In all cases, treatment and referral decisions are to be made in conjunction with the family, and with consideration as to whether the individual is already linked to an existing mental health provider, the geographic proximity of required services, and the intensity of services required. After the individual is stabilized and/or linked to additional services, the mobile crisis team continues to treat and monitor the individual for up to two weeks, as needed, to ensure that stability is maintained.

In those extreme cases where establishing community stability is not possible, the mobile crisis team would facilitate admission to an inpatient unit or a partial hospitalization program. The mobile crisis team would follow up with the individual and hospital personnel within twenty-four hours to facilitate the quickest possible discharge to the community with the support of wraparound services.

c) Response to Emergency Room

Clearly, even with the availability of the hotline and mobile crisis team, some individuals would continue to self-refer to the local ER when faced with a psychiatric crisis. In these cases, the crisis response system via the mobile crisis team is available to consult with ER personnel to offer the full array of diversion services listed above. In those cases where hospitalization is deemed necessary to ensure safety, the role of the mobile crisis team is to be available to facilitate the earliest possible discharge through access to alternative resources. Although diversion is not always possible, immediate involvement of the mobile crisis team would help reduce the number of days children and adolescents spend in inpatient units, thus facilitating family preservation, community-based treatment, and more cost-effective service delivery. All of the services provided during this crisis period last only as long as necessary, with the goal of appropriate linkage to local mental health resources within a two-week period.

3. One-to-One Supervision

The mobile crisis team may determine that some youth could benefit from one-to-one in-home supervision and support. This enhanced service is available in the child's home, or to support a crisis foster home or group care placement. One-to-one supervision can be deployed up to twenty-four hours per day to assist the child in attaining or maintaining stabilization outside of an acute care setting.

4. In-Home Intervention

In-home interventions are designed to offer crisis intervention, intensive counseling, parent/guardian coaching, consultation, and ongoing de-escalation and behavior management supports. These services could be initiated by the mobile crisis team, in consultation with the child/adolescent and the parent/guardian, at any point in the course of treatment.

In-home intervention services are available on a twenty-four-hours-a-day, seven-days-a-week basis to support the mobile crisis team's plan for diverting or abbreviating the hospitalization of a youth. The primary role of the in-home intervention specialist is to provide ongoing crisis management support, conflict resolution strategies, behavior management consultation, and crisis prevention planning to stabilize the youth and his/her family. When not in the home delivering services, the in-home specialist is available to respond to the family within one hour of a request for support. If a crisis bed placement is determined to be the appropriate diversion service, the in-home intervention staff can be accessed to assist in the child or adolescent's transition home. The successful transition back to the home and family and the preparation of a crisis plan for future incidents is the focus of such an intervention.

The in-home intervention specialists are individuals who are experienced in providing family support and behavior management training to youth and families experiencing emotional and behavioral crisis. The specialists are experienced in identifying the individualized needs and goals of each family and in empowering families to access resources available to them in their community. The in-home specialists work in concert with the members of the mobile crisis teams. They assist parents in developing skills for detecting the antecedents of their child's crises and developing plans for responding earlier to de-escalate symptomatic behavior. Specialists are also skilled in assisting families in the development of a crisis plan that could be implemented if there is a reoccurrence of crisis behavior.

5. Crisis Beds—Therapeutic Foster Care

During the past two decades there has been an increasing emphasis on keeping severely disturbed youth in "natural environments" rather than in institutions (Brook, 1973; Brook et al., 1976; Polak & Kirby, 1976). A foster home alternative program was developed by Walker and Brook (1981) at the Southwest Denver Community Mental Health Center for runaway youth. This was modeled after the center's adult alternative community home network. As early as 1958, Winnicott wrote about placing the burden of the treatment on the family and treating a youth at home, and was positive about the use of foster care combined with case management.

In fact, treatment foster care is increasingly viewed as a viable alternative to residential and hospital care, and is an integral component to the range of services provided by the crisis response system. Three residential crisis beds are maintained in three licensed therapeutic foster care homes in Baltimore City. The time limit for this intervention is, again, up to two weeks. The homes are staffed by caregivers who, in addition to meeting the pre-service and ongoing training requirements for therapeutic foster care, receive specialized training in recognizing and managing psychiatric crisis symptoms in children and adolescents. The therapeutic foster care homes are available to the mobile crisis teams, twenty-four hours a day, seven days a week. The families that offer this service are required to have an adult caregiver in the home at all times and the primary caregiver is not permitted to work outside of the home.

The therapeutic foster care case manager is responsible for assisting the family caregivers in implementing the treatment interventions established in the initial Individualized Treatment Plan (ITP) by the mobile crisis team. The case manager also handles the completion of all of the necessary documentation required to meet state regulations for the use of crisis beds. All youth referred for crisis placement receive psychiatric services through the mobile crisis team.

6. Crisis Beds—Group Care

In addition to the three crisis beds that are available through the specially trained therapeutic foster family homes, the crisis system provides three other crisis beds that are housed in a more structured group setting. These are located in a self-contained unit within a Children's Diagnostic Treatment Center. Although designated staff are recruited and trained to work with the youth who are placed in crisis beds, the fact that these beds are located in a larger residential program that operates twenty-four hours per day, seven days per week, provides built-in backup support if needed. This service is also accessed through the mobile crisis team and is designated for those youth who require a structured crisis placement as an alternative to hospitalization. The group-based crisis beds are available twenty-four hours per day, seven days per week, for placements of up to two weeks, or as clinically indicated. The primary goal of this service is to effect immediate resolution to the most critical presenting problem and to develop a permanent and safe plan of discharge by coordinating with caretakers, crisis response system partners, and the mental health community.

COORDINATION AND ADMINISTRATIVE STRUCTURE OF THE CRISIS RESPONSE SYSTEM

A crisis response system, such as the one described above, offers enormous advantages by combining the strengths and talents of four mental health providers. Successful implementation of this type of system requires extensive coordination and cooperation among the partner organizations. To facilitate collaboration and integration, the partnership created an administrative oversight committee and a clinical management team. Both groups consist of representatives from each of the four partner organizations.

The crisis response system is managed and controlled by the administrative oversight committee. This committee is composed of two representatives from each partner organization. The administrative oversight committee employs a full-time project coordinator to oversee and coordinate all aspects of the crisis response system. This individual coordinates the quality improvement, risk management, data collection, patient tracking and documentation, marketing, public relations, and reporting functions for the partnership. In addition, the project coordinator leads the clinical management team and is responsible for coordinating program evaluation efforts. In order to meet the demand for public accountability, program evaluation has been given careful thought. As has been described by Paul and Turner (1976), the rising demand for accountability and consumer protection places increasing pressures on community mental health centers and crisis services to empirically validate their programs. The administrative oversight committee meets as often as necessary to manage all aspects of the crisis response system. The clinical management team meets regularly, to plan and track service delivery to all youth receiving services. The clinical management team is composed of eight individuals: the project coordinator, the medical director, and one lead worker from each service offered by the system. The team is responsible for overseeing treatment planning, monitoring the integration of service delivery, evaluating the progress of open cases, linking with other providers, and planning discharges from the crisis response system.

The partnership also established an advisory board for the child and adolescent crisis response system. This board includes consumers of mental health services (specifically parents who had accessed services for their children), appropriate stakeholders in the Baltimore City service delivery system, and advocates in the area of mental health and other children's issues.

COLLABORATIONS

1. Collaboration with Public Agencies

Prior to issuing a request for proposals for a child and adolescent psychiatric crisis response system, Baltimore City's Mental Health Authority conducted an extensive needs assessment. One of the most compelling findings was that a significant number of the youth who were appearing in crisis at hospital emergency rooms, and who were subsequently being referred for psychiatric hospitalization, were children in the care and custody of public agencies. Based on this information, the administrative oversight committee established as one of its top priorities a close collaborative relationship with the Department of Social Services, the Department of Juvenile Justice, the Department of Education, and the city's Police Department. Key representatives of each of these city agencies were recruited as members of the crisis response system's advisory board. Each of these agencies played a key role in designing, implementing, and evaluating the operation of the crisis response system.

Members of the administrative oversight committee and the clinical management team, accompanied by leadership from the Baltimore City Mental Health Authority, conducted orientation and training sessions for managers and staff from each of the four public agencies. Initial training sessions provided information on access and use of the crisis response system. A follow-up session focused on how to recognize a psychiatric crisis and ways to mobilize resources to hopefully avoid unnecessary use of the emergency rooms. These training sessions provided an opportunity for the personnel of the crisis response system to learn each public agency's particular needs and issues related to child and adolescent mental health.

During the first four months of operation the crisis response system was permitted to limit the number of referral sources that could access the crisis hotline, and thus restrict the number of children who were being referred for service. This period allowed the staff from the four partner organizations a chance to coalesce, and enabled the clinical management team to further refine and clarify procedures. Furthermore, it provided time for the staff of the crisis response system to establish relationships with liaisons within each of the public agencies.

2. Collaboration with Emergency Rooms

The system's project coordinator initially conducted an extensive campaign to notify and educate all city emergency room providers as to the existence of the hotline, mobile crisis service, and other alternatives to hospitalization that are available through the crisis response system. Members of the administrative oversight committee also worked closely with the city Mental Health Authority and the Administrative Service Organization (which was under contract with the state to manage access to the public mental health system). This was important to ensure that the crisis response system is notified of all children in psychiatric crisis who are being evaluated for potential hospitalization. The crisis response system attempts to work cooperatively with all hospitals to provide alternatives to hospitalization, when appropriate, and to ensure timely and effective discharge planning. Its goal is to have ER staff contact the mobile crisis team for consultation prior to recommending a child or adolescent for psychiatric admission, and to facilitate access to nonhospital crisis intervention services, when clinically indicated.

The project coordinator, clinical management team, and administrative oversight committee share responsibility for linkage, liaison, and networking with the city ERs. Outreach and linkage efforts included direct contact with the directors of all city emergency departments, and presentations for appropriate ER personnel regarding the functions of the crisis response system and its interplay with ER services. The presentations focus on the capability of the mobile crisis team to respond directly to all emergency rooms and to collaborate with ER staff to help assess the appropriate level of care for children and adolescents in need of urgent mental health services.

The expectation is that all children presenting to the ER will be evaluated for somatic problems by a pediatrician. The crisis response team is to be activated only upon completion of the somatic and psychiatric evaluations. In some ERs the psychiatric evaluation is completed by the resident physician, and in others by other mental health professionals with the backing of an on call psychiatrist.

The following scenarios outline the most frequent dispositions:

- The youth is stabilized and discharged home.
  - If the youth is currently receiving mental health services, ER personnel attempt to contact that provider to advise them of the situation.
  - If the youth does not have a current mental health provider, he or she is referred to a community mental health provider for follow-up care, as deemed necessary.
- The youth is not stable and additional services are required.
  - The mobile crisis team offers one or more of the crisis intervention services available, including one-to-one supervision, in-home intervention, and/or a crisis bed placement in a foster or group care setting.
  - If the evaluating clinician in the ER believes that the youth is acutely dangerous to him/herself or others, psychotic, and in critical need of hospitalization, then the ER proceeds with an inpatient admission. In this case, the mobile crisis team checks back within twenty-four hours to assess the need for continued hospitalization and, if appropriate, collaborates with hospital staff and with the family or guardian to facilitate a timely discharge with community-based supports.

The crisis response system is predicated on the belief that immediate access to a coordinated continuum of community-based resources will prevent unnecessary hospitalizations. The needs assessment conducted by the Baltimore City Mental Health Authority prior to the development of a request for proposals confirmed that a number of children referred for inpatient admission could have been more appropriately treated in a less restrictive community-based service, if such a service had been accessible. The crisis response system is designed to provide intensive, time-limited, community-based crisis stabilization for youth and their families and to ensure that long-term services, when needed, are in place prior to discharge. The child and adolescent crisis response system is expected to divert unnecessary hospitalizations, and to decrease the lengths of stay for those who presented in acute crisis and needed to be hospitalized.

3. Linkage to Ongoing Mental Health Treatment

Successful linkage, marketing, and coordination with the mental health provider network in the city was critical to the initial program development, implementation, and continuous operation of the system. Ruffin et al. (1993) have described two significant problems in implementing such a crisis program. Other professionals in the community need much education to convince them that a community-based alternative would be adequate for their patient. In their experience this has been particularly true for physicians in the ER and other mental health professionals who have always viewed an inpatient unit as a safe haven for their patients.

The project coordinator and members of the administrative oversight committee have developed relationships with other child and adolescent mental health providers in the city. These providers serve as a source of referrals to the crisis response system and are included on the list of aftercare resources that families can access for service upon discharge from the crisis system. These providers are also contacted for feedback on the efficacy of the system and their input is incorporated into the performance improvement process.

Upon discharge from the crisis response system, youngsters who were already receiving mental health services are referred back to their existing provider for follow-up care if possible. When planning aftercare services for children and their families who did not have a preexisting relationship with a mental health provider, the youth and his/her family are given a list of providers and sites to select from. In this way, consumers are provided with choices, and are able to make treatment decisions based on geographic proximity and personal preference. As a measure of consumer choice, and as a way of documenting that the crisis response system is not inappropriately referring cases to its own partnership agencies, data is collected to document case disposition and referrals made both to partnership organizations and other providers. This data is reviewed periodically by the administrative oversight committee.

4. Collaboration with Existing Child and Adolescent Crisis Response Systems

The staff of the crisis response system received extensive training prior to being deployed. Resources were appropriated from each of the partner organizations and a comprehensive training and orientation curriculum was developed. Initial training focused on the philosophy, values, and mission of the crisis response system. Subsequent training included topics such as team building, risk management, and maintaining personal safety. Other systems from around the nation were consulted to identify state-of-the-art best practice models. Representatives of each of the partner organizations visited another East Coast city to gain firsthand exposure to an existing psychiatric crisis response system for children and adolescents. Several national experts were hired as consultants to assist with the preparation of the staff.

OUTCOMES

A systematic process of measurement and assessment was instituted in order to track the performance of the crisis response system along several clinical and administrative indicators.

Clinical Indicators:

- Reduction in the number of children hospitalized as a result of psychiatric crisis
- Reduction in the patient length of stay for approved hospitalizations
- Sustained stabilization post–crisis response system intervention
- Customer satisfaction with the crisis response system
- Linkages of discharged youth/families to mental health resources
- Incidents of harm to self or others

Administrative Indicators:

- Twenty-four-hour hotline "pickup time" within four rings
- Mobile crisis team response time within one hour from call to action
- Utilization review of appropriateness of crisis response system's determination of acuity and required level of care
- Referral to mental health providers, including partnership and nonpartnership organizations.

In addition to tracking these indicators that are reported to the Baltimore City Mental Health Authority, the project coordinator is also responsible for monitoring a host of other performance improvement measures. These include quality-of-care and integration-of-treatment issues that are addressed expeditiously by the clinical management team, and risk management and resource utilization issues that are addressed by the administrative oversight committee. This would include the identification of, and collection of data specific to, indicators and sensors, which would be tracked and reported on a regular basis. These indicators and sensors would include the occurrences of: self-harm, community endangerment, property damage, and violation of the law.

SENSITIVITY TO CULTURAL AND INDIVIDUAL NEEDS

The four partnership organizations made a commitment to provide services that were responsive to the cultural and individual needs of all youth and their families residing in Baltimore City. The city is composed of a rich network of neighborhoods and communities that provide a population of diverse racial, cultural, religious, and ethnic affiliations. Each community has unique structures, textures, and "cultures," resulting in unique needs. It was important for the staff of the crisis response system to work with these community structures to identify the best way to let people know about these services, to destigmatize the services, and to help people feel comfortable enough to use them. Fortunately the four partner organizations were already very familiar with Baltimore City and had well-established relationships in most communities around the city. Community leaders from different areas of Baltimore were contacted to acquaint them with the philosophy and values of the system and to elicit their input and support. The partnership organizations were also successful in recruiting a culturally diverse and highly qualified workforce, reflective of the population served.

Family involvement is critical to the successful de-escalation, stabilization, and long-term functioning of youth in the community. It is considered imperative for the mobile crisis team to engage families, legal guardians, and foster families, kinship-care families, extended family members, and/or other significant support systems in the community. Families are involved in every aspect of a child's treatment. Family members are encouraged to participate in all treatment planning discussions and are provided with choices for all referral and discharge options. Evaluative feedback is elicited from families through formal consumer satisfaction surveys and informal discussions with staff and consumer advocates. Feedback from families is of paramount importance in the ongoing evaluation and performance improvement process. The administrative oversight committee monitors the perceptions of families regarding the demeanor and cultural sensitivity of the system's staff as well as their responsiveness and the efficacy of their interventions.

Successful linkage, marketing, and coordination with the mental health provider network is critical to the initial program development, implementation, and operations of the project. Furthermore, there are costs involved in the development of such programs, even though there is much in the literature to suggest that community-based programs are less expensive and as effective as inpatient care (Friedman, 1985; Keisler, 1982; Mosher, 1983; Gutstein, 1988). While some of the marketing strategies identified above also target the mental health provider network, those public, private, and nonprofit customers are encouraged to invite system staff to appropriate meetings for more detailed, face-to-face training as well.

In addition, the crisis response system sought membership on appropriate advisory committees, boards and advocacy organizations such as the Mental Health Association, Alliance for Mentally Ill, National Alliance for Mentally Ill, and Parents Involved Together. Other agencies such as the Department of Parks and Recreation, the Police Department, juvenile courts, MCOs, neighborhood health clinics, and community/neighborhood associations received written materials and the request to schedule a presentation of the system to their staff. Ongoing and persistent contact with the community and the service delivery system followed initial education and marketing.

CONCLUSION

The crisis response system described in this chapter was created in response to a request for proposals issued by a midsize city on the East Coast. It is hoped that this system can serve as a model for other organizations or public agencies that are contemplating this type of service. For such a system to be effective and accountable, it is crucial to take into account the strengths of the city in terms of its population base, ethnic diversity, and cultural nuances. It is important for such a system to be committed to a collaborative approach that involves a close working relationship between the staff of the crisis response system and the broader network of mental health providers. The system is predicated on the belief that immediate access to a coordinated continuum of community-based resources will prevent unnecessary hospitalizations, reduce inappropriate use of emergency rooms, and decrease the lengths of stay of children who are hospitalized. Services are designed to be accessible and responsive; they comprise a comprehensive array of complementary services that can be creatively blended based on the needs of a particular child and his/her family.

The system is rooted in a set of core values that include: (a) treating youth in the least restrictive, most clinically appropriate setting; (b) delivering services in a culturally sensitive manner that focuses on the strengths of each family; (c) making services available and responsive to the needs of the families; (d) offering consumers choice and factoring feedback into improvement efforts that address all aspects of the service delivery; and (e) collaborating closely with stakeholders in the community.

Such a system design does have some inherent vulnerabilities. There is potential redundancy and ambiguity in administrative and clinical leadership roles due to the fact that several organizations are involved in governance and service delivery. Accountability for record keeping and data collection might pose a challenge when shared among staff in four agencies. In addition, there is a risk of communication problems between the partner agencies. One needs to be cognizant of these potential limitations during the development of such a system and make a commitment to proactively address them if they emerge as such a system is being developed.

A mobile crisis response system should not be viewed as a panacea, but as an essential component of a comprehensive, community-based system of care for emotionally disturbed youngsters and their families. We believe that when such a system is carefully and thoughtfully put into place it will accomplish the goals that it sets out to achieve.

References

Beachler, M. (1990). The mental health services program for youth. *Journal of Mental Health Administration, 17,* 115–121.

Behar, L. (1988). An integrated state system of services for seriously disturbed children. In J. G. Looney (Ed.), *Chronic mental illness in children and adolescents.* Washington DC: American Psychiatric Press.

Brook, B. D. (1973). Crisis hostel: An alternative to psychiatric hospitalization for emergency patients. *Hospital and Community Psychiatry, 24,* 621–624.

Brook, B. D., Cortes, M., March, R., & Stirling, M. S. (1976). Community families as alternatives in psychiatric hospital intensive care. *Hospital and Community Psychiatry, 27*(3), 195–198.

Chu, F., & Trotter, F. (1974). *The madness establishment: Ralph Nader's study group report on the National Institute of Mental Health.* New York: Grossman.

Duchnowski, A. J., & Friedman, R. M. (1990). Children's mental health services: Challenges for the nineties. *The Journal of Mental Health Administration, 17*(1), 3–12.

Frank, R. G. (1989). The medically indigent mentally ill: Approaches to financing. *Hospital and Community Psychiatry, 40,* 799–804.

Friedman, R. M. (1985). *Serving seriously emotionally disturbed children: An overview of major issues.* Research Training Center for Improved Services for Seriously Emotionally Disturbed Children. Florida Mental Health Institute.

Gutstein, S. E., Rudd, M. D., Graham, J. C., & Rayha, L. L. (1988). Systematic crisis intervention as a response to adolescent crisis: An outcome study. *Family Process, 27,* 201–211.

Keisler, C. (1982). Mental hospitals and alternative care-noninstitutionalization as potential public policy for mental patients. *American Psychologist, 37,* 349–360.

Mosher, L. R. (1983). Alternatives to psychiatric hospitalization. Why has research failed to be translated into practice? *New England Journal of Medicine, 309,* 1579–1580.

Paul, T. W., & Turner, A. J. (1976). Evaluating the crisis service of a community mental health center. *American Journal of Community Psychiatry, 4*(3), 303–308.

Polak, P. & Kirby, M. (1976). A model to replace psychiatric hospitals. *Journal of Nervous and Mental Disorders, 162*(1), 13–21.

Ruffin, J. E., Spencer, H. R., Abel, A., Gage, J., & Miles, L. (1993). Crisis stabilization services for children and adolescents: A brokerage model to reduce admissions to state psychiatric facilities. *Community Mental Health Journal, 29*(5), 433–440.

Saxe, L., Cross, T., Silverman, N., Batchelor, W., & Daugherty, D (1987). *Children's mental health: Problems and treatment*. Durham NC: Duke University Press.

Stroul, B. A., & Friedman, R. M. (1986). *A system of care for severely emotionally disturbed youth*. Washington, DC: Georgetown University Child Development Center, CASSP Technical Assistance Center.

Stroul, B. A., & Goldman, S. K. (1990). Study of community-based services for children and adolescents who are severely emotionally disturbed. *Journal of Mental Health Administration, 17*(1), 61–77.

Walker, P., & Brook, B. D. (1981). Community homes as hospital alternatives for youth in crisis. *Journal of Pscyhosocial Nursing and Mental Health Services*, March, 17–19.

Winnicott, D. W. (1958). A case managed at home. In *Collected Papers* (pp. 118–126). New York: Basic Books.

Yank, G. R., Hargrove, D. S., & Davis, K. (1992). Toward the financial integration of public mental health services. *Community Mental Health Journal, 28*(2), 97–108.

CHAPTER EIGHT

Home- and Community-Based Treatment Programs for Severely Emotionally Disturbed Treatment-Resistant Youth and Their Families: The Child Mobile Team

Harinder S. Ghuman, M.D., Eileen Hastings, R.N.C., L.C.S.W.C., and Marsha Gorth, L.C.S.W.C.

INTRODUCTION

During the last decade there has been increased interest and emphasis on providing psychiatric services to youth in their homes and communities. This is due to a growing awareness of the limitations of clinic-based treatment for seriously emotionally disturbed youth and their families, especially for youth and families with multiple needs and involvement in multiple agencies and systems. Out-of-home placement in hospitals, residential facilities, and group settings is costly, disruptive to the youth and the family, and has an unclear long-term outcome. Various concepts and models of home- and community-based treatments are summarized in chapter 6. In this chapter, we present a description of a home- and community-based program for youth and families.

HISTORY OF CHILD MOBILE TREATMENT

The University of Maryland Walter P. Carter Clinics (WPCC) have for over twenty-five years traditionally served youth with severe emotional/behavioral problems with multiple psychosocial and psychoeducational issues. Clinicians working in these outpatient clinics found that a large part of their work with these youth and their families required extensive case management services such as coordination with the Department of Social Services (DSS), schools and the Department of Education, probation officers, and court and other agencies. These case management services were time-consuming but essential, as many emotional and behavioral problems of youth were rooted in, or exacerbated by, inadequate or inappropriate community or educational services. These case management demands often required the outpatient clinician to perform activities in the community and to develop liaisons with community resources. However, due to the large caseload size, an inability to bill for these services, and lack of transportation, it became necessary for the traditional outpatient program to look at alternatives in care delivery. In 1994, the WPCC responded to a request for a proposal (RFP) to develop comprehensive case management services for children by Baltimore Mental Health Systems, Inc. (a citywide core service agency), and the clinics were granted one-time funds in the amount of $87,500. This award to WPCC resulted in the establishment of a case management team in January 1995 to serve as a complement to an already existing outpatient clinic–based team.

Initially youth and family had a primary therapist from the child outpatient clinic, who provided therapies in the clinic, and the case management team, which provided case management services in the home and community. After the first year, in order to improve coordination and utilization of the services, it was decided to establish an independent child mobile team (CMT) with its own caseload with responsibility for both therapeutic and case management services. Another major step in providing more home and community services was the establishment in 1996 of a special program in coordination with the Department of Juvenile Justice (DJJ) for adjudicated juvenile delinquents, with the majority of these youth being referred to the CMT.

CHILD MOBILE TEAM PRINCIPLES AND MODEL

The CMT incorporated some of the common elements of other community- and home-based models of treatment described in detail in the previous chapter, including: (1) major treatment efforts were home- and community-based; (2) there was thorough evaluation of the youth, the family, and the school and community environment regarding needs, strengths, and resources; (3) the youth and families received individualized supports and services; (4) the youth, immediate and extended family, school staff, and other agency (or agencies) staff were sought to be actively involved in the treatment process; (5) the CMT established close contact with school personnel, Board of Education staff, DJJ and DSS staff, legal advocacy agencies, family support agencies, respite, inpatient, and day treatment and recreational facilities by attending formal meetings and through informal contacts; (6) the CMT provided a wide range of treatment and case management services; (7) services were available on a twenty-four-hours-a-day, seven-days-a-week basis; (8) the CMT staff carried small and shared caseloads and engaged in intensive team work; (9) the home-based services were provided for as long as necessary until the youth and the family were ready to make the transition to traditional outpatient treatment; and (10) outcome studies were conducted.

Some of the major differences in the (WPCC) CMT model from other home- and community-based models were: (1) A child and adolescent psychiatrist had ultimate responsibility for the clinical care and focus of treatment. (2) Interventions were broad-based and included family systems, various behavior therapies and psychotherapies, and medical models of treatment. The results of some of these interventions were easily measurable, while others were not. The CMT was not wedded to any one type of approach but rather looked at what were the youth's and family's needs and what interventions the youth and the family could utilize. (3) Although the CMT tried to develop close working relationships with school systems and various agencies, at times when a particular agency was unresponsive to the youth's or family's needs the CMT assertively tried to involve the agency hierarchy or sought legal aid. The CMT considered the needs of youth and the family paramount. (4) Although the primary goal of the CMT was family preservation, there were certain cases where the team worked with the family to obtain out-of-home placement and maintain the youth in the home until placement was secured. Out-of-home placement usually was recommended in cases where the youth was chronically in danger to him/herself or others and/or when the family situation was too dangerous to the youth despite the CMT interventions over a considerable time or, obviously, when the youth and family were unavailable for treatment despite repeated efforts by the CMT. In such cases, the CMT did not consider placement of the youth in a residential or group setting as treatment failure but rather as a necessary step in healthy growth. (5) The CMT staff paid special attention to safety issues when working in dangerous home or neighborhood environments and also worked in pairs with aggressive juvenile offenders, had a cellular phone available, visited families during certain hours of the day, and set clear guidelines with the youth and family regarding acceptable behaviors.

The CMT staff conceptualized the use of intensive team approach and milieu treatment as the basis for their work (Ghuman & Sarles, 1998). This involves a "core" of the CMT members with the support of "associate" team members including teachers, DSS workers, mentors, and probation officers (if any) all working together in providing containment, support, and structure to the youth and family.

CMT ADMINISTRATION

The child mobile team functioned under the overall direction of a program director with a nursing and social work background. The program director was assisted by a senior social worker who was designated as the child and adolescent services coordinator. The program director, with the help of the child and adolescent services coordinator, was responsible for setting the budget, staff hiring and evaluation, overseeing compliance with regulatory agencies, and insurance. The child and adolescent services coordinator played a pivotal role in the functioning of the CMT by overseeing and linking all the child services within the program.

The Team

Within the team, there was an identified team leader (masters'-level social worker or nurse), a part-time child and adolescent psychiatrist who also served as medical director, two staff social workers, one mental health counselor, and a part-time addiction specialist. In addition, general psychiatry residents in their senior year elected to have training and clinical experience in home-based services for youth. The caseload expectation for a CMT clinician was 1:12, with a minimal twenty-four hours per week of direct service.

Staff Recruitment, Personnel Orientation, and Supervision

The CMT program used a "committee" model of recruitment for non-medical staff in which the program director, child and adolescent services coordinator, and team leader interviewed all prospective candidates. The team psychiatrist then interviewed the top two or three candidates. The final decision was collaborative. This process allowed the candidate to meet the primary administrative staff and provided validation for the interviewers (Hastings, Gorth, & Ghuman, 1998).

The interview was focused on assessing the candidate's depth of knowledge and clinical experience, on his or her motivation and interest in working in the community with youth and families with special needs, and on his or her cultural competence. For example, two of the CMT clinicians were hired because of their special interest in working with juvenile delinquents, one of them with experience as a probation officer.

The newly hired staff received a fairly lengthy and detailed orientation. This took place at three levels. The University of Maryland medical system (UMMS) conducted an orientation explaining benefits/compensation, mission and values, personnel policies, infection control, and fire safety. The second level of orientation took place at the WPCC, where the new staff met with other program directors or their designees to better understand the role of their program and the interface with the various other WPCC programs. The new employees also met with support staff and other key clinical and administrative staff, and were introduced to specific program policies and procedures, such as the use of the CMT van and petty cash. The third level of orientation took place at the CMT level, which included several meetings with the child and adolescent service coordinator, team leader, medical director, and other CMT clinicians to clarify the role and expectations of the new staff, the weekly schedule, and medical record documentation policies and requirements. CMT staff oriented the new employees to assigned youth and their families by providing them with information and taking them to homes, schools, and communities.

The emphasis of the orientation was not just to provide information to new staff but to convey a sense of belonging and security. Important issues such as office assignment and parking were addressed carefully, and a clinical supervisor closely mentored the new staff.

Role of the Team Leader

The team leader provided day-to-day administrative leadership to all the clinicians, helping them structure their day and setting priorities in dealing with issues related to their assigned youth and their families. Cases in crisis were given top priority. The team leader helped the CMT clinician to develop a schedule so that all the youth and families were seen regularly and so that the clinician had a plan of action. Other responsibilities included scheduling new admissions and treatment plan revisions, patient assignments, supervision of the clinicians in the team, and recording of the key events form and Child and Adolescent Functional Assessment Scale

(CAFAS). The team leader's role was to act as an intermediary between administration and the CMT staff to implement program objectives, to monitor productivity, to provide staff training and retraining, to monitor medical records documentation, to measure staff morale, and to manage personnel and administrative priorities.

Role of the Team Psychiatrist

The team child and adolescent psychiatrist provided overall clinical leadership to the CMT staff as a medical director. The role of the team psychiatrist was fourfold: (1) to provide clinical supervision and teaching. The team psychiatrist provided individual clinical supervision to the team leader and psychiatry resident trainee and provided education and training to all the CMT staff during team meetings and via day-to-day consultation. In addition, the team psychiatrist facilitated the monthly clinical case conference with outside expert consultation; (2) to provide support to the team leader and clinical staff. The team leader, who provided leadership for day-to-day program and personnel issues, and the psychiatrist, who provided clinical leadership, shared the leadership responsibilities for the team. It was important that the team leader and the psychiatrist work together in setting priorities and tasks, resolving staff conflicts, and presenting CMT staff needs to higher administration. As working with severely disturbed youth and their families often resulted in staff feeling frustrated, helpless, and demoralized, the team psychiatrist helped them in dealing with these feelings and helped them focus on plans of action; (3) to monitor and provide clinical care. The team psychiatrist conducted weekly rounds on the entire caseload to evaluate progress and emerging issues, to oversee the quality of the treatment provided, and to develop treatment strategies. The team psychiatrist was responsible for the initial psychiatric evaluation and for arriving at a working diagnosis or diagnoses, making treatment recommendations, and providing psychopharmacological treatment; and (4) to work with the program, division administration, and department. This was important as a way to educate others regarding the CMT program and needs, to develop linkage, to develop referral resources, and to update the CMT staff regarding departmental and divisional activities.

Team Meetings

The CMT staff had three weekly formal meetings. An intake/admission/diagnostic meeting was held each Monday to review all the new cases referred to the CMT. The referral staff was invited to attend this meeting to briefly present the case and to describe reasons for referral to the CMT. If the case was deemed appropriate for the CMT, it was scheduled for admission. In this meeting, new admissions from the previous week were presented to finalize the diagnosis/diagnoses, the treatment plan, and case assignment. Also, a treatment planning meeting was held on Wednesdays to review the treatment plans of active cases. The youth, the family, and staff from other agencies (DJJ, DSS, and school staff) were invited to this meeting. Often a CAFAS was obtained by the team group consensus. Finally, weekly rounds were held on Thursdays to briefly go over each case to assess the progress, availability, and involvement of the youth and the family in treatment, to examine any crises or critical issues encountered that week, and to develop short-term strategies.

REFERRAL PROCESS, ADMISSION CRITERIA, AND INTAKE PROCEDURE

Initially, the child and adolescent services coordinator was responsible for coordinating CMT intakes. Later this responsibility was shifted to the CMT leader as the CMT became better established. Two separate intake procedure were established depending upon referral source:

1. Referrals of active cases in WPCC outpatient clinics
   When an active clinic case was identified as needing more intensive home-based services, the following procedure was followed:
   a) Youth had to meet the admission criteria as described below.
   b) A CAFAS was completed on the youth by the current therapist with input from the psychiatrist, team leader, and/or supervisor.
   c) The therapist discussed the youth's condition and reason for referral with the clinical supervisor and the treating psychiatrist. If they concurred with a referral, the case was discussed briefly with the team leader, who had to agree with the decision. If there was disagreement regarding referral, the case was discussed in the clinic team meeting for additional input.
   d) If all involved felt that a referral was appropriate, the therapist called the CMT intake coordinator.
   e) At times, further treatment team recommendations were made to the clinic team to implement before the youth was accepted by the CMT, for example, medication adjustment or change, obtaining certain information from family or agencies, and involving other agencies.
   f) If the youth was accepted for the CMT, the clinic therapist in-

formed the youth and the family and obtained their consent for home interventions.

g) The clinic therapist was responsible for setting up and facilitating the intake appointment and bringing all the documentation up to date, including a transfer form.

2. Referrals from outside clinics or agencies
At times, the child and adolescent team intake screener was able to identify youth that met CMT admission criteria on the telephone or during a walk-in screening. When this occurred, the intake screener was to complete the intake screening form and a CAFAS to assist in determining the severity of psychiatric illness and the intensity of treatment needs. Screening information that suggested that the youth was likely to benefit from CMT interventions was triaged to the CMT for the intake interview after consultation with the clinic team leader and the coordinator of child and adolescent services. Youth triaged to the CMT were expected to have a scheduled intake no later than five days from the intake call. Immediate and aggressive outreach was done for youth who had missed the intake appointment. The CAFAS was again administered as a part of the intake. If the interview and CAFAS score indicated that the youth did not meet the criteria for CMT admission, the CMT team leader contacted the clinic team leader to share the findings and request assignment of the youth to the outpatient clinic. The youth was then assigned and scheduled to see a child therapist within one week of the transfer.

CRITERIA FOR ADMISSION

Admission to the CMT required the following criteria:

a) A primary DSM-IV diagnosis other than mental retardation or developmental disorders.
b) Age from four to eighteen years.
c) Residence within the catchment area. Those who resided out of the catchment area were admitted if there was some connection with the lead agency, such as when youth were already in treatment in one of the university clinics, one or both parents were in psychiatric treatment in one of the university clinics, or if some compelling clinical reason was present. These decisions were made jointly by the child and adolescent services coordinator, the CMT medical director, and the CMT leader.

d) Moderate to severe psychiatric symptoms, likely to have a GAF <50 and a moderate to severe rating (score above 40) on the CAFAS.
e) Three or more of the following treatment problems:

1. A history of multiple or lengthy psychiatric hospitalizations, residential treatment, or other out-of-home placements.
2. Frequent acute and/or severe clinical crises that required additional support to manage or prevent removal of the child from the home, or to prevent the psychiatric hospitalization of the youth or caregiver.
3. Chronic or frequently recurring family or social crises that required extensive interventions.
4. Extremely chaotic family situations that interfered with meeting the basic needs of the youth and resulted in noncompliance with psychiatric treatment.
5. Involvement with several agencies or entities requiring extensive coordination and/or case management intervention.
6. Impulsivity of the youth and/or family complicating the clinical picture, such as financial mismanagement, substance abuse, frequent moves, running away, illegal activities, and chronic truancy.
7. In-home assessment and intervention being a necessary and ongoing requirement to manage treatment adequately.

CMT ADMISSION AND ASSESSMENT

In most cases, the youth and the family were seen for admission to the CMT within five working days after the initial referral and intake screening on the phone. The CMT admitted up to one new youth per week. Priority for admissions was set by the child and adolescent services coordinator and the CMT leader. For the cases already active in the WPCC outpatient clinics, the CMT clinician and psychiatrist met with the youth and the family to review information in the chart, to update the mental status examination, to revise the diagnosis, to assess the current family situation, and to revise the plan of care. As documentation requirements and forms were identical for cases in the WPCC outpatient clinics and the CMT, it was easy to transfer paperwork, substantially reducing staff time.

The new cases admitted from outside sources required more extensive orientation to the WPCC setting and the CMT program. One of the administrative support staff met with the youth and the parents to obtain demographic data and information regarding insurance coverage. The mental health insurance provider was contacted to obtain approval for the initial evaluation and several follow-up visits. The CMT clinician met with the youth and the parents both separately and together to obtain the history of present illness, past history, family history, and developmental and medical history. In addition, the clinician assessed the quality of the youth's relationship with peers and adults, school functioning and the appropriateness of school placement, extracurricular interests and involvement, and involvement in any drugs and/or other illegal activities. The family assessment included the parents' relationship with each other, the youth, and the extended family. And there was also an assessment of the family's basic needs for food, housing, and physical and mental health. The clinician was to identify other agencies currently involved or needing to be involved to best serve the youth and the family.

The clinician then presented the history and assessment findings to the CMT psychiatrist, who subsequently met with the youth and the family to confirm or clarify the clinician's findings, to record mental status, to make a preliminary diagnosis/diagnoses and treatment recommendations, and to initiate, adjust, or renew medications if necessary. For all new youth admitted to the CMT, the CAFAS, Child Behavior Checklist (CBCL), and Connors and Child Depression Inventory (CDI) were completed, and all had screening for substance abuse. Referral for psychological testing, speech and language evaluation, medical consultation, and lab work was made as necessary.

The CMT had a weekly intake meeting to review newly admitted cases, make clinician assignments and to formulate the initial treatment plan. The youth, family, and other involved staff (e.g., DSS, DJJ) were invited. All intake paperwork was required to be completed by this meeting. Intake logs were completed weekly and forwarded to the program director to assure that cases were properly entered in the system.

CMT SERVICES

The services provided by the CMT can be categorized under treatment services and case management services. All youth in the CMT program were eligible to receive the full range of services, which were tailored to each youth's and family's individual needs. Although the majority of services were provided in the home, school, and community, some, such as various group therapies, took place in the clinic. Due to the psychiatrist's limited time in the CMT, medications were prescribed primarily in the clinic and provisions were made for the psychiatrist to see the youth in the home or community during a crisis or due to the youth's refusal or inability to come to the clinic. In addition, the CMT clinician helped the parent with transportation and to make other arrangements as necessary.

Treatment Services

These services included: (1) behavior management, including the development, implementation, and monitoring of behavior programs at home and school; (2) individual verbal and play therapy; (3) family therapy; (4) various group therapies, including a parents group, substance abuse group, teen group, social skills group, and a group for pregnant teens; (5) medication prescription and monitoring; (6) crisis interventions; (7) substance abuse treatment; and (8) psychoeducation.

Case Management

These services included: (1) school advocacy, including helping parents in dealing with the school and the board of education to get appropriate school placement for the child. This might involve writing a letter defining the youth's educational and emotional needs, attending school and board of education meetings, and sometimes helping parents obtain legal assistance. The CMT clinician also facilitated communication and interaction between the youth's parents and teachers by attending parent-teacher conferences and by keeping in regular contact with both parties; (2) liaison with the Department of Social Services (DSS), if applicable. This included updating the DSS worker regarding the needs of the youth and family, treatment progress, and compliance; (3) liaison with the Department of Juvenile Justice (DJJ), if applicable. This included updating the probation officer regarding the youth's condition, enforcing compliance with treatment and probationary conditions, and appearing in court to present treatment recommendations to the master or judge; (4) liaison with day hospital, inpatient, residential setting, and after-school programs, and other health services; (5) attending youth-centered case conferences, such as local coordinating council, a hospital or day hospital team, or a discharge meeting; (6) referral to and liaison with vocational, recreational, and legal services; (7) assessment of family budgeting and financial needs; (8) obtaining and maintaining entitlements; (9) assistance with food, housing, and transportation needs; and (10) referral and coordination of the physical and mental health needs of the parents.

ISSUES, CHALLENGES, AND RISKS

Following are some of the challenges and risk encountered while providing home-based treatment:

1. Dependable relationship versus dependency on the clinician. One of the major challenges is to help the youth and family engage in a trusting, close, and dependable relationship with the home-based treatment staff without becoming too dependent. Mordock (1998) wrote that one of the dangers of in-home treatment is that parents can become dependent upon the practitioner to perform responsibilities that can eventually undermine their own executive role. Such a problem can be avoided: (a) by careful and ongoing assessment of the youth and family regarding their skills and resources that can aid the practitioner to know when and how to respond to family needs. As the youth and family show increased ability to function, treatment staff gradually turn over more responsibilities to the youth and family while still being available; (b) by the youth and family being actively involved in problem solving and decision making rather than having the treatment staff provide solutions for them; (c) by the clinician carefully monitoring for proper use any funds provided to the youth and family; and (d) by the clinician setting reasonable limits to unreasonable demands.

2. Therapeutic versus case management needs. Most home- and community-based programs encounter multiproblem and multi-need families; thus the emphasis is usually on case management. However, the therapeutic (individual, group, and family therapies and medication) needs for the youth and the family may then receive lower priority or be overlooked. It is important for any home-based program to clearly define its focus. If the focus is solely on case management, then arrangement should be made for the proper assessment and delivery of the therapeutic needs. If the focus is on both case management and therapeutic services, the home-based treatment staff then need to have the interest and skills to provide both of these services under proper supervision and training.

3. Dealing with youth and family resistance and dysfunction. Although providing in-home services to youth and families increases compliance with treatment, this does not completely eliminate noncompliance and resistance to change. The CMT staff noted an approximately 25 percent noncompliance rate with appointments to be held in the home and school. Therefore the clinician needed to carefully assess the motivation of the youth and the family, and of the referral agency, prior to initiating in-home services. Clinicians also needed to be sensitive to the youth's and family's level of trust and their particular way of interacting with others. For example, some families did not mind or even preferred or welcomed if the clinician came to their home unannounced. Others were very particular about the time of the appointment and who participated. Similarly, some very needy and isolated families welcomed any interaction, whereas others, especially those in which the parent has emotional difficulties that interferes with trust, may prefer limited interaction and may like to be present whenever the clinician meets with the youth. Individual families are such that some families like the clinician to know about their problems and needs, while others are too embarrassed to tell.

4. *Dealing with staff's countertransference and feelings of hopelessness, despair, frustration, revulsion, and insecurity.* Working with highly dysfunctional youth and families often results in intense feelings in the treatment staff. The staff need to identify, understand, and ventilate these feelings, otherwise they could become overly active or paralyzed by them. For example, one of the staff who had experienced loss in her early childhood had a great deal of difficulty providing services to a child whose mother was dying from drug abuse and HIV-related health problems. The staff member's ability to talk with her supervisor helped in mobilizing resources to deal with this very difficult situation.

Home- and community-based staff often work in poverty-struck, drug-ridden, dangerous neighborhoods. The homes of poor and disorganized families are sometimes filthy and infested. There have been times when CMT clinicians encountered situations where roaches were crawling over the furniture and sometimes on the family members. These situations may result in the staff feeling repulsed, and they may start avoiding such homes. Despite these discomforts, the clinician must address such issues with the family and develop a plan of action to make the home environment healthier, including seeking outside assistance. It is not uncommon for the staff to encounter active drug dealing, shootings, and even experience personal threats. It is important for the administrators of the program and the clinical team to openly address safety and security issues and actions to be taken. Working in pairs, easy accessibility to cellular phones, wearing identification badges, notifying local police, and visiting homes only at certain times of the day are some of the precautionary measures necessary. In cases where active drug dealing or violence is taking place in the house, the clinician may not be able to provide services until the home situation changes or provisions are made to meet with the youth and family in a different, secure place in the community.

5. *Administration and leadership.* Many home- and community-based treatments for youth are organized under the direction of administrators with adult psychiatry background. Community-based programs for seriously mentally ill adults such as Assertive Community Treatment (Santos, Henggeler, Burns, Arana, & Meisler, 1995) have been in practice for some time with good results. These programs are focused primarily toward chronic psychotic disorders. Due to youths' developmental issues, the complexity of their behavioral problems, and various systems' involvement, as

well as availability of different treatment options, program administrators need to educate and familiarize with youth issues and need to be flexible in their approach in dealing with youth. It is important that staff working with youth and families are involved in the decision-making process and thus feel empowered to create and transfer this sense of empowerment to their charges—a major goal of treatment.

CONCLUSION

Home- and community-based care for seriously emotionally disturbed youth and dysfunctional families is essential to meet various therapeutic and case management needs. Administrators of such programs need to assure that all staff are motivated to provide home- and community-based treatment, are culturally sensitive, interpersonally skilled, and are trained in the basics of therapeutic and case management skills. Issues like pay, safety, support, training opportunities, supervision, quality of leadership, and organizational function play an important role in attracting and retaining high-quality staff. Ongoing careful assessment of the program to assure efficiency and effectiveness is essential. Finally, training programs in general and child psychiatry, psychology, nursing, and social work should include experiences in home- and community-based interventions in order to prepare the trainees for working with seriously emotionally disturbed youth and their dysfunctional families.

References

Ghuman, H. S., & Sarles, R. M. (1998). Ambulatory services: Clinical, administrative, and training issues. In H. S. Ghuman & R. M. Sarles (Eds.), *Handbook of child and adolescent outpatient, day treatment and community psychiatry*. Philadelphia: Brunner/Mazel.

Hastings, E., Gorth, M., & Ghuman, H. S. (1998). Child and adolescent services in a community mental health center: Transition, organization, and staffing issues. In H. S. Ghuman & R. M. Sarles (Eds.), *Handbook of child and adolescent outpatient, day treatment and community psychiatry*. Philadelphia: Brunner/Mazel.

Mordock, J. (1998). In-home treatment. In N. E. Alessi, J. T.Coyle, S. Harrison & E. Spencer (Eds.), and J. D. Noshpitz (Editor-in-chief), *Handbook of child and adolescent psychiatry* (Vol. 6). New York: John Wiley & Sons.

Santos, A. B., Henggeler, S. W., Burns, B. J., Arana, G. W., & Meisler, N. (1995). Research on field-based services: Models for reform in the delivery of mental health care to populations with complex clinical problems. *American Journal of Psychiatry, 152*(8), 1111–1123.

CHAPTER NINE

Family-Driven Treatment: Families as Full Partners in the Care of Children with Psychiatric Illness

Ann Vander Stoep, Ph.D., Marilynn Williams, and Charles Huffine, M.D.

A family is a child's most valuable asset. Although on the face of it this assertion appears undeniable, it has not always been accepted as true for children with psychiatric illness. This chapter describes the movements that have returned families to their rightful place as full partners with professionals in the care of children with psychiatric illness and in the evaluation of programs designed to help such children. The principle of full partnership is illustrated in a description of the innovative King County Blended Funding Project and its evaluation.

THE FAMILY SUPPORT MOVEMENT

The family support movement began in the 1960s in the form of grassroots, self-help efforts to increase the strength of family social networks. In their book *Building and Evaluating Family Support Initiatives*, Carl Dunst and colleagues (1993) take a retrospective look at the evolution of the family support movement. They identify five distinct stages that have occurred.

- The first stage was initiated by families who demanded support services when institutions closed their doors to children, and children who had been placed in institutions returned home (Cohen et al., 1989).
- The second stage involved the adoption of state family-support initiatives. By the mid-1980s, over 60,000 families were receiving family-support services through state-level, government-sponsored programs in twenty-two states (Agosta, Jennings, & Bradley, 1987).
- The third stage was heralded by the development of family-centered health care practices, aimed at mobilizing supports and resources needed by families of children who were health-impaired and medically fragile. Underlying the family-centered health care movement was the recognition that, while the roles of service systems and professionals in children's lives change, the family remains constant.
- During the fourth stage, family-focused early intervention practices were established to meet the needs of infants and toddlers with special needs. The focus was on enhancing the capacity of parents to provide specialized care to their young children.
- The latest stage involved the development of family-support programs for persons with developmental disabilities. A set of guiding principles that prioritized maintaining children at home, building support for the entire family, and family empowerment was promoted to guide policies toward families of children with developmental disabilities.

Underlying all phases of the family-support movement was the recognition that strong family functioning is vital to healthy child development and that strengthening families should be a major outcome of social and health care programs (Dunst et al., 1993). The emphasis on supporting families has been related to efforts to change the orientation of children's mental health services from viewing parents as impediments to children's well-being or patients in need of treatment to viewing families as allies or partners in the care of their children (Armstrong & Evans, 1992).

FAMILY-CENTERED MENTAL HEALTH SERVICE MODEL

Historically, family members of children with mental health problems have been excluded from determinations of what their children need (Knitzer, 1982; Donner, 1986). This was due to the tradition of maintaining "therapeutic distance" between professionals and clients and to the common belief that children's emotional problems were primarily a result of the pathological unconscious drives of parents (Caplan & Hall-McCorquodale, 1985). Because traditional psychoanalytic theory held parents responsible for the problems of their children, parental participation in treatment was discouraged. Just as Dunst et al. (1993) described the evolution of the family-support movement, Barbara Friesen and Nancy Koroloff (1990) have traced the development of family-centered services within the children's mental health system. They also point to the 1960s as having spawned new theories, which brought the family into focus as the unit of treatment. According to family systems theory, children's symptoms were seen as expressions of family conflict (Bateson, 1972). "Sick families" gave rise to "sick children." Thus, interventions targeted the ailing family system and assumed that improvement in family functioning would lead automatically to improvement in child health.

More recently our understanding of the etiology of children's emotional and behavioral disorders has been expanded. Childhood mental illness is now believed to arise from a complex set of transactions between the child's biological and psychological makeup and his or her ecological (family, school, neighborhood, peer) context (Sameroff & Fiese, 1990; Moffitt, 1993; Susman, 1993). In keeping with the new understanding, the ideal system of care for children's mental health, first described in the 1980s, is family-centered and ecologically based (Stroul & Friedman, 1986). The role of the parent in the system of care has followed a linear trajectory toward empowerment: from patient, to resource, to expert in understanding and providing for the child's needs (Friesen & Koroloff, 1990). A primary technological development that has emerged from system of care thinking is the wraparound service model.

THE WRAPAROUND PROCESS

Describing the evolution of the wraparound process within the ideal system of care, John VanDenBerg wrote in 1998, "The wraparound process is an organized way that humans in communities support other humans who need help. The basic tenets of the wraparound process are as old as humankind." Around the world, cultures have created methods of supporting community members who need assistance, and of providing support when members are in trouble. In modern technological society, these supportive traditions have been formalized into institutions and service systems. Children in our country with complex needs have access to a complex array of services delivered by child welfare, juvenile justice, mental health, special education, public health, and other organizations. Each of these systems has distinctive theoretical approaches and goals, a different array of providers and services, and a unique funding stream. Thus a family whose needs cross multiple system boundaries is faced with a barrage of uncoordinated, oftentimes conflicting sets of categorical offerings that may or may not approximate the supports needed to achieve the family's goals.

Wraparound is a process in which a family creates a "think tank" to problem-solve, plan, and build caring capacity on the basis of existing strengths. The wraparound process is reliant on members of a natural support system being available at all times (day or night) to respond to the primary caregiver's needs for advice, brainstorming, reassurance, and physical presence. Inherent in wraparound is a shift from reactivity to immediate crises to orientation toward long-term normalized needs. Making this shift requires a very comprehensive understanding of the child's historical patterns and existing resources. Crises become something to prepare for, rather than react to, and the plan incorporates a vision of supporting slow, steady progress toward maximizing normalized goals across multiple life domains. Best theories and practices from a variety of perspectives are consolidated and refined in response to the specific needs of the individual child and family.

MENTAL HEALTH SERVICES IN A FAMILY-CENTERED CARE MODEL

For years traditional clinical service providers and agencies have been caught between the competing needs of families with children who have serious problems and those who fund the services. Within our communities, the need for mental health services has overwhelmed available resources and has led to an ever more tightly managed mental health system (Dangerfield & Betit, 1993; Minkoff, 1994; Pires et al., 1996). As managed care models have been applied to public mental health programs, caseloads have increased. The workforce is less experienced and less educated (Durham, 1998). Psychiatrists and other advanced clinicians have smaller roles in mental health systems, as more people are served with less funding (Inglehart, 1996). Psychiatrists often find that their last remaining role in the system is as medication monitors (Domino et al., 1998). Sadly, their skills and interests may narrow accordingly.

In a family-centered system, if a child has a need identified in the wraparound process that would be best served by a traditional mental health service, families have the power to identify a provider and assure that a quality service is delivered. In order to operationalize that power, the family's think tank, or the wraparound team, must have advice from a mental health consultant who knows the territory in the local mental health service system. Clearly, every child does not need to be on medications, nor will many children profit from formally structured psychotherapy.

A true wraparound process will enable a family to meet the clinical needs of a child by utilizing any number of conventional and unconventional methods that address issues identified as critical to the child. Expert mental health advisers, especially comprehensively trained, community-savvy psychiatrists, have a major role in assuring that the needs of children for advancing their mental health will be met with quality services. But to be effective in assuring such clinical quality, psychiatrists must be able to understand the wraparound process and strength-based approaches and adopt a collegial approach to working with families and their teams. In our communities are many excellent, skilled, and empathic mental health practitioners eager to relate to families and a family-centered system of care. By using a wraparound process that utilizes good expert advice, child and family teams can assure that families and good services can be brought together, either within or outside the traditional provider networks that have grown up under our traditional systems.

PARTICIPATORY RESEARCH

In 1997 Koroloff and Friesen pointed out the implications of changes in service provision on evaluation design. They wrote, "With a greater understanding of the underlying principles of family-centered services has come the realization that evaluating services under such a system severely tests the capability of traditional research approaches." Similar to the traditional value of maintaining "therapeutic distance" in the clinical setting, the traditional research paradigm posits that maintaining distance between scientists and their subjects enhances objectivity, and thereby validity. Yet questions have been raised regarding the ethics of tapping communities' scanty resources for the sake of obtaining scientific knowledge in the absence of any direct benefit to the community being researched. The participatory research model was promoted in developing countries in response to these ethical concerns. According to Van Vlaenderen (1993), participatory research:

1. Requires full and active participation of all involved;
2. Focuses on resolving current problems;
3. Acknowledges the importance of indigenous knowledge and resources;
4. Applies traditional and innovative techniques;

5. Involves a combination of social investigation, education, and action; and
6. Aims at empowerment.

Implementing participatory research raises tensions between the traditional requirements of scientific rigor and the demands put on the research process by community stakeholders. Participatory research combines scientific inquiry, education, and action and provides for alternative measures of validity, emphasizing face validity as much as construct validity.

The role of the scientist is transformed under the participatory research model. Since a basic requirement is commitment to the community's chosen process, rigorous scientific objectivity is but one of a number of important methodological considerations. Participatory researchers work with community members, who historically have been subjects, not designers, of research studies. The researcher facilitates critical understanding of conditions that interfere with the community's ability to address recognized problems. Whereas traditional research methods are predicated upon the assumption that certain people are incapable of articulating their own needs, the participatory model stipulates respect for the capability and potential of community groups to produce knowledge and to analyze it. The role of the scientist is one of activist, observer, and technician. A goal is for the scientist to pass skills to the community participants such that the community gains research proficiency.

FAMILY PARTICIPATION IN CHILDREN'S MENTAL HEALTH SERVICES RESEARCH

The participatory research model was developed in the Third World and has found a foothold in the family-support and family-centered mental health services movements (Van Vlaenderen, 1993). By the same logic that it takes a village to raise a child, it also takes a village to name, study, and meet its challenges. One of the applications of participatory research is the evaluation of efforts to provide services and support for children with mental health concerns and their families. A new research paradigm is emerging from a clearer comprehension of the reality of the life experiences of persons with mental illness. Increasingly, research agendas, priorities, questions, methods, and outcomes are being set with this comprehension as a necessary condition. Evaluations that are constituent-led may generate knowledge that is more likely to improve the ability to effect outcomes. Traditional approaches to evaluation that incorporate "hit and run" methodologies seldom serve the interests of the community.

Specific implications of applying these perspectives and principles to mental health services research have been outlined by Koroloff and Friesen (1997). The range of outcome variables will be wider, as various constituents have their say. More complex processes will be specified, as comprehension of the factors affecting the lives of children and their families increases. Process evaluation will be emphasized, as communities need to understand how program characteristics, family characteristics, and outcomes are linked. New research methods will evolve, as complex family and program questions are addressed. Koroloff and Friesen conclude that "the central challenge for the researcher is to support the change agenda of family members without letting that change agenda bias the research effort," and that "this kind of balance will not be easy to strike" (p. 136).

This introduction to recent developments in family-centered mental health care and family-centered mental health services research sets the stage for a description of the King County Blended Funding Project service model and evaluation.

THE KING COUNTY BLENDED FUNDING PROJECT

The King County Blended Funding Project (BFP) is a new way of doing business for children with mental health concerns who are receiving services from multiple public agencies (Figure 9.1). The project is built on the assumption that families, with the involvement of community-based teams and appropriate supports, can manage their children's care. The BFP in King County is a partnership between the Washington State Federation of Families (FOF), and three services systems: child welfare, mental health, and special education (Williams, 1997). Each service system partner contributes its highest rate for severely troubled youth into a single pool. This large pool of funds is available to each child and family team to be spent flexibly on categorical or noncategorical services and supports. Families are assigned a care manager, a professional who functions as a facilitator/staffer to child and family teams. Families participating in the BFP are encouraged to build a team and initiate a wraparound process. Families use blended funds to implement the wraparound plan to meet the child's needs across multiple life domains (safety, family, physical health, mental health, educational, legal, financial, social, recreational, cultural, spiritual, and residential).

The creation of child and family teams is the basis of the wraparound process. Families entering the Blended Funding Project are generally in the midst of a crisis and are not able to engage their attentions and energies in a discussion of normalizing needs, assessing strengths, or mobiliz-

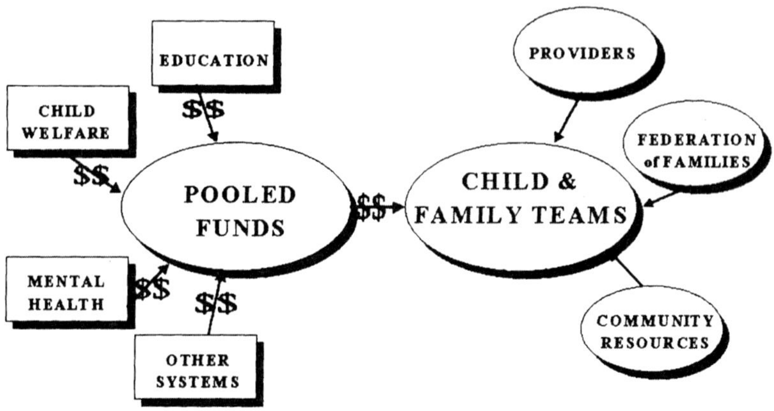

FIGURE 9.1. King County Blended Funding Project.

ing family and community resources. They want immediate solutions to the problems at hand and focus their demands on professionals. Tending to immediate needs is critical to the establishment of an effective wraparound process. As the frustrations with conventional resources emerge in this crisis-oriented phase, the promise of more effective care through a wraparound process is introduced as a more effective and lasting solution to problems.

It is the promise of accessing the funds and of having control over these resources to create a more effective "system of care" for a child that moves even the most desperate family to take a leap of faith and identify people who can form a child and family team. Initially, most teams are composed primarily of professionals, a legacy from a King County interagency service project that most BFP families have participated in. Some families begin to move to approximate the ideal of a community-based team that includes family, friends, neighbors, and community leaders. As families move toward taking control of their children's care, teams include ever fewer professionals. The relationship between teams and professionals shifts. Teams hire professionals who are then accountable to the family, not the agency or the traditional categorical funding source. This shift in accountability is more similar to a traditional (pre–managed care) private model where each practitioner is primarily accountable to children and their families.

What does the family-centered Blended Funding Project look like in action? An illustration of the paradigm shift from professional-centered to family-centered services is the case of Roxanne.

During her infancy, Roxanne lived with her birth mother, where she was neglected and abused physically by both parents. Removed from her home by Child Protective Services, Roxanne was placed in foster care, where she was subsequently raped. At age six Roxanne was placed with her grandmother, who became her legal guardian. She displayed psychotic symptoms, was hospitalized and then placed in a residential program.

At the time she entered the BFP her grandmother was attending meetings at the residential program. Professionals told the grandmother that the child needed to be discharged into a specialized foster home because she was judged as not up to the task of handling this troubled girl. The grandmother was terrified that her child might be harmed in foster care a second time, but she was told that there was no other choice. The grandmother invited two friends and Roxanne's aunt and uncle to undergo training as a Child and Family Team by the Federation of Families (FOF), a local affiliate of a nationwide advocacy group. The team assumed control of the funding for the proposed foster home placement. They asked the social service and mental health professionals exactly what were the critical elements of the proposed care in a therapeutic foster home. As they learned about this therapeutic program, the team focused on the specifics of how Roxanne's needs were to be targeted.

Led by her grandmother, Roxanne's team was able to determine how each of her needs might be met as well or better in the grandmother's home. Because of the grandmother's lack of parenting skills, a highly skilled, experienced parent, who met the test of cultural competence, was hired as a parent trainer and coach to spend ten hours a day in the home for four months. As expensive as this was, it was less costly in the long run than if Roxanne had remained in residential care. The living space in the home was rearranged to allow Roxanne to have her own room. Roxanne had previously tried to molest her younger sister, so alarms were purchased to assure that she didn't roam the house at night. Her Individualized Educational Plan (IEP) was rewritten to place Roxanne in a small kindergarten classroom and to provide a home tutor. A certified restraint teacher was hired to train the grandmother and others to safely constrain Roxanne. Mental health treatment was arranged that more specifically addressed her rape and multiple losses. The original team of professionals could not accept the Child and Family Team's plan and withdrew from the case. New professionals, accountable to the team, were hired. Roxanne has remained in the community for the past two years with lessening requirements for external controls. The costs of her services have been reduced dramatically.

THE BLENDED FUNDING PROGRAM AND CLINICAL SERVICES IN THE COMMUNITY

In King County, like many other communities, a set of mental health service agencies has developed since the 1963 Comprehensive Mental Health Centers Act launched the community mental health movement. Community mental health centers and specialized child-serving agencies constitute the system's provider network under the county's Health Care Financing Administration (HCFA) waiver managed care plan. Some of these agencies have excellent staff, good psychiatrists, and effective programs and subscribe to the concepts of family-centered care and integrated services. Blended Funding children received services from these agencies directly or through the interagency coordinating teams prior to joining the Blended Funding Project. It has been a goal of the BFP to hold disruptions in care to a minimum. Thus, when existing treatment relationships were perceived by families to be working well, children stayed with the provider agency and their trusted staff. The BFP enabled agencies to be much more flexible in their provision of care, and many have partnered well with their client's families and with the FOF advocates. Other agencies have not been able to adapt to dealing with empowered parents and have resented the emergence of a powerful parent advocacy organization. Some of these agencies have chosen not to participate in providing services to BF children. Those in the leadership of the BFP have sought to educate and nurture agencies toward working more closely with family teams to develop more meaningful treatment plans.

Some elements of a comprehensive service package had not been economically viable under the old system. The BFP has allowed for the emergence of new types of services independent of mainline agencies. Therapeutic foster homes, case aides who specialize in mobilizing community resources, parent trainers, tutors, and activities coaches all can be developed, hired, and funded under the BFP. The child and family team's assessment of needs is driving this aspect of service development. The child and family teams assure that all the treatment elements, mental health therapists, and support workers are functioning according to a comprehensive care plan devised by the team with the support of a care coordinator and input from professionals.

With flexible funding, families are also able to reach out to local treatment specialists. There is great interest in establishing a highly structured program for children with fetal alcohol spectrum disorders due to the great number of such children referred to the project. A number of children with severe PTSD due to chronic abuse are able to obtain highly skilled psychotherapy from community specialists. Some children in the program have utilized pioneering work in treating borderline personality disorder, and receive dialectic behavior therapy (DBT). Fortunately, through expertise developed at the University of Washington, our community has tremendous resources in these areas.

Much more needs to be done to knit the system of care together. Many psychiatrists and agency therapists/case managers have yet to feel the advantages of working closely with a powerful group of parent advocates and empowered parents. They still feel threatened and confused, not quite believing that with the adequate support, a mother they had known to be disorganized and overwhelmed could be thoughtful and articulate about her child's strengths and clearly define the child's needs. Active efforts are under way to provide all agency staff with training and experience in family-centered care.

PSYCHIATRIC CONSULTATION

When faced with confusing or serious issues that build to a crisis, families will still need intensive psychiatric services. To address ongoing mental health issues, they need effective clinical interventions. With the responsibility to purchase services, how can they evaluate the quality and relevance of interventions? Clinical advice is a critical element to team functioning. Teams often seek professional counsel. Credentialed mental health workers who have been involved with a child may be asked initially to be part of the child and family team. They may also be invited as resources to the team.

It is an unfortunate but common experience that families will report having had disappointing, or perhaps demeaning, encounters with psychiatrists in mental health agencies. They have experienced psychiatrists as rushed and prone to recommend medications for their children without adequately explaining their purpose or possible side effects. Many parents enter the Blended Funding Project having developed fearful or even hostile reactions to all psychiatric treatments. These parents needed some credible assurances regarding the appropriate role of psychiatry in the care of their children.

The King County mental health authority provides consultation to families in achieving good psychiatric care through their medical director for child and adolescent programs. The medical director has had an informal supportive role with the FOF from its inception and has been available by phone continuously to the director of the federation. The core staff of the FOF, through their alliance with this psychiatrist, are able to teach and empower parents to be good consumers of psychiatric services in the agencies serving their children. If they feel services within the public provider network are inadequate, they may take their share of the blended funding pool outside the network and purchase private psychiatric services.

Formal monthly consultative sessions have been instituted by the FOF director as a key aspect of the relationship between the FOF and the county mental health authority. The director invites parents to talk to the psychiatric consultant, or may have the consultant conduct a brief consultative psychiatric evaluation of a child from the Blended Funding Project. This consultation is conceptualized in a manner consistent with the writings of Gerald Caplan in his many papers on psychiatric consultation to social agencies and schools (Caplan & Caplan, 2000). The principles are adapted to the special circumstances of a parent advocacy organization. This direct clinical support from a program medical director helps assure the safety of children and their families who use community-based plans in circumstances where, in a conventional service system, residential care might have been sought.

Roxanne's grandmother has used psychiatric consultation during the course of her participation in the BFP. She had not been satisfied with psychiatrists in years past, but the "house psychiatrist" of the FOF is trusted because of his close relationship with the director and many of the other parents. For example, the psychiatric consultant was able to assure her that a medication plan for Roxanne, offered by a psychiatrist from a community agency, should be supported. In other cases, the plan might be deemed dubious and the child in need of reevaluation. The consultant can help build a bridge of trust between the families and their existing mental health professionals. This helps them to be full partners with these professionals in providing care for a child and better evaluators of the care the child receives.

THE BLENDED FUNDING PROJECT EVALUATION

A team consisting of family advocates and research scientists conducts the Blended Funding evaluation. In initial evaluation team meetings, research scientists assumed that they would be leading the way in designing and implementing evaluation methods. From the start, however, family members made it clear that they had developed an evaluation agenda and that following their agenda would turn the traditional research approach on its head. Inappropriate measures would be tossed, offensive questions would be revised, and irrelevant outcomes would be overlooked. What began as a concession on the scientists' part to political correctness and self-preservation evolved into their enthusiastic acceptance of an approach that has generated more useful results.

The parent-led Blended Funding evaluation team designed and implemented the evaluation in a series of logical steps that are outlined below.

1. Create a Model of Change

As a first step, the evaluation team created a model of change that clearly articulated how children and families who enter the project were expected to attain an improved state of health and functioning. The model of change served as a compass guiding the design of the Blended Funding Project and its evaluation. The model of change stated that with the support of the child and family team and with the ability to purchase and create needed supports:

- Families will become empowered;
- Everyone—the child, family, care manager, community team, and systems—will become more hopeful and motivated to change;
- Service systems and families will collaborate more effectively on behalf of children;
- Children's base of support within their natural communities (family, school, neighborhood) will strengthen;
- Children's needs will be better met across multiple domains;
- Children will stabilize in less restrictive residential and educational settings;
- Children's behavior and functional status will improve;
- Cost of care will decrease.

2. Identify Relevant Outcomes

The second challenge was to decide what would best reflect improvement in children's behavior and functioning. Deciding which outcomes to measure is a very political process. Outcomes can be used to create pressure for reform, to hold systems accountable, to inform administrators how to modify programs, to inform clinicians how to modify treatments, and to inform consumers so they can decide whether to take their business elsewhere. Traditionally, in mental health services research, outcomes are selected from a short list of measures of problem behaviors that have good psychometric properties and that have been used in previous studies (Weiss & Jacobs, 1988).

Within the Blended Funding Project, "success" meant something different to each stakeholder group. For the King County blended funders (the service system stakeholders), indicators of success had to do with school attendance and achievement, arrests, psychiatric hospitalizations, permanency plans, and out-of-home placements. For parents, indicators of success had to do with concrete and individualized behavioral indicators—for example, a child punching only *one* hole in the wall every month or riding the school bus for five successive days without incident. For the program director, indicators of success had to do with increasing the strength of connections between the child and the community and meeting children's needs across multiple domains. For the scientific community, changes in functioning would be more credible if they were assessed with already standardized instruments. The central challenge was to develop a list of outcomes that reflected the interests and needs of all the various stakeholders.

In the Blended Funding Project evaluation, the list of outcomes is long. All of the outcomes of interest to the blended funders are measured. Participating families are allowed to define individualized concrete behavioral indicators that reflect their child's unique issues. Outcomes commonly measured in children's mental health service evaluations (e.g., child's level of functioning) have been incorporated. In addition to these "ultimate outcomes," a number of process outcomes (e.g., strength of community connections, family empowerment, service coordination, parent-professional collaboration, motivation to change, satisfaction, cost of care) are also measured.

3. Choose Measurement Tools

The third task was to select instruments to be used in measuring the process and outcome variables. The research scientists provided a starting point by accumulating evaluation tools that had been used in previous children's system of care evaluations. Family members waded through stacks of instruments and documentation, asking themselves and the research scientists such questions as:

- Could most parents understand these questions?
- What might we learn from administering this questionnaire?
- Does this measure reflect an anticipated outcome of our project?

Often, individual questions or entire instruments were judged to be demeaning, offensive, unclear, or pointless. The team accepted some measurement tools "as is." Others were modified with permission from their original developers. As an example of where an existing tool was modified, the Oregon Partners Family Empowerment Scale (Koren, DeChillo, & Friesen, 1992) included these items:

- "I feel I have the RIGHT TO APPROVE all services my child receives."
- "I know steps to take when I am CONCERNED my child is receiving poor services."
- "I tell professionals what I think about services being provided TO my child."

Families felt that these particular empowerment questions needed to be rewritten to better reflect the unique role of families in the Blended Funding Project.

- "I have the RIGHT TO APPROVE services" became "I am an active participant in formulating my child's care";
- "I know steps to take when I am CONCERNED my child is receiving poor services" became "I feel I am a full partner in providing for my child's special needs";
- "I tell professionals what I think about services being provided TO my child" became "When service systems do not have existing services which would benefit my family, I believe my team can create or find the needed supports."

At the same time that the team wrestled with the problem of trespassing the sanctity of already validated instruments, the American College of Mental Health Administration (ACMHA, 1998), which had convened a group of prominent services researchers, including Barbara Burns from Duke University, Sonja Shoenwald from the Family Services Research Center in South Carolina, and Kimberly Hoagwood from the National Institute of Mental Health (NIMH), wrote a set of research guidelines. The most vexing challenge faced by the group was that of reconciling measurement-related concerns with ACMHA's commitment to brevity, pragmatism, simplicity, and relevance—"attributes likely to be valued in the marketplace, where the burden and costs associated with the collection of outcome data will be borne by providers and consumers." Noting that most well-validated symptom checklists, diagnostic interviews, and multidimensional functioning measures are lengthy and difficult to administer, the group recommended the use of *subscales* from instruments with demonstrated validity, despite the violation of psychometric rigor this strategy represents.

In the end, the team borrowed heavily from the work of other system of care research projects. The Vermont System for Tracking Client Progress (Burchard, Schaefer, Rogers et al., 1991), originally developed by John VanDenBerg for the Alaska Youth Initiative, could be used by families to identify and track individualized progress indicators. The Fort Bragg Evaluation spawned widespread use of the Child and Adolescent Functional Assessment Scale (CAFAS) (Hodges, Bickman, Kurtz, & Reiter, 1991). The Oregon Partners Project (Regional Research Institute for Human Services, 1996) provided the starting point for many of the process measures, including family empowerment, service coordination, and parent-professional collaboration.

Some tools were invented. The model of change posited that improvements in the child's functioning would rest on the success of the child and family team to build a strong network of informal supports that could endure beyond the child's tenure in the project. This warranted incorporating into the evaluation design a method to assess this process variable. The Oregon Partners Project had begun to develop a Service Fit Questionnaire. The team used this as a basis for creating the Community Connections Questionnaire (CCQ) (Federation of Families, 2000) to assess the nature and strength of the child's formal and informal connections within the community.

4. Implement Evaluation Design in the Field

Once the evaluation protocol had been established, the fourth task was to decide who would implement it. Advocates argued that family members should be sent to the field to conduct in-person interviews in the homes of Blended Funding Project participants. Their rationale for this was that families would be more receptive to participating in the evaluation, more comfortable during the interview, and more willing to share their candid impressions of the efforts of service providers and of their children's well-being. Scientists were concerned about standardization of evaluation procedures. The compromise that emerged from this part of the design was that parent advocates conduct interviews only after having undergone intensive evaluation training conducted by a research scientist. During the training, the interviewer and trainer read the training manual aloud together, interviewers observe trainers conducting in-home interviews, and trainers observe interviewers while they conduct their first two in-home interviews. Thereafter, periodic supervisory "spot checks" are conducted in the field.

5. Disseminate Results

The last step involves disseminating evaluation findings in ways that maximize usefulness to child and family teams, the Blended Funding Project, and the blended funders. Each stakeholder is interested in different aspects of the evaluation and puts the results to use for different purposes. The project director wants to use the findings to guide the development of the intervention. This requires giving feedback to care managers about how effective they are being. The blended funders want to use the findings to make determinations about the appropriateness of their funding contributions. This requires very careful framing of the results of the cost study. National child services leaders and legislators want to learn about the effectiveness of this best practices model program. This requires submitting abstracts for presentation to national meetings and writing briefs for lobbyists.

Child and family teams desire comprehensible depictions of children's progress. This means finding clear and accessible ways of communicating evaluation results. One response has been that the Blended Funding evaluation team has worked with participating parents and care managers to develop simple formats for displaying the type, number, and strength of the child's connections within the community. Each quarter, evaluators take information directly from each child's Community Connections Questionnaire (Federation of Families, 2000) and create pictographs that give feedback to the child and family teams showing how the child's ecology is changing (Figure 9.2).

What does the participatory Blended Funding Project evaluation model look like in action? Lisa is the mother of a large seventeen-year-old boy

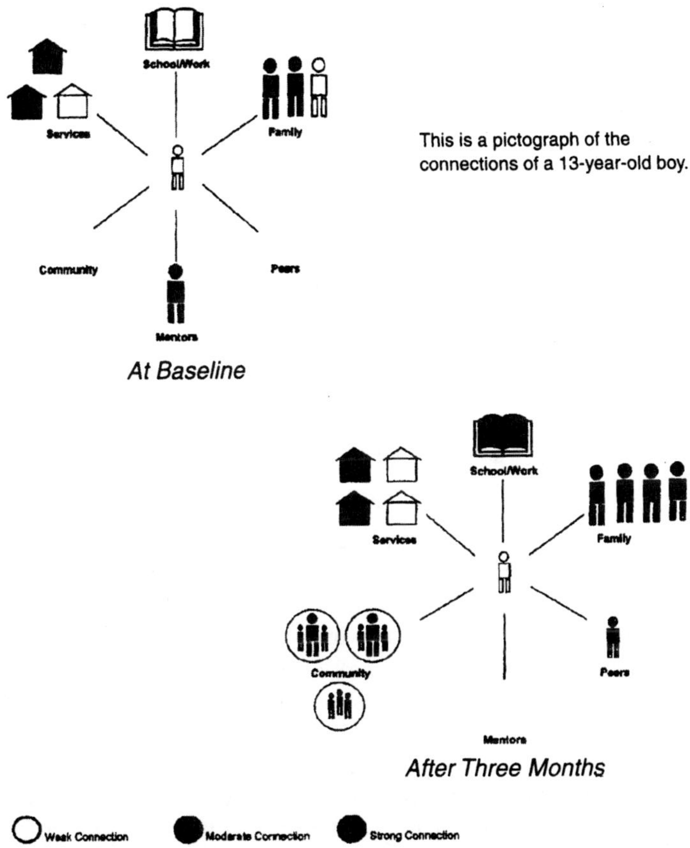

©1997 King County Federation of Families

FIGURE 9.2. Community Connections

who has bipolar disorder, is volatile, and is often out of control. Lisa has been through innumerable crises with him throughout his life. He has spent many of his days in mental health or correctional facilities. She has confronted the many problems of single mothers faced with daunting problems and minimal supports. As the years go by, Lisa has felt that nothing much changes as she deals with frequent manic crises.

Lisa was put off by the idea of participating in the evaluation process. She had no time or patience for an evaluation process that didn't have any immediate relevance to her son's situation. Lisa participated reluctantly in the baseline and three-month interviews. In the "Needs Met Questionnaire" we have developed, domains of need (mental health, physical health, education, safety, legal, family, residential, cultural, recreational, social, spiritual) are represented by individual tulips. If the child's needs are being fully met in a domain, the tulip is colored red. If they are met somewhat, the tulip is colored yellow. White means "a little," and gray means "not at all." As results began to accrue and were presented to her in user-friendly pictograph formats, Lisa became more interested in the evaluation process. She eventually shared her delight as she saw that despite the crises there was solid evidence, shown by pictographs of tulips turning ever more brilliant colors, that her son's needs were indeed beginning to be met. Lisa was able to use evaluation results to advocate for her son in a more credible manner, as she gained evidence of what was helping him. She became a strong advocate for the participatory research process as she felt the benefits for her. She is now a member of the Blended Funding evaluation team and is an articulate spokesperson for the project as she uses evaluation results to attest to its value.

IMPLICATIONS OF PARTICIPATORY RESEARCH FOR CARE OF CHILDREN

Returning to the implications of participatory model applied to mental health services research, in our experience, Koroloff and Friesen (1997) had predicted correctly. The range of outcome variables *did* widen, as various constituents had their say. More complex processes *were* specified. Process evaluation *was* emphasized. New research methods *did*, indeed, evolve. The funny thing is that while the participatory research model was developed out of regard for ethical considerations, it also makes sense to conduct research in this way because of our obligations to science. One might imagine that the participatory researcher is constantly weighing decisions with scientific integrity (validity) on one hand and moral integrity on the other. On the contrary, participatory research offers a win-win solution to both. Working together with multiple constituents to carefully specify a model, carefully choose appropriate constructs and questions, and carefully frame results improves research validity.

SUMMARY OF BLENDED FUNDING EVALUATION RESULTS

Preliminary evaluation results have shown that the Blended Funding Project is effective in producing many desired outcomes. Furthermore, the Blended Funding model of change was substantiated. Statistically significant improvements were demonstrated in a number of domains, including family empowerment, service coordination, number of community connections, meeting children's emotional, residential, and social needs, and stabilization in community-based residential and educational placements. Twelve-month evaluation results are summarized briefly below for the first twenty-five Blended Funding Project participants, who ranged in age from four to seventeen (Vander Stoep, Green, & Williams, 2000).

Empowerment. Families have changed from feeling "somewhat" empowered to feeling "mostly" empowered. The greatest changes occurred in the following areas:

- Getting the kinds of supports they need.
- Being able to choose services they need.
- Better responsiveness from the service system re: requests for support.
- Ability to create or find needed supports when they don't exist within service systems.

Service Coordination. Services have changed from being "somewhat" coordinated to being "mostly" coordinated. The greatest changes occurred in the following areas:

- Families don't have to run all over to get services.
- New providers are aware of the child's situation.
- Different providers agree on what care the children should get and on a single plan.
- Different providers involved with the child cooperate with one another.

Family/Professional Collaboration. Although families report significant improvement in collaborating with several systems, after a year in Blended Funding, families rated:

- Blended Funding and Mental Health as "somewhat" collaborative.
- Education and Juvenile Justice "a little" collaborative.
- Child Welfare (DCFS) as "not at all" collaborative.

Community Connections. The average number of children's connections have increased:

- From 2 to 4 formal services.
- From 1 to 4 community-based activities, peers, and mentors.
- From 2 to 5 family members.
- From 0 to 1 school connection.
- Children have on average only two peers, one group activity, and no hobbies.
- Eleven children still have no peers.
- Four children still have no activities or hobbies.

Needs Met. Children's needs have been met more completely (from "a little" to "some") in these domains:

- Mental/emotional health
- Safety
- Residence
- Social/recreational

Children's needs continue to be met only "a little" in these domains:

- Educational
- Cultural/spiritual

Home and School Setting.

- The proportion living in a community home setting increased from 24 to 64 percent.
- The proportion going to school in the community increased from 48 to 84 percent.
- Two children moved to more restrictive home settings.
- Two school-aged children were not attending school.

Child Functioning.

- Overall functioning has not improved significantly according to the CAFAS.
- For the Blended Funding children, the CAFAS may not be sensitive enough to detect functional improvements, particularly in the areas of home, school, and community performance where a child is rated as "severely impaired" when either s/he has to be sent to an out-of-community placement *or* receives exceptional supports to be maintained in a community placement. The project would draw a distinction between the two.

Costs of Care.

- Sixty percent have experienced a decrease in the cost of care.
- The average cost of care per child has decreased by $1,166 per month.*

---

*The Blended Funding partners pool over $5,000/child/month. This amount reflects the combination of the highest rates available for group care, mental health services, and special education. The money that is pooled over all twenty-five

Blended Funding Model of Change.

- The degree to which families feel empowered has a strong positive association with the extent to which services are coordinated and children's needs are met.
- The extent to which the family feels empowered during their first three months in Blended Funding is positively related to how the child is functioning nine months later.
- The extent to which a child's needs are met is also related to the child's functional status.

CONCLUSIONS: FAMILIES AS FULL PARTNERS

The full involvement of families in the care of their children seems on the surface to be a logical and easy concept to endorse. It is a testimony to how distorted our systems of care have become that so many families had been excluded from any real sense of control when their children's difficulties involved them with many service systems and agencies. The Blended Funding Project in King County, Washington, is one example of a program designed to rectify such system distortions. The results of the project evaluation are still preliminary, but they look very promising. The King County Project is one of many similar programs around the country that adhere to the principles of the ideal system of care.

The evaluation of nationwide system of care projects is producing a large amount of data that have not been fully analyzed. Some early studies have raised doubts about the impact of family-centered practice on clinical outcomes. It has been suggested that these studies may not have measured relevant outcomes or may not have been able to impact enough of the intermediate factors (e.g., mental health agency, mental health intervention, practitioner, informal support structure) that affect an individual child's clinical course. Which practices are most helpful to improved care have yet to be determined, but the measures used by the King County Project strongly support parent empowerment through full involvement as a key factor in improving care for the most difficult children in our communities.

Do Blended Funding results clearly indicate that children are "getting better"? Not necessarily in the traditionally accepted way, that is, that

children covers all costs for placement, treatment, school, recreation, and so on, as well as the administrative costs of the Project. On average, for their first three months in the Project, cost of care averaged $6,359/child/month. One year later, their cost of care averaged $5,193/child/month.

the child has fewer symptoms and more skills. What they do indicate is that families and communities are "getting better" at caring for challenging children. With blended funding, flexible spending, and a group of earnest people thinking "outside the box," a family can hire a case aide to provide full-time supervision and strike a "deal" with the local beauty school to accept an adolescent with an interest in hair styling. A single parent can make an arrangement with a judge to obtain a book of "go to jail free" tickets for when her daughter violates her probation. A parent with two children can receive support to find a house that has sufficient space and privacy to bring the children home. A foster parent can pay a case aide overtime to accompany a sexually aggressive youth to his first high school prom. A teacher can be hired to teach private dance lessons to a group of children in a Blended Funding parent's home. Children can join the local Y and go to summer camp.

The greatest challenge to creating any truly integrated form of care for our children is in getting our public agencies to buy off on such efforts. This involves administrators taking a "leap of faith" by giving over sections of their budgets to projects where they will have a more difficult time accounting for all expenditures. Administrators are bound to protect their agencies from being sued or hounded by the press when a crisis occurs. Clearly state legislative support is needed to facilitate administrative efforts on behalf of family-centered programs. Federal agencies will need to waive categorical constraints on systems of care for children and adolescents if families are to be enabled to take control of federally derived funds for their children. Empowering families is often threatening to service agencies. The more a case worker or care manager is subject to huge caseloads and inadequate supervision, the less secure they are in their practice.

Having families in charge of treatment decisions is often felt by professionals as undercutting and a final blow to any sense of control over their jobs. Teaching our workforce of mental health professionals, including psychiatrists, the advantages of a family-driven system of care will take a revolution in training and practice orientation. Until then, tension between providers and child and family teams can be expected. Unfortunately, the resistance to full involvement of families by administrators and professionals often kills efforts at system of care reform.

It is also important to acknowledge that many families are not ready to participate in an empowering process such as we have described. Some children don't have available families and either must lead their own teams if they are older teens approaching emancipation, or must await some stability in a long-term guardianship or foster arrangement. Parents who have too many problems of their own, who cannot tend to their own children's problems, and who cannot bond with a support group of other parents may maintain a posture of trying to get professionals to fix their problems. If they can work with a family advocacy group that views them with patience and understanding, some will come around eventually. But many will never buy into family-driven care, learn the team-building process, nor embrace participatory evaluation. Children in such families may end up being "system kids" even after family-driven treatment takes hold in a community. Family advocacy groups who ally with the professionals and foster parents caring for these children can still make an impact by forming teams that can mobilize community resources and offer normalizing experiences. Clearly family-centered treatment, which places parents in the driver's seat in organizing care for their own children, has wide applicability and must be considered as a "best practice" for the future in child and adolescent mental health. Lisa, the mother of a difficult adolescent, expressed this best in her comments after reviewing the six-month evaluation report.

> *The Blended Funding program empowered me as a parent. Before my son and I were a part of the program, systems people told me what to do. Professionals had all the answers and laid all of our choices out for us. I followed blindly. As one choice after another failed to bring desired outcomes, I began to lose hope. I began to stop caring what we did. It all amounted to failure anyway. But the Blended Funding Project told me I was the team leader. They taught me how to build a supportive team. They encouraged creative thinking around making a crisis plan, building an educational program, and designing a job opportunity. And there were funds to make these creative ideas possible. By having flexibility in the use of funds, my team was not limited in where they looked for solutions to problems.*
>
> *Once, in a difficult legal situation, where my son's probation officer wanted him incarcerated in a juvenile justice center, we convinced the judge that stabilizing him in a hospital before returning him to the community was an option we had the funding for and was a choice that would better meet his psychological needs. Instead of his usual "detention pattern" of refusing meds, becoming psychotic and unstable and creating more problems for himself, his meds were balanced during a two-week hospital stay, and he reentered the community ready and able to try a small summer job. With the Blended Funding Project, I went from feeling hopeless to believing my child, with the proper supports, could be a stable participant in the life of the community.*

ACKNOWLEDGMENTS: Parts of this chapter appeared in an article by Ann Vander Stoep, Ph. D., Marilynn Williams, Robert Jones, M.S.W., Linda Green, and Eric Trupin, Ph.D., in the *Journal of Behavioral Health Services & Research,* Volume 26 (3), copyright © Sage Publications entitled "Families as Full Research Partners: What's in It for Us?" Reprinted by permission of Sage Publications, Reference #SRN 0606000028. The paper won a Distinguished Research Paper Award at the 11th annual research conference titled "A System of Care for Children's Mental Health: Expanding the Research Base." This conference is sponsored annually by the Research and Training Center for Children's Mental Health at the University of South Florida, Tampa. The King County Blended Funding Project was funded originally by a grant from the Robert Wood Johnson Foundation. The evaluation has been funded by the Washington Institute for Mental Illness Research and Training and the King County Mental Health and Chemical Abuse and Dependency Services Division. The authors wish to thank Petra Manns for her editorial contributions to initial drafts of this chapter.

References

Agosta, J. M., Jennings, D., & Bradley, V. S. (1987). State wide family support programs: Results for a national survey. In J. Agosta & V. S. Bradley (Eds.), *Family care for persons with developmental disabilities: A growing commitment* (pp. 94–112). Cambridge, MA: Human Services Research Institute.

Armstrong, M. I., & Evans, M. E. (1992). Three intensive community-based programs for children and youth with serious emotional disturbance and their families. *Child and Family Studies, 1*(1), 61–74.

Bateson, G. (1972). *Steps to an ecology of the mind.* New York: Ballentine.

Bickman, L. (1992). Designing outcome evaluations for children's mental health services : Improving internal validity. In L. Bickman (Ed.), *Evaluating mental health services for children* (pp. 57–68). San Francisco: Jossey-Bass.

Bickman, L. (1996). A continuum of care: More is not always better. *American Psychologist, 51*(7), 689–701.

Bickman, L., Summerfelt, W. T., & Noser, K. (1997). Comparative outcomes of emotionally disturbed children and adolescents in a system of services and usual care. *Psychiatric Services, 48*(12), 1543–1548.

Burchard, J. D., Schaefer, M. S., Rogers, J., Tighe, T., & Welkowitz, J. (1991). *User's guide to the daily adjustment indicator checklist.* Burlington, VT: University of Vermont, Department of Psychology.

Caplan, G., & Caplan, R. (2000). Principles of community psychiatry. *Community Mental Health Journal, 36*(1), 21–23.

Caplan, P. J., & Hall-McCorquodale, I. (1985). Mother-blaming in major clinical journals. *American Journal of Orthopsychiatry, 16,* 31–33.

Cocks, E., & Cockram, J. (1995). The participatory research paradigm and intellectual disability. *Mental Handicap Research, 8*(1), 25–37.

Cohen, S., Agosta, J., Cohen, J., Warren, R., et al. (1989). Supporting families of children with severe disabilities. *Journal of the Association for Persons with Severe Handicaps, 14*(2), 155–162.

Dangerfield, D., & Betit, R. (1993). Managed mental health care in the public sector. *Directions in Mental Health Services, 59,* 67–80.

DeChillo, N., Paulson, R., & Stuntzer-Gibson, D. (1995). Oregon Partners Project Evaluation, Regional Research Institute for Human Services, Portland, OR.

Domino, M. E., Salkever, D. S., Zarin, D. A., & Pincus, H. A. (1998). The impact of managed care on psychiatry. *Administration and Policy in Mental Health, 26*(2), 149–57.

Donner, R. (1986). *Social workers' view of parent of children with emotional disturbances: A problem or partner in the solution.* Unpublished paper.

Dunst, C. J., Trivette, C. M., Starnes, A. L., Hamby, D. W., & Gordon, N. J. (Eds.). (1993). *Building and evaluating family support initiatives.* Baltimore, MD: Paul H. Brookes Publishing.

Durham, M. L. (1998). Mental health and managed care. *Annual Review of Public Health, 19,* 493–505.

Federation of Families, Washington State Organization of the Federation of Families for Children's Mental Health. (2000). Community Connections Questionnaire.

Friesen, B. J., & Koroloff, N. M. (1990). Family-centered services. Implications for mental health administration and research. *Journal of Mental Health Administration, 17*(1), 13–25.

Hodges, K., Bickman, L., Kurtz, S., & Reiter, M. (1991). Multidimensional measures of level of functioning for children and adolescents: In A. Algarin & R. M. Friedman (Eds.), *A system of care for children's mental health: Expanding the research base.* Tampa, FL: Research and Training Center for Children's Mental Health, Florida Mental Health Institute, University of South Florida.

Inglehart, J. K. (1996). Health policy report: Managed care and mental health. *New England Journal of Medicine, 334,* 131–135.

Knitzer, J. (1982). *Unclaimed children: The failure of public responsibility to children and adolescents in need of mental health services.* Washington, DC: Children's Defense Fund.

Koren, P. E., DeChillo, N., & Friesen, B. J. (1992). Measuring empowerment in families whose children have emotional disabilities: A brief questionnaire. *Rehabilitation Psychology, 37*(4), 305–321.

Koren, P., Paulson, R. I., Kinney, R. F., Yatchmenoff, D. K., et al. (1997). Service coordination in children's mental health: An empirical study from the caregiver's perspective. *Journal of Emotional and Behavioral Disorders, 5*(3), 162–172.

Koroloff, N. M., & Friesen, B. J. (1997). Challenges in conducting family-centered mental health services research. *Journal of Emotional and Behavioral Disorders, 5*(3), 130–137.

Mason, R., & Boutilier, M. (1996). The challenge of genuine power sharing in participatory research: The gap between theory and practice. *Community Mental Health, 15*(2), 145–152.

Minkoff, K. (1994). Community mental health in the nineties: Public sector managed care. *Community Mental Health Journal, 30*(4), 317–321.

Moffitt, T. E. (1993). Adolescence-limited and life-course-persistent antisocial behavior: A developmental taxonomy. *Psychological Review, 100*(4), 674–701.

Pires, S. A., Stroul, B. A., Roebuch, L., Friedman, R. M., McDonald, B. B., & Chambers, K. L. (1996). *Health Care Reform Tracking Project: The 1995 state survey.* Research and Training Center for Children's Mental Health, Tampa, FL.

Regional Research Institute for Human Services. (1996, March). *Oregon Partners Project evaluation. Final report to the Office of Mental Health Services.* Oregon Mental Health and Developmental Services Division, Portland, OR.

Sameroff, A. J., & Fiese, B. H. (1990). Transactional regulation and early intervention. In S. J. Meisels & J. P. Shonkoff (Eds.), *Handbook of early childhood intervention.* New York: Cambridge University Press.

Stroul, B. A., & Friedman, R. M. (1986). *A system of care for severely emotionally disturbed children and youth.* Washington DC: Georgetown University Development Center.

Susman, E. J. (1993). Psychological, contextual, and interactions: A developmental perspective on conduct disorder. *Development and Psychopathology, 5,* 181–189.

VanDenBerg, J. (1998). History of the wraparound process. In B. J. Burns & S. Y. Goldman (Eds.), *Promising practice in wraparound for children with serious emotional disturbance and their families.* National Technical Assistance Center for Children's Mental Health. Georgetown University.

Vander Stoep, A., Green, L., & Williams, M. (2000). *Blended Funding Project pilot evaluation report. 12-month follow-up of children enrolled in 1998.* Federation of Families, the Washington State Organization of Federation of Families for Children's Mental Health.

Vander Stoep, A., Williams, M., Jones, R., Green, L., & Trupin, E. (1998). Families as full research partners: What's in it for us? *Journal of Behavioral Health Services & Research, 26*(3), 329–344.

Vander Stoep, A., Green, L., Williams, M., Jones, R., & Trupin, E. (2000). *Parents as evaluators: King County Blended Funding Project evaluation pilot results.* In 12th Annual Research Conference Proceedings, A System of Care for Children's Mental Health: Expanding the Research Base (pp. 149–154). Research and Training Center for Children's Mental Health, Louis de la Parte Florida Mental Health Institute, University of South Florida, Tampa, FL.

Van Vlaenderen, H. (1993). Psychological research in the process of social change: a contribution to community development. *Psychology and Developing Societies, 5*(1), 95–110.

Weiss, H. B., & Halpern, R. (Eds.). (1989). *The challenges of evaluating state family support and education initiatives: An evaluation framework.* Cambridge, MA: The Public Policy and Family Support and Education Programs Colloquium.

Weiss, H. B., & Jacobs, F. H. (Eds). (1988). *Evaluating family programs.* New York: Aldine De Gruyter.

Williams, M. (1997, January). *King County Blended Funding Project.* Burien, WA: Puget Sound Educational Service District.

Williams, M., Vander Stoep, A., & Jones, R. (1998, Summer). Families as full research partners. *Claiming Children* [national newsletter of the Federation of Families for Children's Mental Health].

CHAPTER TEN

Institutional Treatment Transferred: Narrative Family Therapy Approach to Acute Services

Thomas Hebeisen, Ph.D., and Michael Longo, M.A.

INTRODUCTION

In 1995, the State of Delaware's psychiatric center for children, the Terry Children's Psychiatric Center, was mandated to reorganize its services with the implementation of Delaware's Medicaid managed care waiver. Though the Terry Center had provided a continuum of care in Delaware since 1969, state officials had decided to close the outpatient unit, change the twenty-five-bed inpatient hospital unit into a thirteen-bed residential treatment center, and develop a community-based crisis program. The center's day program and statewide consultation program were left unchanged. Staff were reassigned to the new crisis unit and to the division's managed care office. Despite the fact that these programs have a history of change, the overall approach was fairly traditional in that the major therapeutic agents were considered to be family therapy (both in the center and in the community), a structured therapeutic milieu, and the use of psychotropic medication. There was also a strong sense of pride in the work being done and the consistently positive feedback from families. On the other hand, the patient population has continued to change in the direction of increased environmental chaos and trauma. In point of fact, most all of current admissions to Terry Center programs were those with very long treatment histories in all levels of care. There was a feeling by staff that they were getting others' "treatment failures." Not surprisingly, this led to a sense of frustration and diminished optimism. Staff were challenged to improve services while under pressure to do so without hospitalization.

Given the above changes and demands, leadership was faced with developing a model for crisis intervention or hospital diversion and rethinking models appropriate for the more chronic cases being admitted to the Residential Treatment Center (RTC) or Day Program (DP). Narrative therapy (White & Epston, 1990; Hart, 1995) offered a fresh "out of the box" approach that is more hopeful, more respectful, and, perhaps most importantly, significantly different from the pathologizing approaches to which our clients have been exposed. Bill Ohanlon (1994) writes, "The appeal of Narrative Therapy involves much more than a set of techniques. To my way of thinking it represents a fundamental new direction in the therapeutic world. Narrative approaches get therapists out of unproductive struggles and enable them to avoid one of this profession's great occupational hazards—being captured by our clients' own despair." Moreover, its application to acute services in Massachusetts (Longo & Tolomicenzenko, 1991) and Baltimore (Joseph, 1995) had been demonstrated. Narrative therapy is described by White and Epston (1990) as an approach that "centers people as experts in their own lives and views problems as separate from people." Narrative refers to the emphasis that is placed upon the stories of people's lives. A narrative approach is interested in looking at "problems" and people's experience of them in the broader context of their life, including their relationships with family and community. It focuses on telling and retelling someone's "story" in order to develop new meanings that emphasize competency, relationships with others, and the possibility for new solutions. At the Terry Center we have experienced this approach as detoxifying the climate of crisis and failure and opening up opportunities for change in our most difficult cases.

Philosophy

There are several "core" elements that make up the foundation of this approach as it has been developed at Terry Center. Treatment philosophy is the most basic and focuses on the development of a collaborative relationship between clinicians, children, family members, and other outside treating professionals. Harlene Anderson (1996) describes collaboration as "processes that foster respectful, humane, positive and fruitful interactions." This collaborative approach is critical to promoting change quickly. Without a shift in power from treating professionals to families, families cannot be empowered to take those steps necessary to ensure a child's rapid return to his/her home and community. In order to implement a collaborative approach the treatment team must set aside several ideas about change and adopt others. First, the team must view the client as an expert on his/her own problems. In defining the client as the expert, the clinicians set aside their acquired knowledge based on previous treatment experiences and become students, *prepared to learn from a family instead of teach them*. This shift in clinicians' point of view encourages an entirely new treatment dynamic. It opens the door for a new description of events that is based on the child and family's point of view. When clinicians take a position of *curiosity instead of certainty*, it widens the possibilities for change. Instead of re-creating the same treatment process that has occurred in every other treatment situation, it gives everyone the message that "this is something different."

When treating children and families, we cannot possibly create a different ending if we do not first take steps to create a different beginning experience for everyone. This new stance immediately gives children and families the message that they have an expertise that is valued. Carlos Sluzki (1992) believes that the therapist should "maintain a stance of interest and curiosity about the family's ideas" and "favor an optimistic stance of positive connotation." Acknowledging the family's expertise creates an opportunity for the family to find their own solution and then act on it. In viewing the child and family as expert, the treatment team creates a framework in which the responsibility for change shifts to the family. The team becomes a resource, responsible for facilitating a process of change, rather than for fixing the problem presented by the child and family. This shift supports families in becoming less dependent on mental health systems and more active in taking those steps that will lead to long-term stability.

The Use of Language in Communicating with Families

The first step in utilizing a philosophy that views the family as expert is using *their* language to describe events. In order to do this we must first set aside the familiar language for describing problems that is utilized in most diagnostic assessments. While the ideas contained in such language might be completely accurate, talking about the problem in this manner is not helpful to the family in defining their own experience. When we expand our use of language to include the family's description of events, we can also be curious about how they have handled them. This curiosity develops a foundation from which the family can better uncover areas or times of desired functioning that White and Epston (1990) describe as "unique outcomes." Helping a family find their own unique outcomes reveals those ingredients that can be utilized to fashion a new and more positive ending. These become the building blocks for new interventions, for a new story of success.

Uncovering the family expertise with a unique outcome is best utilized when we have a different understanding of the problem. Separating the person from the problem through the use of what White and Epston (1990) describe as externalization is another building block that opens up possibilities for change. Its use broadens the understanding of events and creates a context in which the child's behavior takes on new meaning. Chasin and Roth (1994) describe the aim of extenalization as "to release people from experiencing the problem as internal." Instead, it provides people with an experience of the problem as external. They believe that "this promotes their capacity to act in relation to it." Externalizing problems in an institutional setting is very different from the problem descriptions staff are used to. Linear problem descriptions encourage us to focus only on the child and what he or she must do to recover from his or her "problem." Externalization, on the other hand, encourages people to use their imagination and think beyond what is before their eyes. Describing things differently changes the relationship they have to each other, the presenting problem, and those events that have contributed to it. Accessing such imagination when working with children plays to their strengths and engages them in entirely new ways. It creates a partnership in which the child, clinical team, and family collaborate on a new solution. Accessing a child's imagination creates a playful approach to serious problems that energizes the treatment process, bringing hope into situations that have typically experienced crisis and failure.

Jimmy is a nine-year-old boy who had recently referred for treatment due to encropretic behavior and angry outbursts. His mother reported a history of sexual abuse by his stepfather. Professionals and family alike had been frustrated by the lack of progress with the encropresis. A new kind of conversation was begun with Jimmy and his family when a therapist began an interview by asking them what they called the encropresis. They immediately replied, "Making a mess." The therapist followed by asking, "When did you first realize that there was a mess in your family?" Jimmy's mother immediately began to talk about the sexual abuse and the attempts to recover from it. "How will you begin to 'pick up this mess'?" asked the therapist. Jimmy's mother began first, talking about what needed to be done and what action she would take. Jimmy was attentive as others in his family followed suit. When it was his turn he talked about "not making any more messes." The encropretic behavior was now seen in the larger context of sexual violence in which everyone could speak about how they were affected by it and what steps they would take to find a solution. By locating the problem outside of Jimmy, the family and treating professionals were now "free" to talk about the underlying trauma and treatment strategies that would give them a chance for protection and recovery. Jimmy could feel more a part of his family and certainly part of a new kind of treatment experience. Encropresis could be addressed, but it was no longer located inside of Jimmy where no one could get to it. It was now part of something serious and dangerous that required everyone's involvement to "pick things up" and begin the process of recovery.

View of the Problem

How we see problems determines how we will act on them. Traditionally, the problem is viewed as residing *inside* of someone. Children are hospitalized because they are afflicted with something that must be cured. This view presents serious difficulties in the treatment of children who have experienced a variety of "deep end" services. If we only look at what might be contained in the child's experience, we ignore the impact of successive crises, failed treatment attempts, family turmoil, and out-of-home placements. These events impact not only the child but also everyone involved in the child's life. It is critical for the treating professionals to recognize the link between the presenting problem and the way that everyone, including professionals, has been impacted over time in trying to solve it. This is especially true for children who have experienced multiple crises, hospitalizations, and treatment attempts. In order for treatment to be successful, it must acknowledge these realities and look beyond the child to the entire treatment context, which includes the presenting crises/problems and the efforts to solve them over time (Itzkowitz, 1996). Understanding the children and their community in this context helps everyone to "step back" and identify patterns and develop new ideas for treatment. In taking the problem out of the child and acknowledging it as part of the family's community, a new experience is created in which everyone may reorganize their work together (Oseroff, Longo, & Joseph, 1998). This builds on the view of the client as expert, values his/her description of events, and allows greater access to experiences of success.

Teamwork and Supervision

Often, multidisciplinary teams look for the "correct" approach to providing treatment and operate hierarchically—handing down supervision from a clinical leader to less experienced staff. This "top down" approach to generating ideas can narrow the view of the problem and limit possible solutions. In contrast, our team model focuses on what has been most difficult in providing treatment. Complicated cases often pull treatment professionals in different directions or produce intense feelings of frustration, anger, or hopelessness. Our supervision process looks at how the reactions, ideas, and choices of the current treatment team compared to others attempts to solve the problem. Because it is inevitable that, in forming a new treatment relationship, the team will be pulled to replicate past patterns, it is useful to step back and look at the *team's* relationship with the problem, the family, and the treatment system. Anderson and Gooloshian refer to the last as a "problem determined system" (Anderson, Gooloshian, & Windermand, 1991). Families do not cause or make problems—communicatively shared problems mark and define the system. Thus we must position ourselves, if we are to be useful in our consultation with those who are actors in the drama of struggle and change called therapy. By identifying patterns of difficulty that surface within the team and then understanding these patterns as replications of previous turmoil and failure, the current team is better able to change directions and avoid previous failures. By focusing on their own reactions, team members are able to understand the treatment impasse without passing judgment, and then use this experience to generate new ideas. This "democratic" process encourages the sharing of diverse experiences and ideas and establishes a collaborative process that encourages a "fresh look."

As Fine and Turner (1991) put it, therapists are likely to step back from their work sufficiently to develop a more acute awareness of their ideas, and hence into a position of increased choice with respect to the revision of ideas.

CRISIS UNIT

When Terry Center operated an inpatient unit, there was tendency for everyone involved in a child's life to pass on the responsibility for treatment and change to the hospital. Now the hospital staff had suddenly become mobile, and treatment was brought into the community. Because treatment was no longer occurring inside the hospital walls, the difficulty and danger in each child's life was there for everyone to see. The responsibility for change was now everyone's to share. In order to create a safe and successful treatment experience, we knew that we had to create a framework that allowed everyone to not only work together but also to share responsibility for change. Developing a new model for collaboration that acknowledged the needs of all of our clients was paramount.

First and foremost we needed to redefine our relationship with the children and families referred to us. The ability of the program to restore safety and promote change is dependent on the degree to which a successful collaboration is established between the family and our staff. Often children in crisis have a complicated history of previous treatment that includes past crises and placement. The treatment process is laced with conflict and confusion. For us, this meant that we had to take steps to create a ***different beginning*** experience for the child and family. In this new beginning, we immediately give the child and family the message that they have an expertise that is valued. Acknowledging the family as a valued customer who has a specific expertise creates an opportunity for the family to find their own solution to the crisis and then act on it. In viewing the child and family as expert, the treatment team also creates a framework in which the responsibility for change shifts to the family. The team becomes a resource, responsible for facilitating a process of change, rather than fixing the problem presented by the child and family. This shift supports families in becoming less dependent on mental health systems and more active in taking those steps that will lead to ending the crisis and promoting long-term stability. The only exception to this is when the family is not able to reestablish safety for the child. In these cases, the team takes the stance of making the decisions to ensure safety, much like it did when the child was hospitalized. Although the family is making the decisions, it is critical to engage the school and other providers in a way that creates a new understanding of the problem and potential solutions. The structures that we installed to solicit everyone's input early and involve them in a collaborative treatment process with the family are key.

Only Thirty Days!

A major challenge for the Crisis Unit was how to restore safety and promote dramatic change outside a hospital and in only thirty days. This was considerably different from our previous mission of providing acute services until they were complete and a child and family could step down to a less intensive model of care. As a wraparound service treating difficult and dangerous cases in the community, we had to change the focus and expectations of our treatment. Our limit of three days of crisis bed care and thirty days of community-based treatment defined that for us.

In order to work within this time frame, the psychiatrist and the rest of the team needed to make a rapid assessment of the child, family, and social system and set reasonable priorities about which interventions needed to occur first. We were pressed to sort out which pharmacological interventions should occur while the child was in a crisis bed and which could occur with the child in treatment in the community. We confronted families early on the issue of whether out-of-home placement for the child was needed and engaged with school and outpatient therapists early on about the kind of supportive services that were needed as an alternative to hospitalization.

While concerns about safety dominate any referral for acute services, the real dilemma in working with many emergency cases is one of understanding repeated treatment failures and impasses. This latter "treatment impasse" may involve community agencies and institutions such as schools, protective services, therapists, and so on. Understanding this treatment impasse in a brief, narrative model involves understanding past patterns of treatment failure, what we call the "second order crisis" (Bobele, 1987).

Triage

Triage is the entry point into the crisis service. While triage has always been designed to obtain demographic information and assess the level of risk, the Terry Center approach entails much more. The triage clinician always speaks to at least one responsible family member and one involved professional during each triage contact. This first contact with a family member, school personnel, or treating professional is a time to establish a framework for collaboration. The triage clinician asks the caller about the reason for the referral, the caller's experience of either receiving or providing treatment, and their ideas about what they would like to happen. This is a critical first step in developing a collaboration between the Terry Center and everyone involved. The triage clinician begins to carefully develop a language with the caller that contains an accurate but new description of the problem and the ideas for a solution. Within this new conversation the triage clinician asks about who else is involved and the caller's understanding of how their experience compares to their own. This approach takes the demographic information and expands it to develop a systemic picture of how the child, family, and treatment system have been impacted by this crisis and every other crisis over time. This conversation is used to plan the initial assessment. The callers are asked who should attend the assessment, and their assistance is requested to get them to the initial evaluation, which must happen within one hour. (Due to the life-threatening nature of many requests for service, the State of Delaware Department of Children, Youth and Families requires an on-site response by a mobile team within one hour of the initial telephone call.)

Assessment

The initial session often occurs in the community, with a team of two clinicians going to the most appropriate location. A thorough risk assessment is conducted at this time, including the risk of suicide, harm to others, fire-setting, running away, and substance abuse. The assessment is designed to understand not only the presenting problem and the level of risk but also the experience of past struggle and crisis that has surrounded family members and treating professionals. In moving to a systemic assessment, the team looks beyond the child to the "child in context" of their family and community and the effort to find a solution. In broadening the assessment, the team seeks to expand the collaboration developed in the triage telephone conversation and develop a foundation for an intervention that will help everyone end both the presenting crisis as well as the pattern of crisis over time. The two clinicians assigned to the case now follow the child and family, and treating professionals bring the interventions to them in the community.

Crisis Bed

The option to treat a child in a crisis bed allows for a fuller assessment of the risk issues and closer monitoring for more aggressive pharmacological interventions. Seeing the child in a crisis bed on a daily basis in effect extends the assessment, intensifies the intervention, and helps everyone develop an understanding of whether the child can return home. The ability of the mobile crisis team to continue the intervention begun in the crisis bed directly in a community, without the need to pass the case off to someone else, maintains the framework for collaboration and treatment intensity necessary to make something different happen. The short length of stay in the crisis bed creates a very useful pressure on everyone involved to find out what it will take to restore safety.

Intervention

Techniques focus on helping family members start to look at the problem and themselves differently, so they can feel differently about themselves. This process involves, first, uncovering the meaning that problems have for children and families, and then helping them consider alternative ways to understand their present difficulty. Highlighting the manner in which a family makes meaning of a particular crisis, deconstructing it, and codeveloping a new meaning that builds on the family's existing competence, is at the heart of a narrative therapy intervention. These changes often begin in small steps, so it is important to help families notice and then expand changes when they occur. Generally, at the outset of treatment in crisis situations, family members experience little hope that change can occur. Useful conversations facilitate changes in this belief through discussions of past successes, the development of ideas about life in the future, and encounters during therapy sessions that are consistent with the changes family members want to experience.

All of the elements listed above help clarify the goals families have for treatment. But it is important to make these goals explicit, preferably in the first session. And it is important to recognize that the goals and the problems can appear independent of one another. Such goals emerge from discussions of the meaning of problems, past successes, and visions of the future. The family's participation in creating these goals fosters a sense of ownership of them. This ownership of new ideas facilitates meaningful changes in interactions between people and a focus on achieving short-term goals.

The team of two clinicians works with the child, family, and treating professionals for thirty days by organizing and facilitating a series of interventions that have been custom designed during the assessment phase by the child, family, and involved professionals. Clinicians work in teams so that they may pay attention to both the content of the session and the process by which solutions have been attempted over time. Expanding the focus to include both the first order (content) and second order (processes) is best done with two clinicians because of the complexity of the information. Expanding what we pay attention to in a session greatly accelerates the treatment process. It is critical that this occur, especially when the children and families referred have experienced treatment as not working in the past. Rather than focusing the treatment on just helping the child "get better," the team attends to helping the family and community be more successful in their efforts to find a lasting solution to the problem(s) that have most concerned them. Working in teams increases everyone's understanding of the crisis and the treatment impasse that may have contributed to it. Teammates pay attention not only to each other's ideas, but also look at how their experience of the treatment process compares to everyone else's over time. By noting their place in the system as it is identified by ideas, attitudes, and experiences, the team is better able to map the way in which the system of child, family, and professionals has become organized in its effort to find a solution that works. Including their own experience as a "mirror" to hold up to treatment, the team is able to help everyone look at their process of working together and develop new ideas about how the impasse might be broken by "changing the approach to change."

RESIDENTIAL AND DAY PROGRAM

Unlike the Crisis Unit, which had the opportunity of developing a program from "scratch," the Residential Treatment Center (RTC) and Day Program had a nearly thirty-year history of operation. Perhaps the first and most significant change in the program was one that developed slowly. In the context of observing the Crisis Unit develop its own narrative approach, there ensued a sense of intrigue by RTC and Day Program staff. As narrative training and consultation was expanded to these units, there also developed a sense of excitement and increased hopefulness about our ability to help families make positive changes. Traditional interventions can be made more meaningful when done in the context of children's stories. This led to the development of a core set of beliefs which stressed that children and their families can make relatively rapid but significant and lasting positive changes by looking at their past successes and current strengths. In so doing, they begin a process of reauthoring their lives that enables them to break free from past patterns of failure and rediscover effective and powerful ways of dealing with problems. *Collaboration* between the families and Terry Center staff around the structured milieu of the RTC and Day Program was also seen as essential for maximum progress and for the reauthoring process. While outcomes are incomplete with the Residential and Day Treatment programs, the Crisis Unit was able to show an immediate, positive outcome. Only 3 percent of all children referred for evaluations were hospitalized. Twenty-five percent of children utilized a crisis bed, but the average length of stay was only 2.5 days. Because of this, the cost of treating children in crisis was reduced by 65 percent compared with hospitalization. Day treatment costs were reduced by 35 percent.

Out of the Box: Free at Last

With the option of narrative thinking, the more traditional "linear" approach was broken down and replaced with a nonlinear and more systemic one. Whereas the linear approach fostered a hierarchy of treatment, narrative thinking has led to greater collaboration and "permission" for staff to experiment with new techniques, new approaches, and—most importantly—new ways of interacting with families. This newfound sense of freedom seemed to expand the possibilities for children, families, and staff. Permission to experiment has allowed everyone to discover ideas, interventions, and experiences that have been previously hidden from view. It has also led to a significant increase in community interventions of all types, ranging from traditional family sessions held in the home to outreach efforts with the family to other resources in the community, such as Boys and Girls Clubs, the family's local church, and so on.

The Language

When we receive the inevitable one to two inches of records on a child prior to his or her admission into either the RTC or Day Program, they are replete with professional terminology and perhaps even some "psychobabble." In order to satisfy state reporting requirements we must make DSM-IV diagnoses. While we have these conversations with the clinical reviewers, we do not talk to the family in such terms. Instead, we use the family's language and seek to identify words and phrases that are meaningful to them. Thus, rather than talking about the child's "oppositional defiant disorder" or his or her "ADHD," we may end up talking about the "temper tantrum monster" or "Mr. Hyper" that is interfering with not only the child but the entire family. As various authors have noted, this can have a very dramatic effect because it creates a structure of alliance instead of one in which the child is the problem. As White and Epston (1990) say, "the person is not the problem, the problem is the problem. When a child and family discover that their own words are being used by staff to discuss problems and solutions, it breaks down the gap between family and professionals. In addition, it has the effect of "authenticating"—rather than "marginalizing"—the child and family. It helps to establish them as "experts" on their difficulties and related possible solutions.

The Team

In the past, the RTC and Day Program had several multidisciplinary treatment teams. When bringing a narrative perspective to the programs, the idea of the team was expanded so that all staff felt some degree of "ownership" for all cases. As was true in emphasizing nonlinear thinking, the expanded team led to the breaking down of boundaries so that staff have become more flexible in their roles. Rather than a setting in which teachers teach, counselors manage, nurses nurse, therapists "therapize," and so on, staff began to move beyond their traditional roles, which in turn led to a significant increase in *possibilities* for change and *opportunities* for success. This enhanced model for collaboration within the team accelerates the treatment process. Instead of carrying out interventions designed by clinicians, milieu staff take part in creating them. Such interventions have involved not only the family and extended family but all disciplines of

Terry Center staff, including therapists, counselors (direct-care staff), nurses, and teachers. This fosters integration across the various disciplines and shifts and helps to create a seamless experience for children and families.

Assessment: Problems versus Solutions

In the more traditional approach to treatment employed prior to the integration of narrative approaches, a great deal of emphasis was given to clarifying diagnoses and performing various professional assessments. As narrative thinking has taken hold, understanding the family's and child's stories has become the major focus, with traditional assessment and diagnosis taking a "back seat." The stress on the family's story is, of course, a key component in any narrative work; however making it a primary task for *all* staff in an institutional setting is unique. Narrative approaches stress solution-focused approaches rather than dwelling on problem-saturated descriptions. At Terry Center now, the search for "unique outcomes" begins before admission and continues throughout. Moreover, it is the responsibility of *all* staff to participate in this process with the family. Consider the case of one ten-year-old boy (we will call him Tommy) who had a "problem" with angry outbursts. Through narrative conversations with various direct-care staff, we came to understand that he related his outbursts to "worry." He named (externalized) this as the "worry monster"; he even drew a picture of it in relation to his own body. As conversations continued, various "unique outcomes" were discovered. He began to talk about the "worry monster" more and more and share his successes in defeating it with staff. This experience was subsequently formalized by means of a videotape that he made about himself, the "worry monster," and his successes. The tape was first shared with staff while he narrated it; he subsequently felt proud and able to share it with his family, which he had not been willing to do before for fear of their response. As this process evolved two things happened: (1) his outbursts all but disappeared, and (2) his self-esteem/pride was observed by many to be noticeably better. We would also say that he had begun a reauthoring process in which he saw himself as strong and "in control" of himself.

Management versus Treatment

Traditionally, professionals (often "doctors") *prescribe* treatment. This is in line with the hierarchy involved in a traditional perspective (e.g., doctor to patient), and it tends to make both the child and family and many of the institution's staff more passive in treatment. With the narrative perspective, the family and *all* members of the Terry Center team develop interventions together. Obviously, this provides a greater sense of investment in various ideas and "things to try" and fosters a genuine sense of respect and empowerment. This has led to a shift away from the duties of direct-care staff being viewed as basically management of children and reporting to "professional staff." Now direct-care staff help develop and implement all aspects of treatment. This has resulted in equal standing with other disciplines but also an increased responsibility. (See the case of Tommy above.)

CONCLUSION

We have learned that, in order to successfully change our services at Terry Center, we had to also change the way in which we think about services. Key to this have been several pardigm shifts that are easier said than done, but once done are surprising in their results. First we had to believe that treating children and families in acute distress in the community could work. This was a step that made all of us a little nervous. In order to take it we had to begin to believe that sudden change was possible. This is an idea that we welcomed but were also very skeptical of given the history of difficulty and crisis with all of our cases. Changing the way in which we understood both families and their problems was a significant first step that helped us to make this shift. We have always respected families, but once we began to see children and families as experts in their own struggle we felt liberated. We gave up our role as problem solvers, and instead became students of the child's and family's experience. Treating a crisis that had become familiar to us had often drained our energy and our hope. Now chronic difficulties suddenly became explorations where our understanding of ideas and relationships was suddenly "fresh." Our shift away from pathology and to the language and ideas of each family member opened us to interventions that were unique. This created a sense of discovery and adventure for both staff and children and their families. Everyone was now more involved, and it changed the way we worked with each other. It especially changed the way our team worked together. The democratic, collaborative approach we had established with families was now transferred to our team. We aknowledged the expertise of all team members and used it to strengthen our interventions. We came to rely on each other more than ever and staff felt valued, included, and empowered. Our sense of team has been strengthened, and our understanding of problems and possible solutions forever changed.

References

Anderson, H. (1996). A reflection on client-professional collaboration. *Families, Systems, and Health, 14*(2), 201.

Anderson, H., Gooloshian, H., & Windermand, P. (1991). Problem determined systems: Towards transformation in family therapy. *Journal of Strategic and Systemic Therapies, 5*(4), 374.

Blumberg, S. (1999). *An integrated hospital diversion model: A narrative systems approach in conjunction with biological and behavioral approaches.* Unpublished.

Bobele, M. (1987). Therapeutic interventions in life-threatening situations. *Journal of Marital and Family Therapy, 13*(3), 227.

Chasin, R., & Roth, S. (1994). Externalization–linguistic key to new approaches in family therapy. *Psychiatric Times, 3.*

Fine, M., & Turner, J. (1991). Tyranny and freedom: Looking at ideas in the practice of family therapy. *Family Process, 30,* 227.

Hart, B. (1995). Re-authoring the stories we work with by situating the narrative approach in the presence of family therapists. *Family Therapy, 16*(4), 183.

Itzkowitz, A. (1996). Children in placement: A place for family therapy. In *Children in family contexts.* New York: Guilford Press.

Joseph, I. (1995). Research Project, Baltimore Mental Health Systems and the Children's Guild, Baltimore, MD. Unpublished.

Longo, M., & Tolomicenzenko, G. (1991). Research Project, Massachusetts Department of Mental Health. Unpublished.

Ohanlon, B. (1994). The third wave. *Family Therapy Networker, 81,* 19–29.

Oseroff, C., Longo, M., & Joseph, I. (1998). Finding our way home: Home and community based care. In H. S. Ghuman & R. Sarles (Eds.), *Handbook of child and adolescent outpatient, day treatment, and community psychiatry.* Philadelphia: Brunner/Mazel.

Sluzki, C. (1992). Transformations: A blueprint for narrative changes in therapy. *Family Process, 31,* 215.

White, M., & Epston, D. (1990). *Story, knowledge and power: Narrative means to therapeutic ends.* New York: W. W. Norton & Company.

PART THREE

Special Issues

CHAPTER ELEVEN

Children's Mental Health: Partnering with the Faith Community

Christine A. Prodente, Ph.D., Mark A. Sander, Psy. D., Alvin C. Hathaway, MACM, Tom Sloane, LCPC, and Mark D. Weist, Ph.D.

INTRODUCTION

Media coverage of recent tragedies, such as the violence that occurred in two California schools in 2001, has served to focus the nation's attention on the unmet mental health needs of its youth. In today's world it is difficult to find a school-aged child who has not been exposed to, experienced, or been affected by the realities of divorce, violence, depression, suicide, substance abuse, teen pregnancy, or AIDS (Thomas & Texidor, 1987). Thus, it may not be surprising that one in five school-aged children present with an emotional or behavioral disturbance severe enough to warrant intervention (Shaffer et al., 1996). Unfortunately, less than one-third of these youth actually receive treatment (Leaf et al., 1996).

The current political climate is ripe to facilitate a surge forward in establishing more collaborations between mental health agencies and the faith community. President Bush has clearly shown his strong support with his 2001 campaign for "charitable choice" and by creating the Office of Faith-Based and Community Initiatives, which is under the leadership of John Dilulio, a well-respected political science professor from the University of Pennsylvania. Single agencies or organizations are often not prepared to address the tremendous mental health needs of youth. One strategy for keeping pace with this trend is for children's mental health agencies to develop collaborative partnerships with faith-based organizations. The fact that such linkages may seem counterintuitive signifies several barriers to such a collaboration that will need to be addressed in order to establish effective partnerships.

The goals of this chapter are fourfold. First, reasons for establishing collaborative partnerships between mental health agencies and faith-based organizations will be discussed. Second, barriers to forming such linkages will be identified. These include: (a) limited awareness of the positive impact of religious commitment on youth mental health; (b) a lack of information about the role that clergy currently serve in the mental health field; (c) the distrust of mental health professions by many faith traditions, and in turn, the view of some in mental health that strong faith is irrational or even psychotic; (d) language barriers; (e) cultural barriers, (f) limited awareness of youth mental health issues; (g) narrow views of mental health services; (h) concerns about client confidentiality; (i) concerns about maintaining the separation of church and state; and (j) the varying ministry perspectives of faith-based organizations (FBOs). Third, suggestions for addressing these barriers and for developing effective partnerships will be provided. Finally, some examples of promising collaborative endeavors involving the faith community will be highlighted.

THE FAITH COMMUNITY: AN UNTAPPED RESOURCE

Religion is important to Americans, and faith-based organizations constitute one of the largest service resources in this country. In a 1997 CNN/*USA Today* Gallup poll, 97 percent of adults surveyed reported believing in God or a universal spirit. In another poll, 76 percent of adolescents in the United States believe in a personal God, 74 percent report praying at least occasionally, 48 percent report having attended church or temple weekly, and 27 percent report a higher interest in religion than their parents (Gallup & Bezilla, 1992). There are approximately 500,000 churches, temples, and mosques represented in almost every community across the United States (Weaver, 1998). American congregations contribute approximately \$6.6 billion to community causes each year, \$500 million more than corporations donate (Goodstein, 1993). Churches alone are responsible for 37 percent of the volunteer activity in America (Samuelson, 1994).

The U.S. government has long recognized the potential of partnering with the faith community. The Salvation Army, Catholic Charities, and Lutheran Family Services regularly contract with the government to provide child care, foster care, and other services (Shirk, 2000). As mentioned previously, President Bush's 2001 campaign for "charitable choice" recognizes and seeks to capitalize upon the possibility for government partnerships with faith-based organizations in addressing community needs.

BARRIERS TO COLLABORATION

Limited awareness of the positive impact of religious commitment on youth mental health. Given the high levels of volunteerism and charitable donations by the religious community, why have children's mental health programs been slow to capitalize on this resource? For one, clinicians may not be aware that religious commitment is associated with a host of positive mental health outcomes for youth. In a 1995 literature review, Donahue and Benson found that religiousness is the second strongest inhibitor of both suicide ideation and attempts for adolescents. Furthermore, religiously involved youth, as compared with noninvolved youth, were 50 percent less likely to abuse substances or engage in violent behavior (Donahue & Benson, 1995; Elkin & Roehlkepartain, 1992). Benson, Williams, and Johnson (1987) found that the importance of religion, church attendance, and orthodoxy are consistently correlated with youth measures of caring and prosocial behavior (e.g., concern for the poor, helping behavior). It has also been estimated that religiousness may decrease the probability of premature sexual behavior of adolescents by as much as 50 percent (Spilka, Hood, & Gorsuch, 1985).

Consistent with the above findings, many of the assets identified by the Search Institute (1997) as promoting positive youth development directly reflect or are strongly related to faith. These developmental assets, or resilience factors, for youth include: involvement in religious activities one or more hours per week; positive values such as caring, integrity, honesty, and responsibility; a perception of being valued by adults in the community; serving others in the community one or more hours per week; feeling safe in the community; exposure to adults who model positive, responsible behaviors; belief in a life purpose; and a positive view of the future. The Search Institute found that youth with the most assets were least likely to exhibit negative behaviors such as depression, attempted suicide, violence, alcohol use, illicit drug use, sexual activity, and school problems. Having more assets was also associated with a variety of positive behaviors (e.g., success in school, maintaintenance of good health, and ability to delay gratification).

Other research has shown that involvement in meaningful activities was related to lower levels of aggressive and delinquent behavior in males (Tashman, Weist, Nabors, & Shafer, 1998). One way to increase an individual's likelihood of involvement in meaningful activities would be through activities often sponsored by faith communities (i.e., Habit for Humanity projects, volunteering in homeless shelters, mentoring programs). Many times, the faith communities offering these activities do not require that an individual be a member of the congregation, but only that he/she be willing to commit time to work on the specific project.

These research findings suggest that young people are empowered through religious involvement. Positive values in direct opposition to violence and crime, for example, are modeled and reinforced by the faith community. It is not uncommon for youth today to complain of feeling hopeless and depressed, and to have difficulty envisioning a positive future. Spirituality can offer hope and a sense of life purpose. Furthermore, strong religious connections help youth feel safer and more invested in their communities. These supportive connections also assist in alleviating feelings of loneliness and depression.

Lack of information about the role that clergy serve in the mental health field. Clinicians may also be uninformed as to the primary role that clergy serve in the mental health field as counselors for millions of Americans. In the United States, there are more than 400,000 clergy and religious workers allotting 10–20 percent of their time (approximately 148.2 million hours annually) to providing mental health services (Weaver, 1995, 1998). Clergy are among the most trusted professionals in society (Gallup, 1990). Due to the cultural stigma associated with receiving mental health services, youth in distress may be more likely to consult with a clergy member before speaking to a mental health professional. Clergy also tend to establish long-term relationships with congregation members and their families and are in a unique position to provide support, observe early warning signs of emotional disturbance, and pave the way for other mental health providers to assist individuals in crisis who would not otherwise seek psychological services (Weaver, 1998).

Mental health and religion: uncomfortable bedfellows. A third barrier to collaboration has to do with the fact that mental health professions and religion have a long history of mutual mistrust. Sigmund Freud (1953), the father of psychoanalytic theory, linked religiousness with mental illness, claiming that religion is a "universal obsessional neurosis." Skinner ignored religious experience to focus exclusively on observable behavior. Albert Ellis, the founder of rational emotive (cognitive) therapy, equated religion with irrational thinking and emotional disturbance: "The elegant therapeutic solution to emotional problems is to be quite unreligious. . . . The less religious they are, the more emotionally healthy they will tend to be" (1980, p. 637).

Similarly, the faith community has long had concerns that mental health professions promote a divergent value system. While religion tends to emphasize personal responsibility for behavior, mental health professions often focus on other explanations for misbehavior, such as genetics or unfortunate childhood circumstances. Some Christian critics of psychology, for example, have expressed concerns that therapy is unbiblical, may undermine the local pastor's authority, and implies that the confession of sin and recognition of the need for salvation are less important than the pursuit of self-actualization (Rabey, 1996).

Language barriers. Some of the reticence of mental health professionals and clergy (or people of faith) to collaborate may be due to language differences. Psychologists, psychiatrists, and social workers, for example, have a professional language that may be unclear or misinterpreted by lay people. Similarly, each religious tradition has a certain way of conceptualizing or talking about issues. It is not uncommon for persons in the faith community to communicate using parables, metaphors, or phrases associated with their religious traditions or books (Plante, 1999). These language differences can lead to increased tensions when attempting to forge ongoing alliances. Even a common psychological term such as "self-actualization," for example, may be off-putting to certain people of faith concerned with de-emphasizing the "self" in an effort to maintain a God-focus. Diagnostic terminology (e.g., "anxiety disorder") also may increase tensions, since some faith communities eschew medical or psychological etiologies, seeing individual difficulties as resulting from a spiritual crisis or a lack of enlightenment.

Cultural differences. These communication barriers may not be easy to breach since religious persons tend to be underrepresented in the mental health professions when compared with the general population (Bergin, 1991). Fifty percent of psychologists in an academic setting reported having no religious preference, as compared with 7 percent of the general population (Shafranske, 1996). Furthermore, while most graduate training programs in psychology include courses on cultural diversity, only 5 percent of clinical psychologists report having had training in religious issues prior to licensure (Shafranske & Malony, 1990). There is also a scarcity of articles in professional journals describing psychologist-clergy collaboration (Weaver et al., 1997). Thus, for many mental health professionals, the perspectives and cultural traditions of the faith community are outside their life experience (Weaver, 1998).

Limited awareness of children's mental health issues. In general, public awareness of children's mental health issues is limited. For many there is a basic lack of understanding about the magnitude and severity of the unmet mental health needs of today's youth, and it is not uncommon for people to minimize or underreport youth mental health problems. This may be particularly true for faith communities who tend to view mental health problems as manifestations of spiritual issues. People of faith may feel that mental health services are unnecessary, since religious leaders are available to provide counseling services. In order to establish effective partnerships, however, it will be important for clergy (e.g., pastors, rabbis, ministers) to be aware of their limitations and to establish appropriate referral guidelines. For example, if the pastor has offered three or more counseling appointments to a congregation member and the difficulties persist, then it may be appropriate to make a formal referral for mental health services.

A narrow view of mental health services. Mental health care is often narrowly defined to include the diagnosis and treatment of existing problems rather than on children at risk for developing mental health problems (e.g., due to exposure to violence, abuse, or neglect). Focusing on building protective or resilience factors (e.g., support from positive adults, community involvement) for at-risk youth may be critical in preventing mental health problems in youth—and, therefore, an appropriate goal for mental health care providers (Weist, Ginsburg, & Shafer, 1999). As mentioned previously, faith-based organizations are ideally situated to foster developmental assets or resilience factors in youth. Religious organizations provide a means for mobilizing the community's assets to address youth mental health needs. The faith community, for instance, may have access to the human resources or the funding necessary for establishing much-needed wraparound services for youth (e.g., after-school programming, community mentors for at-risk youth). Broadening the public's view of mental health services to include prevention efforts will be key in gaining support for partnerships between mental health and faith-based agencies.

Confidentiality concerns. One of the challenges of collaborating with outside organizations has to do with maintaining client confidentiality. In the interest of helping, the faith community may expect the mental health provider to share information regarding the client. Psychologists, psychiatrists, social workers, and other mental health providers, however, are bound by strict confidentiality guidelines set forth in their professional codes of conduct. For example, psychologists are not even permitted to reveal that someone is a client unless a written release-of-information form is obtained beforehand (American Psychological Association, 1992). In the faith community the emphasis tends to be more on information exchange. It is not uncommon for members of the faith community, for example, to share concerns for one another so that many will pray for the person in need. Thus, without knowledge of the ethical/legal obligations of the mental health provider, the faith community may begin to view the clinician as aloof and unwilling to collaborate. Similarly, tensions may arise if the mental health provider is not educated as to the policies and professional standards of the clergy.

Separation of church and state. The American ideal of limited religious involvement in governmental agencies is very ingrained and may be difficult to overcome. Many agencies fear legal repercussions should they attempt to partner with a faith-based organization. The concept of church and state separation hails from the First Amendment of the U.S. Constitution. This amendment safeguards religious freedom by prohibiting the establishment of a state or national church—as well as laws that aid one religion, all religions, or one religion over another. However, as long as the religious agency is not attempting to indoctrinate people or proselytize and is seeking to engage in activities or provide services that any nonsecular organization would do or provide (e.g., child care, foster care, and other services provided by agencies such as the Salvation Army, Catholic Charities, and Lutheran Family Services), the First Amendment is not at issue (e.g., *Bradfield v. Roberts*, 1899). If faith-based organizations are going to provide such services they must adhere to governmental and professional guidelines with regard to licensure, peer review, and liability. It does not necessarily constitute a violation of the First Amendment, for example, for a faith-based organization to provide wraparound services for youth (e.g., after-school or mentoring programs). Yet a lack of awareness about the scope of the First Amendment will lead to increased tensions, making it difficult to establish these types of partnerships.

DIFFERING MINISTRY PERSPECTIVES

A mistake potential partnering agencies make regarding faith-based organizations (FBOs) is a generalization of their role in community development. Most agencies operate from the perspective of their agenda and fail to understand the ministry agenda of the FBO. This is due primarily to the perception that the location of the FBO determines its mission, when in fact the agenda of the FBO has to be viewed from *that* institution's perspective. The ministry objectives of FBOs tend to fall into four basic models: (1) The FBO as temple—this organization's ministry is to provide a safe haven from the problems, predicaments, and situations of the present day. It is seen as a place of prayer and contemplation. It has an "otherworldly" view of the present age. (2) The FBO as evangelical—this organization's ministry is to bring the "lost" into their fold and to aid them in reordering their thought patterns. It would reason that the primary need in the present age is salvation from sin. It also has an "otherworldly" view of the present age. (3) The FBO as community center—this organization's ministry is to use the resources of the private and public sector to provide services to the community it serves. It will be a highly structured organization with a "this world" view that allows it to cooperate with agencies and individuals to assist it in accomplishing its goals and mission. (4) The FBO as social activist—this organization's ministry is to confront the systems that oppress and to be an advocate for the poor and dispossessed. It has a "this world" view that will tend to be distrustful of being seen as ineffective if it cooperates with representatives or agents of systems that oppress (Bakke, 1987). While FBOs may possess all of these elements to varying degrees, one element will typically be dominant.

To know and respect the role and ministry model of the FBO is paramount. In partnering with FBOs, three understandings are required: (1) Do we seek a relationship or simply want them to perform a task or role? A relationship will be defined as involving "quid pro quo." What can we offer to assist them in their ministry mission? And the answer to this question needs to be more than just getting them involved in our particular project. You have to be willing to invest the time into developing a long-term sustainable relationship that understands mutual self-interest. (2) Do you respect the ministry model of the FBO? This is important because, from the perspective of the FBO, they are fulfilling a God-given mandate to minister in the manner they do. Who are we to change or reinterpret their role? Collaboration implies respect for the goals and objectives of the other party. In some instances alliances may develop, while in others only mutual respect may evolve. (3) Do you recognize the validity of the leadership of the FBO? This is important when there may be an imbalance of professional credentialing. If all the professional and academic training is on one side of the table and only "mother wit" is sitting on the other side, a person may feel uncomfortable or possibly intimidated. Do you recognize the validity of the leadership of the FBO that has and can provide access to the people you seek to serve? The "3 R's" of collaboration are recognition, relationship, and respect. If the partners bring this understanding to the table, the potential for a successful collaboration is high.

OVERCOMING BARRIERS AND BUILDING SUCCESSFUL PARTNERSHIPS

Despite the potential advantages of collaboration, the challenges discussed above must be overcome before mental health and faith-based organizations will be able to forge successful partnerships to benefit youth. The following strategies will assist mental health providers in this endeavor.

1. Clarify goals. It is important that the mental health agency determine beforehand what needs are to be met through a partnership with the faith community. One method for making this determination is to conduct a needs assessment to determine if the mental health needs of the youth in the community are being adequately addressed with the available resources (Acosta et al., this volume). This type of assessment will assist in identifying gaps in services that may serve as the focus of community partnerships. Also, it will be important for the FBO to articulate what their goals are in ministering to the youth in their community.

2. *Network.* Once the decision to pursue a partnership with a faith-based organization has been made, it will be important for key persons in the mental health agency to become visible within the faith community. The appointed liaison to the faith community should focus on getting to know faith leaders in the community by attending services and participating in other meetings sponsored by the faith organization (Budd, 1999; Plante, 1999). When the mental health agency is perceived as actively interested in the faith organization, the faith community will be more receptive to collaborative endeavors.

3. *Convey respect and appreciation.* When interacting with the faith community, it is important to express an understanding of the positive impact of religiousness on youth mental health. Mental health providers also should demonstrate respect for the important role clergy serve in the mental health field and for their expertise in this regard. In doing so, the mental health agency will be seen as valuing the role of religious faith. This will help alleviate concerns the faith community might have that mental health providers will attempt to discourage others from their faith by suggesting that religiousness is a manifestation of neurosis or that faith is a crutch for the weak-minded (Budd, 1999).

4. *Form reciprocal relationships.* Successful partnerships tend to be characterized by mutual support. With this in mind, it is suggested that the mental health organization offer culturally sensitive services to the faith community (e.g., parenting workshops, educational presentations on specific childhood difficulties, informational packets with referral information) (Plante, 1999). Mental health providers are also encouraged to make information regarding faith-based referral sources available to clients and to invite a clergy member to sit on the agency's advisory board. This investment of time on the part of the mental health care providers will increase the likelihood that the faith community will invest the resources, time, and effort required to partner with the mental health agency in establishing youth programs.

5. *Learn the language.* Effective communication is essential to forming reciprocal relationships. In order for productive conversations to take place, mental health providers and the faith community need to develop a common language. Ideally, mental health professionals should gain an understanding of religious terminology and the clergy should develop a lay knowledge of psychological nomenclature. Since it is likely that the mental health organization will initiate communication with the faith-based organization, it is especially important for mental health providers to avoid using professional jargon and to develop an understanding of how their

psychological terminology may be perceived by people in the faith community. One method for exploring this issue is to employ social marketing techniques. Social marketing would involve learning about the faith community and ascertaining what would make them want to support the proposed partnership. Using a social marketing approach, the mental health agency would assess the faith community's understanding of the mental health program, determine the current level of support for such programs, decide what messages the mental health agency would like to convey to the faith community, test these messages using focus groups, review the feedback received, and then refine the messages accordingly (National Association of State Boards of Education, 1999).

6. *Know the religious system and traditions.* Many religious traditions hold specific teachings on issues such as divorce, homosexuality, abortion, premarital sex, contraception, and the role of women that may run counter to values in the mental health system (Bergin, 1991). These issues can be real sticking points for some. Plante (1999) suggests that mental health providers do not need to agree with these traditions, but should be sensitive to these issues and sympathetic to the mission of the faith-based organization.

7. *Establish a common mission.* If the faith-based and mental health organizations are viewed as having disparate goals, there may be reservations about collaborating. In order to initiate a successful partnership, both parties must be seen as having shared goals. Serving others and promoting positive youth development, for example, are primary aims for both faith-based and mental health groups. Thus, coming together and identifying a partnership mission statement will be very important in guiding the development of the collaborative endeavor as well as in enhancing stakeholder support for the program.

8. *Develop a planning committee.* It is recommended that an initial planning committee/advisory board be established. Included on this committee should be representatives from various community groups: faith-based leaders, mental health providers, agency coordinators, parents, educators, etc. This committee will assist in defining the partnership mission, determining the coalition structure (e.g., delineating the referral process, establishing funding and quality improvement mechanisms), clarifying legal/ethical obligations (e.g., client confidentiality, informed consent procedures), and developing other organizational policies (Acosta et al., this volume).

9. *Start small.* Coalitions are encouraged to pilot proposed projects locally before implementing services on a wide scale. For instance, the planning committee might pilot a mentoring program by training volunteers from one church or synagogue to mentor at-risk youth referred by a local school mental health program. These types of pilot projects provide

coalition coordinators the opportunity to identify program strengths and weaknesses and to develop strategies for improvement.

10. Provide training. To ensure service quality as well as the continued growth and development of the coalition, it will be important to provide training for members of the faith community and for the mental health providers. Topics that will be particularly important to cover on an ongoing basis include cultural sensitivity (especially religious sensitivity) and ethical/legal obligations. Suggested training/educational methods include direct supervision, peer support networks, professional conferences, staff development workshops, and written resource materials (Acosta et al., this volume).

11. Assure quality improvement. Quality improvement measures assure that the partnership goals are being met. Data from peer review teams, focus groups, interviews, and questionnaires assist in documenting service efficiency and effectiveness. This type of information is invaluable when attempting to build support (e.g., funding, human resources in the community) for the partnership activities.

12. Provide feedback. Ongoing feedback assists in maintaining coalition vitality. Partners typically remain more highly involved and motivated when there is continuing communication regarding program successes and difficulties. This type of consistent contact also assists in minimizing difficulties by identifying problem areas early, recruiting new members, and delegating leadership responsibilities.

PROMISING COLLABORATIVE ENDEAVORS

While there is a substantial literature base on different aspects of psychology and faith communities, few articles have been published examining collaborations between faith organizations and mental health agencies aimed at promoting mental health in youth. One such collaboration is a faith-based mentoring program. Mentoring programs such as the Big Brother/Big Sister programs, TeamMates, the Church Mentoring Network, and the Baltimore Mentoring Partnership (to name just a few) have been providing one-to-one mentors to children and adolescents. Many companies now have policies that allow an employee to leave early (with pay) one to two hours per week to spend time participating in a mentoring program. Faith-based mentoring programs involve members of a congregation agreeing to mentor a youth. Many congregations probably have several members who would be energetic about the opportunity to be a positive role model and mentor in a youth's life.

Pastoral Partners is a youth mentoring program in Baltimore City. Its mission is to provide Baltimore City youth the opportunity to form healthy and meaningful relationships with adult members of the Baltimore faith community. The University of Maryland School Mental Health Program (SMHP) is partnering with a church in the Harlem Park community, Christ is King, with the goal of providing mentoring relationships for the students at Harlem Park Middle School. The Baltimore Mentoring Partnership's Church Mentoring Initiative (CMI) will provide orientation, training, and technical assistance for this mentoring program. The cost of beginning a mentoring program is fairly inexpensive (e.g., Baltimore Mentoring training is about $100).

Many other cities also are involved in mentoring projects. In Philadelphia, the Church Mentoring Network was established in 1991 and has been providing mentoring services for over a decade. It also provides a Coordinators' and Providers' Network to promote shared resources and support among 130 members of mentoring and other youth-serving programs. Another mentoring program is TeamMates, which is located in Lincoln, Nebraska, and was founded by Tom Osborne, the former football coach of the University of Nebraska, and his wife, Nancy Osborne. TeamMates has been in existence since 1991 and has the support of Lincoln Public Schools, the City of Lincoln, the Lincoln Public Schools Foundation, the Lincoln Education Association, and the Lincoln business community. These are just a couple of the hundreds of mentoring programs throughout the county.

OTHER TYPES OF COLLABORATIONS

Mentoring is just one of many different collaborations that mental health agencies can have with FBOs. Other possible types of collaborations are listed below (the list is clearly not exhaustive).

1. Youth mental health promotion. Partnering with faith communities to provide mental health promotion activities in church settings for youth. These activities can take place as part of a summer Bible camp, ongoing lecture series at the church, period workshops for youth, and so on. The University of Maryland also is partnering with two other area churches to establish a youth mental health promotion campaign. The mission of this venture is to educate youth on aspects of positive mental health.

2. Training summer Bible school counselors. Mental health agencies and university-based faculty could provide some basic training to summer Bible school counselors on warning signs for mental health problems in youth. These counselors could then refer students, as needed, to the mental health agencies for mental health screening. This would provide an opportunity for at-risk and high-risk youth who may not typically have access to mental health professionals to become identified and receive treatment if so determined. This service also may educate parents and caregivers of the mental health resources in their community, and provide them a less threatening opportunity to access those resources. The religious leaders and the staff working with them could provide support and reassurance to families that are uncomfortable or uneasy with receiving mental health services, which may increase the likelihood that families needing services would actually seek out those services.

3. *Periodic presentations.* Staff from a mental health agency could do presentations at churches on various mental health topics (i.e., parenting, ADHD, the impact of violence on youth development, positive mental health, ways to build protective factors in youth). These presentations could take several different forms depending on the FBO, such as "brown bag" or lunch discussions during the week, short presentations followed up with a question-and-answer period, or a facilitated group discussion regarding these different issues.

4. *Peer counseling programs.* Religious leaders and youth directors at the FBO could identify youth who are sought out by their peers for help with problems. These youth could then be asked to participate in a peer counseling program, where they would have weekly meetings over the course of a year. The meetings would focus on training the identified youth how to handle situations (i.e., grief, depression, suicidal ideation) by providing their friend with support and helping their friend become connected with mental health professionals if needed.

CONCLUDING COMMENTS

The unmet mental health care needs of today's youth highlight the fact that the demand for mental health services often exceeds available resources. One solution, proposed in this chapter, is to find and mobilize the resources of the faith community in an effort to promote healthy youth development. Several challenges to developing cross-sector partnerships involving mental health and faith-based organizations have been identified. It has been suggested, however, that these barriers can be overcome when partners convey mutual respect and appreciation, establish effective means of communication, display cultural sensitivity, and invest the time needed to build an ongoing reciprocal relationship.

Nationwide, there remains a need to raise awareness and support for mental health partnerships with the faith community. Presidential support has clearly made a significant positive impact on garnering support for

FBOs working to improve their communities, which has in turn encouraged new and unique collaborations between FBOs and mental health agencies. However, forums in which both religious leaders and mental health providers are afforded the opportunity to discuss collaborative strategies for promoting youth development are needed. These types of dialogues need to occur on a consistent basis in order to alleviate tensions that typically arise when individuals with differing beliefs come together. It also will be important to build support among national mental health and faith-based organizations and to develop and publish integrated theories of mental health and faith. As the number of mental health–faith community coalitions increases, and as advocacy efforts gain momentum, it is believed that barriers will continue to be identified and overcome and community support will be garnered for these programs, as they represent a powerful, healthy, and healing force to combat the challenges and stresses facing today's youth.

References

American Psychological Association. (1992). *Ethical principles of psychologists and code of conduct*. Washington, DC: Author.

Bakke, R. J. (1987). *The urban Christian: Effective ministry in today's urban world*. Downers Grove, IL: Intervarsity Press.

Benson, P. L., Williams, D., & Johnson, A. (1987). *The quicksilver years: The hopes and fears of early adolescence*. San Francisco: Harper & Row.

Bergin, A. E. (1991). Values and religious issues in psychotherapy and mental health. *American Psychologist, 46,* 394–403.

Bradfield v. Roberts, 175 U.S. 291 (1899). Cf. *Abington School District v. Schempp,* 374 U.S. 203, 246 (1963) (Justice Brennan concurring).

Budd, F. C. (1999). An Air Force model of psychologist-chaplain collaboration. *Professional Psychology: Research and Practice, 30*(6), 552–556.

Donahue, M. J., & Benson, P. L. (1995). Religion and the well-being of adolescents. *Journal of Social Issues, 51*(2), 145–160.

Elkin, C. H., & Roehlkepartain, E. C. (1992, February). The faith factor: What role can churches play in at-risk prevention? *Source* [Search Institute, 700 S. Third St., Suite 210, Minneapolis, MN 55315], *8,* 1–3.

Ellis, A. (1980). Psychotherapy and atheistic values: A response to A. E. Bergin's "Psychotherapy and Religious Issues." *Journal of Consulting and Clinical Psychology, 48,* 635–639.

Freud, S. (1953). *The future of an illusion* (W. D. Robson-Scott, Trans.), p. 76. New York: Liveright Publishing.

Gallup, G. H. (1990). *Religion in America: 1990*. Princeton, NJ: Gallup Organization.

Gallup, G. H., & Bezilla, R. (1992). *The religious life of young Americans*. Princeton, NJ: George Gallup International Institute.

Goodstein, L. (1993, June 10). Put the kindness back into public policy, coalitions urge. *Washington Post*, p. A19.

Leaf, P. J., Alegria, M., Cohen, P., Goodman, S. H., Horowitz, S. M., Hoven, C. W., Narrow, W. E., Vadem-Kierman, M., & Reiger, D. A. (1996). Mental health service use in the community and schools: Results from the four-community MECA study. *Journal of the American Academy of Child and Adolescent Psychiatry, 35*, 889–897.

National Association of State Boards of Education. (1999). *Building support for school health programs: An action guide*. Washington, DC: Author.

Plante, T. G. (1999). A collaborative relationship between professional psychology and the Roman Catholic Church: A case example and suggested principles for success. *Professional Psychology—Research & Practice, 30*(6), 541–546.

Rabey, S. (1996, September 16). Hurting helpers: Will the Christian counseling movement live up to its promise? *Christianity Today*, p. 76.

Samuelson, R. J. (1994, March 26). Here's some good news, America. *Washington Post*, p. A21.

Search Institute (1997). *The asset approach: Giving kids what they need to succeed.* Minneapolis, MN: Author.

Shaffer, D., Fisher, P., Dulcan, M. K., Davies, M., Piacentini, J., Schwab-Stone, M. E., Lahey, B. B., Bourdon, K., Jensen, P. S., Bird, H. R., Canino, G., & Regier, D. A. (1996). The NIMH Diagnostic Interview Schedule for Children Version 2/3 (DISC 2.3): Description, acceptability, prevalence rates, and performance in the MECA study. *Journal of the American Academy of Child and Adolescent Psychiatry, 35*(7), 865–877.

Shafranske, E. P. (1996). *Religion and the clinical practice of psychology.* Washington, DC: American Psychological Association.

Shafranske, E. P., & Malony, H. N. (1990).Clinical psychologists' religious and spiritual orientation and their practice of psychotherapy. *Psychotherapy, 27*, 72–78.

Shirk, M. (2000). Faith-based youth work wins more converts. *Youth Today: The Newspaper on Youth Work, 9*(1), December/January.

Spilka, B., Hood, R., & Gorsuch, L. (1985). *The psychology of religion: An empirical approach.* Englewood Cliffs, NJ: Prentice-Hall.

Tashman, N. A., Weist, M. D., Nabors, L. A., & Shafer, M. E. (1998). Involvement in meaningful activities and self-reported aggression and delinquency among inner-city teenagers. *Journal of Clinical Psychology in Medical Settings, 5*(3), 239–248.

Thomas, P. A., & Texidor, M. S. (1987). The school counselor and holistic health. *Journal of School Health, 57*(10), 461–463.

Weaver, A. J. (1995). Has there been a failure to prepare and support parish-based clergy in their role as front-line community mental health workers?: A review. *Journal of Pastoral Care, 49*, 129–149.

Weaver, A. J. (1998). Mental health professionals working with religious leaders. In H. Koenig (Ed.), *Handbook of religion and mental health* (pp. 349–364). San Diego, CA: Academic Press.

Weaver, A. J., Samford, J. A., Kline, A. E., Lucas, L. A., Larson, D. B., & Koenig, H. G. (1997). What do psychologists know about working with the clergy? An analysis of eight APA journals: 1991–1994. *Professional Psychology: Research & Practice, 28*(5), 471–474.

Weist, M. D., Ginsburg, G. S., & Shafer, M. E. (1999). Progress in adolescent mental health. *Adolescent Medicine: State of the Art Reviews, 10*, 165–174, vii.

CHAPTER TWELVE

Children Are Newsworthy: Working Effectively with the Media to Improve Systems of Child and Adolescent Mental Health

Caroline S. Clauss-Ehlers, Ph.D., and Mark D. Weist, Ph.D.

Reports of youth violence have made headline news in virtually all the major news media over the past several years. The "above the fold" section of front-page news has headlined a plethora of child-related mental health issues. Stories report that patterns of violence involve perpetrators who are typically young, White, depressed males (Gabel, 1999), that a copycat syndrome has led youth to imitate school violence (Cohen, 1999), that depression is a recognizable problem in youth (United States Department of Health and Human Services, 1998), and that half a million to one million prescriptions for antidepressants are written for children and teens each year (Chua-Eoan, 1999).

At first glance it appears that the American public has a greater understanding of particular issues that have an impact on childhood development. However, other reports highlight how little is actually known about children's mental health issues. A survey by the Pew Littleton Charitable Trust found that the Littleton, Colorado, incident was one of the most followed stories of the 1990s due to our inability to fully comprehend what occurred (Gibbs, 1999). Similarly, the U.S. Department of Health and Human Services (1998) estimated that while approximately one youth in every ten has a serious emotional disturbance, less than a third receive any mental health care (the percentage of youth who receive effective care is not known, but it is far less than a third). Dryfoos (1994) estimated that at least one-fourth of youths could benefit from mental health intervention when life stress and risk factors are considered. Further, when the definition of mental health is expanded to include enhancing youth strengths and protective factors, a case can be made that almost all youths would benefit from mental health intervention. These prevalence data suggest that despite coverage of a youth sound bite in the popular press, major gaps in understanding and awareness about children's mental health issues remain among the American public.

POOR UNDERSTANDING IS ASSOCIATED WITH SIGNIFICANT STIGMA

The gap between sound bite information and the lack of mental health services for children and adolescents appears to be filled with significant stigma. Stigma refers to an abstract concept that denigrates those with mental health problems and has tangible consequences that take the form of painful and destructive attitudes and behaviors. Often the general public does not consider the impact of mental health problems to be real, or to be comparable to physical health problems. A common perspective is that individuals who struggle with mental health issues have actually caused their problems, or that such individuals should be able to "pull themselves up by their bootstraps."

While stigma is prominent for mental health in general, it is particularly striking in terms of children's mental health issues. There is an historical basis for the stigma associated with childhood mental health. Historically, the mental health profession presumed that children were invulnerable to mental illness and thus did not need treatment (Freud, 1894, 1896). Many clinicians still hold the view that infants, children, and adolescents are unable to get depressed because their ego and cognitive capacities are not yet fully developed (Carlson & Garber, 1986; Wenar, 1994). Without fully developed functions, the belief is that the young person lacks the necessary understanding to interpret or even experience depressive symptomatology. This historical, theoretical viewpoint is reflected in current practices in the mental health field. In the fourth edition of the Diagnostic and Statistical Manual (DSM-IV), for instance, childhood depression is not fully endorsed as a clinical possibility. Thus it is not listed as a disorder that usually occurs in infancy, childhood, or adolescence.

Another reason for the stigma associated with mental illness among youth concerns general sentiment toward childhood in the United States. Ours is a society that prefers to view childhood as a time of carelessness, devoid of worry. When problems do occur, developmental perspectives are often expressed through the belief that the child will "grow out of it." As a nation, we do not want to acknowledge when our children are ill. In a special report, *Time* magazine (Chua-Eoan, 1999) cited a study conducted at Ball State and Columbia universities which asserted that 57 percent of adolescents who attempted suicide suffered from major depression. Of these, however, only 13 percent of the parents had thought that their child was depressed. The cycle of such blindness only increases misunderstanding, which subsequently contributes to greater stigma.

LIMITATIONS IN CHILD AND ADOLESCENT MENTAL HEALTH PROGRAMS, AND THE DEVELOPMENT OF REFORMS

In addition to the public's very limited knowledge about mental health issues among youth (and adults), many other problems make our child and adolescent system a "nonsystem" (see Burns & Friedman, 1990; Weisz & Weiss, 1993). These problems include: (1) a continued reliance on passive forms of mental health care in clinics away from people's neighborhoods; (2) a lack of capacity to respond to the mental health needs of youth and an overreliance on professional staff; (3) the excessive focus on pathology in assessment and intervention approaches; (4) the failure to focus on youth strengths and environmental factors; (5) extremely limited evaluation of clinical programs and the perpetuation of subjective methods of care; (6) poor collaboration between mental health disciplines, and between mental health staff and staff from other disciplines (e.g., health, education); and (7) the failure to develop integrated systems of care (Clauss, 1998a; see Weist & Christodulu, 2000).

However, the good news is that there is a major effort to reform systems of mental health care and education for youth in the U.S. This reform is seeking to move us beyond limiting constructs and approaches in order to develop a full array of effective programs for youth in communities in natural settings that remove barriers to their learning and improve their psychosocial adjustment. Three major developments in this reform effort are: (1) the advancement of programs developed by systems of education to enable student learning, led by the work of Adelman and Taylor (1993, 1999); (2) the national movement toward expanded school mental health programs, which provide prevention, assessment, treatment, and case management services to youth in general and special education, and involve strong collaboration between schools and community agencies (Weist, 1997a, 1999; Flaherty & Weist, 1999); and (3) the progress of prevention research, which is documenting that many broad-based prevention programs in schools lead to long-term positive impacts for youth (Durlak, 1995; Weissberg & Greenberg, 1998).

In many ways mental health prevention and intervention efforts in schools are moving us beyond many of the above-mentioned limitations. Services are proactive and are provided to youth in the most universal natural setting (i.e., schools). We are building capacity to respond to the mental health needs of youth in interdisciplinary efforts that involve professional staff working with paraprofessional and nonprofessional staff (see Cowen et al., 1996; Waxman, Weist, & Benson, 1999). In most programs, youth do not need diagnoses to be seen, and there is a growing emphasis on building youth strengths and resilience factors, and on placing major attention on the role of environmental variables (see Tashman, Waxman, Nabors, & Weist, 1998). Quality improvement and evaluation activities are being prioritized as perhaps the most important set of activities for programs to document that they are in fact helping youth (see the chapter by Ambrose et al., this book; Nabors, Weist, Tashman, & Myers, 1999). Finally, there is significant progress toward developing a system that emphasizes prevention and mental health promotion, while ensuring adequate services for youth showing early signs of problems and those with more serious and established problems (Weist & Christodulu, 2000).

Importantly, there is very inadequate public awareness of the limitations in child and adolescent mental health, or of reforms that are moving us beyond these limitations. For us to build support for increasing capacity in children's mental health, enhancing the focus on prevention, and moving care to natural settings such as schools, the public needs to be involved in the dialogue.

ADVANCING REFORMS IN CHILDREN'S MENTAL HEALTH THROUGH GREATER AWARENESS

To further advance progress that is being made in systems of children's mental health and education (as above), an important first step is to broadly raise awareness. Through greater awareness of children's mental health needs, system limitations, and strategies to improve the system, important steps can be made to bridge the gap between needs and resources. And public education is the vehicle to raise such awareness.

Broadly defined, public education refers to educational efforts that communicate information about key issues in children's mental health (as above) to increase community awareness of the issues, and to build support in communities to do something about the issues. Such information also assists children, adolescents, their families, and concerned citizens in learning about local resources and builds support and advocacy to improve systems.

In public education, teams work with public and private organizations to implement workshops, seminars, and informational sessions in businesses, schools, universities, day care centers, and community organizations. Teams include a range of representatives from mental health, physical health, education, youth, juvenile justice, advocacy, and other organizations.

Public education teams work in a pre-intervention mode where information is disseminated about the vulnerabilities associated with mental health problems among youth, factors that help protect youth from mental health problems, and systems issues that need to be addressed and improved to broaden impacts. A realistic goal of such public education is to increase understanding among diverse community members of what constitutes mental health. We use a framework whereby a child's (or adolescent's or adult's) mental health at a given point in time is a reflection of stress/risk factors and protective factors that are operating in his or her life (Weist, 1997b; Weist, Ginsburg, & Shafer, 1999). Obviously, people under high stress with limited protective factors are at the most risk for emotional/behavioral problems and problems in life functioning (e.g., in school, work). In contrast, those under low stress and with high protective factors are at the least risk for problems in mental health and life functioning.

The framework enables children, adolescents, parents, and community members to better understand mental health, and to immediately learn of some strategies to improve it (i.e., by reducing stress and increasing protective factors). This is facilitated by more in-depth discussion on environmental and stress factors (e.g., neighborhood crime and violence), how they affect people, and how they can be changed, and on the powerful role of both external (e.g., recreational opportunities, support from others) and individual (e.g., spirituality, reading for pleasure) protective factors, and how they can be relatively easily modified. Presenting the framework helps to demystify mental health, and to destigmatize it, as all people have variations in their mental health depending on stress and protective factors that are operating at a given point in time in their lives.

Public education should also include discussion of more serious mental health problems. Parents might not be aware that mental health problems can be caused by biological or environmental factors, or a combination of both. During workshops, for instance, parents often state that they changed their child's diet in attempts to control attentional problems. By clearing up such myths, informational workshops help parents see that biological factors might include genetics, chemical imbalances, and damage to the central nervous system.

But it must be noted that the content of public education efforts critically influences people's response to it. Mental health professionals often give presentations that emphasize pathology in human beings, such as various mental disorders of children and how to recognize them. This approach, without mention of youth strengths, protective factors, or environmental influences, can actually increase stigma, and increase the reluctance of families to seek contact with the mental health system. Similarly, the way a topic gets marketed is critical to either decreasing or increasing stigma around particular content areas. In one instance, a college university scheduled a workshop on suicide during finals week. The concern of the campus health center was that the higher incidence of stress might trigger suicidal ideation and/or attempts among the student body. The workshop, however, was exclusively attended by professionals who worked in the surrounding community. Further inquiry revealed that the seminar was advertised as a suicide workshop. In this context, students did not attend due to concerns and fear that they might be identified by peers, and thus rendered more vulnerable.

WORKING WITH THE MEDIA TO RAISE AWARENESS AND IMPROVE MENTAL HEALTH SYSTEMS FOR YOUTH

Media outreach is a major strategy that can help advance reforms and build systems of care that include mental health promotion and intervention for children, adolescents, and their families. Being responsive to the media takes both public education and advances in children's mental health to a larger, macro-level of communication. It is frequently the case that mental health professionals, advocates, and academics view the print and broadcast media as sources that will sensationalize and incorrectly represent the position of children's mental health. However, given the intrinsic nature of the media in the lives of Americans, this viewpoint fails to recognize the wonderful resource that the media provide. The fact is that Americans receive most of their information through the writings, recordings, and videos of journalists, making the members of this profession the gatekeepers between the struggles that children face and the media outlets that can report them as news (MacEachern, 1994).

The media are made up of radio, television, newspapers, magazines, and newsletters that regularly circulate throughout the country. According to the Radio Advertising Bureau (RAB), Americans listen to the radio for an average of three hours per day. Two out of three Americans listen to the radio while they drive to work, making it a first news source during the day. According to the Roper organization, 65 percent of Americans identify television as their major source of news. Further, Gallup polls found that "watching television" was rated by Americans for the past forty years as their favorite way to spend an evening (Newport, 1999). The Benton Foundation (1991) stated that more than 92 million U.S. households, or

98 percent of all homes, own television sets. Between the ages of two and sixty-five, the average individual will watch nine full years of television. Further, 65 percent of all Americans consider television their main source of health information.

Approximately 1,600 daily newspapers are published daily in the U.S., with an overall circulation of 62.6 million. Many cities have a daily newspaper as well as weekly and special-interest papers. Newspapers are most likely to respond to the particular events that occur in nearby communities and often provide the most local media coverage. There are approximately 8,000 magazines published in the United States, most of which circulate once a month. Weekly news magazines such as *Time* and *Newsweek* cover a broad range of public interest topics. Finally, the newsletter is another form of media that is often distributed to constituencies, employees, or specific interest groups. Community newsletters that target a particular area of interest or theme can be especially responsive to the unique needs of the community (MacEachern, 1994).

As you begin to identify the media sources in your area, remember that the local media can play a powerful role in advocacy efforts. Often when we think of the media, we immediately connect with the major networks or newspapers that circulate in the community. While both local and national outlets are valid sources of communication, remember that each has its unique constituency. Through a local newspaper you might be able to reach a certain audience that would be lost with a national forum. A two-tiered strategy accounts for both levels of media, and encourages you to pitch your story to local and national sources simultaneously. What you help identify as news on a local level might eventually get picked up as news on the national front.

Having summarized the extensiveness of who the media are, the question becomes: How can we leave the media out of the need-resource gap equation in children's mental health? The answer is we absolutely cannot. Perhaps professionals shy away from the media because they are unaware of how to be responsive to the diversity of media sources. Being responsive, or developing an openness to the idea of the media, is a key operating term as professionals begin to negotiate media relations. Individuals often fail to realize that as a credible, reliable source, the media needs you as much as you need them.

BEING RESPONSIVE TO THE MEDIA

The first step in being responsive is to identify the media sources in your constituency. This involves contacting your radio, television, and newspaper sources to identify the names of the reporters who cover your interest, or "beat." For instance, in attempts to get a story covered on childhood depression in the Bronx, it became important to identify a reporter who covers health issues in the Bronx. Media directories such as Bacon's Media Directories are available and list media outlets by type, city, and area of specialization.

Having identified your specific sources, a logical next step is to pitch your story. Several key message principles will facilitate this process. One is to know beforehand the story you want to see in print or on television. In a story presented to a major Spanish television network, for instance, the first author was very clear that the piece was about childhood depression. As you keep to your story, use numbers to give it weight. This establishes a legitimacy of need associated with your story, and subsequently makes it more newsworthy. For the childhood depression story, it was critical to communicate that 9 to 13 percent of children ages nine to seventeen suffer from a serious emotional disturbance such as depression (American Academy of Child and Adolescent Psychiatry, 1998). Statistics are brought to life and made compelling through the use of examples. In this instance, it was important to distinguish between normal sadness, which is a part of growing up, and clinical depression, which severely effects functioning in educational and social arenas.

Language usage is also key in getting your message across (Clauss, 1998b). The average sound bite, or quotable comment to broadcast media, is 7.2 seconds long. This means a good quote is concise, summarizes critical talking points, is presented in the active voice, and is no more than twenty-seven words long (Jahnke, 1998; Substance Abuse & Mental Health Services Administration, 1998). Good quotes convey the humanity of a story and compel viewers and readers to continue their engagement with it long after the story has aired. These principles underscore the fact that it is critical to keep your story simple. Despite some of the highly complex issues associated with child and adolescent mental health, the message will get lost if it is weighted down with complexities.

Keep to three key message points that you communicate throughout the interview. Using three themes makes your message accessible to viewers and listeners. It gives your story "legs," indicating action associated with the topic you cover. The three points for the story on childhood depression were: (a) one in ten youths has a serious emotional disturbance; (b) symptoms of childhood depression include depressed mood, insomnia, decreased appetite, and academic difficulties; and (c) treatment works. These three simple statements give viewers a sense of prevalence, symptomatology, and solution.

Bridging will allow interviewees to sustain their themes throughout the interview. Bridging means that the interviewee provides a direct answer to a question, and then transfers to his or her message point. For instance, a reporter says, "If so many children have depression, why don't more go for treatment?" The interviewee might respond as follows: "There is great stigma associated with getting help. But what I can tell you about treatment is that it is successful 80 percent of the time." The interviewee answers the reporter's question, and bridges to the message strategy. The sequence here is: Hear the question, answer, bridge. In fact, research shows that highly successful corporations consistently reiterate the same messages over time to further their success (Collins & Porras, 1994).

Responsiveness, however, refers to much more than identifying and bridging. A main component is to understand and react to what the media need as the individual clinician, program, or school builds reporter relations. Reporters work under time constraints. If a school says it will call a reporter back with information by a certain time, it should be certain to do so, even if it is to say the school was unable to get the desired information. Know that reporters are under a tremendous push to give stories a human interest appeal. This is where mental health professionals can respond to the media by brokering connections with people. In the childhood depression piece, for instance, the story was only able to air because a clinic was contacted that identified a family who was willing to share their experience.

Mental health professionals can provide an ease of access for the media and connect them with personal sources that make a story memorable. If a reporter has a deadline for a piece on school-based mental health, the piece won't air unless some connection is made with a school program that provides access and story. Thus it becomes important for mental health professionals to be smart about the media opportunities available to them. This also means not making themselves difficult to find. If a reporter has a five o'clock deadline and wants a quote from a mental health professional by four, it is critical that sources have up-to-date contact information. Throughout this process, remember that it is important to cultivate relationships with media personnel. This means not just calling to pitch a story, but also calling to converse as colleagues or to return calls when the media turn to the clinician as a resource.

CONNECTING MEDIA AWARENESS TO CHILD AND ADOLESCENT MENTAL HEALTH

It is hoped that the above description outlines ways in which the media can push forward awareness of youth mental health needs and state-of-the-art approaches to addressing them. Clearly, the media do not have the answer, and are only one piece of a complex, ever-changing puzzle. However, being responsive to the media influences public will, which has a subsequent impact on political will. Greater awareness of child and adolescent mental health and the need for proactive, interdisciplinary, and empirically supported programs in natural settings such as schools takes the conversation out of the individual arena and locates it in the public sphere as a major policy issue.

Such media responsiveness will assist in creating a sense of national urgency, and in so doing will address the tremendous gap between youth mental health needs and resources, as well as excitement about new developments that offer so much potential. This activity will push children's mental health beyond individual intrapsychic functioning, to an ecological model where the totality of the child/adolescent and his or her environment is considered. Through awareness about the range of stressors children and adolescents face today, along with environmental and individual resilience factors that can help them, communities can begin to make more informed decisions about how to structure themselves to promote the positive life trajectories of their youth.

A MULTIMEDIA CAMPAIGN

A multimedia campaign (MC) is one way to respond to the media to advance reforms and systems of mental health promotion and intervention for youth. The authors of this chapter are in the middle of planning for such a campaign. As both practicing child psychologists and academics, the sense of urgency about the MC comes from recognizing that most children with emotional problems are not getting help. In addition, myths abound regarding what is and what isn't a mental health problem. One parent, for instance, only acknowledged that her child had attention problems when he had to stay back a grade. "I didn't want to admit something was wrong with my son," she shared. "I thought if I ignored it and changed his diet, the problem would go away." The MC, then, is an attempt to "give psychology away" through the knowledge, education, and, most importantly, the awareness it aims to provide.

The key point to be made about establishing an MC is that it can be as all-encompassing or as grassroots as the planner wants it to be. The purpose of the MC is to enhance awareness of children's mental health issues through media outreach. This task can be accomplished by clinicians who act on a one-to-one basis, organize a small team, or spearhead a community-wide effort. For the independent clinician, the above points certainly apply to how one crafts and communicates his or her message.

In some ways, individual clinicians who interface with the media have much more flexibility: They are not constrained by agency protocol and do not have to wait for clearance to be interviewed. Waiting can jeopardize a story, since the reporter might be under a deadline. Individual clinicians might also have greater access to children and families who want to share their stories. These relationships are critical, since reporters often depend on the human element so the story will resonate with readers and viewers.

For small teams and clinicians working one-on-one, a dual media outreach strategy is very effective. A dual strategy means that on the one hand, the team or individual pitches stories to local media, while on the other, national media outlets are also contacted. Teams and independent clinicians can develop a media contact list that becomes their virtual Rolodex for events that merit coverage. A particular strength of the media-aware clinician or team is knowledge about particular media outlets in the area. On a slow news day, for instance, local stations might actually be on the lookout for stories to air. This is when the clinician or team becomes a resource for the station.

For those interested in a community-wide effort, the authors aim to sponsor an MC comprised of local and national print and broadcast media; for-profit and not-for-profit organizations; and parents, youth, and community leaders. The MC will further communication about the gap between youth mental health needs and resources and the potential for school-based programs to bridge the gap. The goal of this particular MC is to further responsiveness between media and mental health professionals on various levels.

Organizing a community-focused MC creates a unified network that communicates three key message points about children's mental health: (1) there is a significant gap between children's mental health needs and effective programs and resources for them; (2) children's mental health is much more than mental illness, including the influences of stress and protective factors in their lives; and (3) expanded mental health programs for youth in natural settings such as schools (the most universal natural setting) are the most promising strategy to close the gap.

The hope here is that the MC creates a snowball effect whereby the media and the public clearly pick up on the need for news coverage. Certainly this occurred for the Columbine incident, where suddenly youth violence became a major news story. School shootings have occurred throughout the 1990s, but the Columbine incident spiraled into one of the most reported events of the decade. In contrast, the event where six-year-old Kayla Rolland was shot and killed by her six-year-old classmate received substantially less attention. Kayla was killed at Buell Elementary School in Mt. Morris Township, Michigan, on February 29, 2000. Her classmate had gone to stay with his uncle eight days before the shooting.

It was at his uncle's home that the six-year-old found a loaded gun that he brought to the classroom. Reportedly, the two children had argued prior to the shooting. Unfortunately there was no spiral effect, or media coalition, to move the story forward as a major news piece about gun control. In this instance, there was a lack of responsiveness between mental health organizations and the media.

A final aim of the MC is to have a significant impact on the lives of children and their families. On numerous occasions, parents, grandparents, and even children have called the first author of this chapter after reading a newspaper story on childhood mental health. Frequently the callers reveal that they knew something was wrong, but doubted themselves or were uncertain about how to access systems of care. It was only after thoughtful media coverage raised awareness that such families felt less alone in their struggles and willing to seek intervention.

To maximize the possibilities presented by a community-focused MC, it is important to be savvy about how news conferences work. A good news conference is one where the story is important and thus newsworthy. Because an empty campaign will not propel the desired message, the story must compel and engage participants. The lack of resources amid great need among youth is controversial as it is tragic. In addition, location is a key aspect of any successful MC. Locations must be easy to reach, and, if possible, known to media in the area. Since television assignment editors are unlikely to send a crew great distances for a brief clip, the aim is to have the MC in a central location in a major city.

Choosing the right day of the week is another draw for media sources. Opinions are mixed on this subject. Some say the earlier in the week, the better. Others caution against Mondays and opt for Tuesdays through Thursdays. One option is to schedule a media campaign on a Monday from 10:00 A.M. to 1:00 P.M. so that reporters will arrive promptly and leave with enough time to meet afternoon deadlines to file stories. Once the day is determined, all participants will receive a press kit that includes statements of what speakers will say, and fact sheets that outline the objectives of the MC. Prior to the event, it is important to fax a written announcement of the MC so that reporters are notified in advance. Faxes will be followed with telephone calls to confirm they were received. A media contact list will be generated to document all those who plan to attend. In addition, attempts will be made to get on the "daybooks," or the computerized calendars that indicate what media events are occurring that week.

If possible, the MC will involve parents, youth, and leaders in children's mental health who will amplify the three themes reviewed above. Panelists, including children, adolescents, and their families, will share their knowledge and experience with mental health problems. As mentioned earlier, personal stories give life to the statistics and examples presented by professionals and are thus a key component for any MC. After comments are made, reporters will have time to inquire about the three talking points. After the conference attempts will be made to archive stories developed from the MC.

Children growing up at the turn of the twenty-first century face great vulnerabilities. As technology explodes, so does the gap between the haves and have-nots, as well as the stress and pressure on youth and adults who live in an increasingly fast-paced society. Yet the little attention focused on mental health in general, particularly with regard to youth, leads to limited resources, and thus the message that mental health doesn't matter. Broad constituencies in our nation need to recognize that mental health, especially child and adolescent well-being, is everyone's issue. It is only through this understanding that our nation will truly be in a position to move forward.

ACKNOWLEDGMENTS: Supported by the Maternal and Child Health Bureau, Office of Adolescent Health, Health Resources and Services Administration (project #MCJ24SH02-01-0), and the Agency for Healthcare Research and Quality (grant #RO3 HS02-01-0), U.S. Department of Health and Human Services.

References

Adelman, H., & Taylor, L. (1993). School-based mental health: Toward a comprehensive approach. *Journal of Mental Health Administration, 20,* 32–45.

Adelman, H., & Taylor, L. (1999). Mental health in schools and systems restructuring. *Clinical Psychology Review, 19,* 137–163.

American Academy of Child and Adolescent Psychiatry (1998). *Mental health fact sheet.* Washington, DC: Authors.

American Psychiatric Association (1994). *Diagnostic and statistical manual of mental disorders* (4th ed/). Washington, DC: American Psychiatric Association.

Bacon's Media Directories. Chicago, IL.

Benton Foundation. (1991). *Strategic communications for nonprofits.* Washington, DC: Author.

Burns, B. J., & Friedman, R. M. (1990). Examining the research base for child mental health services and policy. *Journal of Mental Health Administration, 17,* 87–97.

Carlson, G. A., & Garber, J. (1986). Developmental issues in the classification of depression in children. In M. Rutter, C. E. Izard, & P. B. Read (Eds.), *Depression in young people: Developmental and clinical perspectives* (pp. 339–434). New York: Guilford Press.

Chua-Eoan, H. (1999, May 31). Escaping from the darkness. *Time*, pp. 44–49.

Clauss, C. S. (1998a). Cultural intersections and systems levels in counseling. *Cultural Diversity and Mental Health, 4*(2), 127–134.

Clauss, C. S. (1998b). Language: The unspoken variable in psychotherapy practice. *Journal of Psychotherapy, 35*(2), 188–196.

Cohen, A. (1999, May 31). Criminals as copycats. *Time*, p. 38.

Collins, J. C., & Porras, J. I. (1994). *Built to last.* New York: Harper.

Cowen, E. L., Hightower, A. D., Pedro-Carroll, J. L., Work, W. C., Wyman, P. A., & Haffey, W. G. (1996). *School-based prevention for children at risk.* Washington, DC: American Psychological Association.

Dryfoos, J. G. (1994). *Full Service Schools: A revolution in health and social services for children, youth, and families.* San Francisco: Jossey-Bass.

Durlak, J. A. (1995). *School-based prevention programs for children and adolescents.* Thousand Oaks, CA: Sage.

Flaherty, L. T., & Weist, M. D. (1999). School-based mental health services: The Baltimore models. *Psychology in the Schools, 36*, 379–389.

Freud, S. (1894). The neuro-psychoses of defence. In *The standard edition of the complete psychological works of Sigmund Freud* (Vol. 3) (1962) (pp. 43–61). London: Hogarth Press.

Freud, S. (1896). Further remarks on the neuro-psychoses of defence. In *The standard edition of the complete psychological works of Sigmund Freud* (Vol. 3) (1962) (pp. 159–185), London: Hogarth Press.

Gabel, E. (1999, May 31). Patterns of violence. *Time*, pp. 36–37.

Gibbs, N. (1999, May 31). Time: Special report. *Time*, pp. 33.

Jahnke, C. K. (1998). *Conquering the camera* [Media training handout]. Washington, DC: Positive Communications Media & Speaker Training.

MacEachern, D. (1994). *Enough is enough! The hellraiser's guide to community activism.* New York: Avon Books.

Nabors, L. A., Weist, M. D., Tashman, N. A., & Myers, C. P. (1999). Quality assurance and school-based mental health services. *Psychology in the Schools, 36*, 485–493.

Newport, F. (1999). *Television remains Americans' top choice for evening recreation.* Princeton, NJ: The Gallup Organization.

Substance Abuse & Mental Health Services Administration. (1998). *Communicating with the media.* Washington, DC: Office of External Liaison, Center For Mental Health Services.

Tashman, N. A., Waxman, R. P., Nabors, L. A., & Weist, M. D. (1998). The PREPARE approach to training clinicians in school mental health. *Journal of School Health, 68*(4), 162–164.

United States Department of Health and Human Services (1998). *Systems of care: A promising solution for children with serious emotional disturbances and their families.* Washington, DC: Author.

Waxman, R. P., Weist, M. D., & Benson, D. (1999). Toward collaboration in the growing education–mental health interface. *Clinical Psychology Review, 19*, 239–253.

Weissberg, R. P., & Greenberg, M. T. (1998). Social and community competence-enhancement and prevention programs. In. W. Damon, I. E. Sigel, &

K. A. Renninger (Eds.), *Handbook of child psychology, Volume 5: Child psychology in practice* (pp. 877–954). New York: John Wiley & Sons.

Weist, M. D. (1997a). Expanded school mental health services: A national movement in progress. In T. H. Ollendick & R. J. Prinz (Eds.), *Advances in clinical child psychology* (Vol. 19) (pp. 319–352). New York: Plenum.

Weist, M. D. (1997b). Protective factors in childhood and adolescence. In J. Noshpitz (Ed.), *Handbook of child and adolescent psychiatry* (Vol. 3) (pp. 27–34). New York: John Wiley & Sons.

Weist, M. D. (1999). Challenges and opportunities in expanded school mental health. *Clinical Psychology Review, 19,* 131–135.

Weist, M. D., & Christodulu , K. (2000). Expanded school mental health programs: Advancing reform and closing the gap between research and practice. *Journal of School Health, 70,* 195–200.

Weist, M. D., Ginsburg, G. S., & Shafer, M. (1999). Progress in adolescent mental health. *Adolescent Medicine: State of the Art Reviews, 10,* 165–174.

Weisz, J. R., & Weiss, B. (1993). *Effects of psychotherapy with children and adolescents.* Newbury Park, CA: Sage.

Wenar, C. (1994). *Developmental psychopathology: From infancy through adolescence* (3rd ed.). New York: McGraw-Hill.

Contributors

Olga M. Acosta, Ph.D., Chief Clinical Administrator, Safe Schools/Healthy Students Initiative, Child and Youth Services Administration, Washington, DC

Melissa Grady Ambrose, L.C.S.W.C., Program Manager, Center for School Mental Health Assistance, University of Maryland School of Medicine, Baltimore, Maryland

Jennifer Axelrod Lowie, Ph.D., Associate Director, Center for School Mental Health Assistance, University of Maryland School of Medicine, Baltimore, Maryland

Kristin V. Christodulu, Ph.D., Postdoctoral Fellow/Outreach Coordinator, Center for School Mental Health Assistance, University of Maryland School of Medicine, Baltimore, Maryland

Caroline S. Clauss-Ehlers, Ph.D., Assistant Professor of Psychology, Department of Psychology, Rutgers University, Piscataway, New Jersey

Steven W. Evans, Ph.D., Associate Professor of Psychology, Human Development Center, James Madison University, Harrisonburg, Virginia

Robert J. Evert, M.A., M.S.W., Site Coordinator, Linkages to Learning, CPC Health, Inc., Silver Spring, Maryland

Louise Fink, M.Ed., Director, Special Programs, Baltimore City Public School System, Baltimore, Maryland

Harinder S. Ghuman, M.D., Associate Professor of Psychiatry, Medical Director, Child and Adolescent Psychiatry, Walter P. Carter Center Outpatient Clinics, University of Maryland School of Medicine, Baltimore, Maryland

Nancy K. Glomb, M.A., Special Education Consultant, Human Development Center, James Madison University, Harrisonburg, Virginia

Marsha Gorth, L.C.S.W.C., Coordinator, Child and Adolescent Outpatient Services at Walter P. Carter Center, University of Maryland School of Medicine, Baltimore, Maryland

Mark E. Greenberg, M.A., Executive Director, Villa Maria Treatment Center, Timonium, Maryland

Yu Ling Han, Ph.D., Program Manager, CBHJ:PP, Jessup, Maryland

Eileen Hastings, R.N.C, L.C.S.W.C., Deputy Director, Community Psychiatry, Program Director, Walter P .Carter Center Outpatient Clinics, University of Maryland School of Medicine, Baltimore, Maryland

Alvin C. Hathaway, M.A.C.M., Pennsylvania Avenue A.M.E. Zion Church, Baltimore, Maryland

Thomas Hebeisen, Ph.D., Clinical Director, Terry Child Psychiatric Center, New Castle, Delaware

Susan Hill, M.A., Quality Assurance Coordinator, Center for School Mental Health Assistance, University of Maryland School of Medicine, Baltimore, Maryland

Charles Huffine, M.D., Assistant Medical Director, Child and Adolescent Programs, King County Mental Health Division, Clinical Instructor, University of Washington, Seattle, Washington

Paramjit T. Joshi, M.D., Professor and Chair, Child and Adolescent Psychiatry, National Children Center, George Washington University, Washington, DC

Michelle Leff, M.D., Medical Director, Child and Adolescent Services, Johns Hopkins Bayview Hospital, Assistant Professor of Psychiatry, Johns Hopkins Medical Institution, Baltimore, Maryland

Michael Longo, M.A., Director, The Narrative Project for Crisis Intervention, Belmont, Massachusetts

Laura A. Nabors, Ph.D., Assistant Professor, Department of Psychiatry, University of Cincinnati, Cincinnati, Ohio

Jennifer Oppenheim, Psy.D., Project Director, Linkages to Learning, Silver Spring, Maryland

Christine Prodente, Ph.D., Postdoctoral Fellow/Networking Coordinator, Center for School Mental Health Assistance, University of Maryland School of Medicine, Baltimore, Maryland

Eric Proescher, Psy.D., Postdoctoral Fellow, Center for School Mental Health Assistance, University of Maryland School of Medicine, Baltimore, Maryland

Bernice Rosenthal, M.P.H., Medicaid Consultant, Comprehensive School Health Services, Baltimore, Maryland

Mark A. Sander, Psy.D., Postdoctoral Fellow, Center for School Mental Health Assistance, University of Maryland School of Medicine, Baltimore, Maryland

Jennifer L. Sapia, Ph.D., Assistant Professor, Department of Psychology, East Carolina University, Greenville, North Carolina

Richard M. Sarles, M.D., Professor of Psychiatry and Pediatrics, Director of Training, Child and Adolescent Psychiatry Fellowship, University of Maryland School of Medicine, Baltimore, Maryland

Cindy Schaeffer, Ph.D., Postdoctoral Fellow, Center for School Mental Health Assistance, University of Maryland School of Medicine, Baltimore, Maryland

Tom Sloane, L.C.P.C., Mental Health Clinician, Center for School Mental Health Assistance, University of Maryland School of Medicine, Baltimore, Maryland

Ann Vander Stoep, Ph.D., Assistant Professor and Senior Researcher, Department of Psychiatry & The Washington Institute for Mental Illness Research, University of Washington, Seattle, Washington

Nancy A. Tashman, Ph.D., Assistant Professor of Psychiatry, Center for School Mental Health Assistance, University of Maryland School of Medicine, Baltimore, Maryland

Mark D. Weist, Ph.D., Associate Professor of Psychiatry, Director, Center for School Mental Health Assistance, University of Maryland School of Medicine, Baltimore, Maryland

Marilynn Williams, Founder and Director, King County Federation of Families, Co-chair KCBFP evaluation committee and steering committee member, CMHS Children's System of Care Grant, King County Mental Health Division, Seattle, Washington

Index

Acosta, Olga, 6
Adelman, H., 98, 227
Agency for Health Care Policy and Research (AHCPR), 96
Alaska Youth Initiative, 115, 177
Alliance for Mentally Ill, 145
Ambrose, Melissa, 8
American College of Mental Health Administration (ACMHA), 177
Anderson, H., 192, 196
Annie E. Casey Foundation, 2
Anthony, E. J., 10
Assertive Community Treatment, 161
Association for Health Services Research (AHSR), 96
Attention deficit/hyperactivity disorder (ADHD) in a school-based mental health setting, 75, 83–87

Baltimore, City of, mobile crisis response system, 131–146
Baltimore City school-based mental health programs: Baltimore City Health Department (BCHD), 20, 26, 27, 28, 29; Baltimore City Public Schools (BCPs), 20, 26; Baltimore Mayor's Office for Children and Youth, 19, 20; Baltimore Mental Health Systems, Inc. (BMHS), 32–33; Baltimore's Task Force on Mental Health Services, 25–26, 29, 31; Booker T. Washington Middle School satellite program, 26; Caplan model, 20; case management model, 26; collaborative partnerships, 25–26; contract between agencies for SMH funding, 27;Department of Social Services (DSS), 20, 26, 27; development of ESMH services, 25; ESMH/SBHC collaborations, 30; factors critical to ESMH development, 34; Family and Children Services (FCS), 27; Futures Program, 32; impact of managed care, 33; Johns Hopkins University (JHU), 20, 28, 31; Juvenile Services Administration (JSA), 20, 26; maintaining the programs and funding, 33–34; managing children's mental health services, 32–33; *Maryland Meets the Challenge: The Public-Private Partnership for Mental Health,* 25; Maryland Mental Hygiene Administration, 31; Medicaid revenues, 27, 30, 33; middle stage: expanding "stand-alone" ESMH programs, 29–30; organizations in leadership role, 26–27;

Baltimore City school-based mental health programs (*continued*) partnerships with institutions, 27–28; political support for ESMH programs, 28–29; primary care clinical model, 26; school-based health centers (SBHCs), 27, 28–29, 31; School Health Policy Initiative (SHPI), 33; School Readiness Initiative, 31; state community mental health funds, 31–32; State of Maryland DHMH, 20, 24, 25; Task Force on Mental Health Services for Children and Youth, 18, 19–20; third-party billing project (TPBP), 30–31; University of Maryland, Baltimore (UMB), 20, 28, 31–32
Benson, P. L., 211
Bradfield v. *Roberts,* 215
Bridges for Education, 83
Brook, B. D., 137
Building and Evaluating Family Support Initiatives (Dunst et al.), 163
Building Support for School Health Programs: An Action Guide, 63
Burchard, J. D., 115
Burns, Barbara, 177
Bush, George W.: "charitable choice," 209, 210, 221

Caplan, G., 20, 174
Cardinal Principles of Secondary Education (NEA), 22
Catholic Charities, 210, 215
Centers for Disease Control and Prevention (CDC), 7, 59
Chabra, A., 40–41
Challenging Horizons Program (CHP), case example of, 83–87
Chasin, R., 194
Child and Adolescent Functional Assessment Scale (CAFAS), 102; in child mobile team (CMT), 153–154, 155, 156; in family-driven treatment, 177
Child and Adolescent Service System Program (CASSP), 2–4, 130; guiding principles of proactive delivery of mental health services, 3; history of ESMH programs, 19–20; home-and community-based programs, 115; launching of program, 2–4
Child Behavior Checklist (CBCL), 102
Child Mental Health Service Program, 2
Children's Defense Fund, 19
Christodulu, Kristin, 9
Church. *See* Faith-based organizations (FBOs), children's mental health partnering with
Cognitive-behavioral therapy (CBT), in school-based mental health programs, 88–89
Collision, B. B., 67
Comer, J. P., 48, 49
Commonwealth Fund of New York City, 22
Community-change programs, elements of, 8
Community mental health centers (CMHCs): history of ESMH programs, 17–18
Comprehensive Mental Health Centers Act, 171–172
Confidentiality: in faith-based organization/mental health partnerships, 214; in school-based mental health programs, 81–83

Dennis, K., 115
Denver, foster home alternative program, 137
Diagnostic and Statistical Manual (DSM-IV): and childhood depression, 226; eligibility criteria for special education, 78
Dialectic behavior therapy (DBT), 172
Dilulio, John, 209
Donahue, M. J., 211

Doyle, J. C., 114
Dryfoos, J. G., 226
Duca, D. J., 104
Dunst, C. J., 163–164, 165

Educating public about child and adolescent mental health issues, 225–239
Education for All Handicapped Children Act of 1976, 23–24, 25
Elementary school program serving immigrant and minority children: considering elementary schools, 41–42; continuity of care, 51–54; easy transition in comprehensive school-based programs, 44, 45; ecological approaches to treatment, 48–50; effectiveness of programs, 47–51; Free and Reduced Meals (FARMS), 42; funding for, 55; future challenges, 54–55; holistic assessments, 47–48; increased access for children and families, 43–47; increasing generalized behaviors, 50–51; Linkages to Learning model, 42–43, 44; Making the Grade Initiative, 42; multiple entry points for service, 44, 45; prevention programs, 52; providing mental health services, 40–41; Robert Wood Johnson Foundation, 39, 42
Ellis, Albert, 212
Epston, D., 192, 193, 194, 202
Evaluation and quality improvement in school mental health: Agency for Health Care Policy and Research (AHCPR), 96; assessing multiple domains of youth environment and functioning, 99; assessing staff productivity, 100, 101; Association for Health Services Research (AHSR), 96; assuring cultural competence, 99; Child and Adolescent Functional Assessment Scale (CAFAS), 102; Child Behavior Checklist (CBCL), 102; conducting treatment outcome studies, 100, 102–103; developing an advisory board, 104; evaluating student functional improvement, 100; focus groups, 104–105; *Improving Quality of Health Care for Children: An Agenda for Research* (AHSR), 96; institutional review boards (IRBs), 106; National Committee for Quality Assurance (NCQA), 96; Office of Health Maintenance Organizations, 96; outcome evaluation, 97–98; peer review, 106; potential barriers to implementation of QI and program evaluation activities, 106–107; President's Advisory Commission on Consumer Protection and Quality in the Health Care Industry, 95; process evaluation, 97; program evaluation, 97–103; quality improvement and expanded school mental health, 103–106; satisfaction surveys, 105–106, 117; specific measurement strategies, 99; steps in doing ESMH program evaluations, 98–99; targeting program services and the evaluation, 98–99; University of Maryland School Mental Health Program evaluation, 100–103 ; Youth Self Report (YSR), 102
Evans, S. W., 41, 50
Evert, Robert, 8
Expanded school mental health (ESMH), 5–6, 7, 8; in Baltimore City school-based mental health programs, 25–30; evaluations of, 98–99; guidelines and recommendations for, 57–74; history of, 17–20, 21, 22; school-based health centers (SBHCs), 17–18

Faith-based organizations (FBOs), children's mental health partnering with, 209–224; assuring quality improvements, 219; awareness of positive impact of religious commitment on youth mental health, 211; Baltimore Mentoring Partnership's Church Mentoring Initiative (CMI), 219, 220; barriers to collaboration, 210, 211–215; Big Brother/Big Sister, 219; *Bradfield* v. *Roberts*, 215; Catholic Charities, 210, 215; Church Mentoring Network, 219, 220; clarifying goals, 216–217; collaboration, 3 R's of, 216; confidentiality concerns, 214; conveying respect and appreciation, 217; cultural differences, 213; developing a planning committee, 218; differing ministry perspectives and agendas, 215–216; establishing a common mission, 218; forming reciprocal relationships, 217; knowing the religious system and traditions, 218; language barriers, 213; learning the language, 217–218; limited public awareness of children's mental health issues, 213–214; Lutheran Family Services, 210, 215; mental health and religion as bedfellows, 212–213; mental health topic presentations, 221; narrow view of mental health services by public, 214; networking, 217; overcoming barriers and building successful partnerships, 216–219; Pastoral Partners, 219–220; peer counseling programs, 221; promising collaborative endeavors, 219–220; providing training and feedback, 219; role of clergy in the mental health field, 212; Salvation Army, 210, 215; scope of First Amendment, 215; separation of church and state, 214–215; social marketing, 218; starting small, 218–219; TeamMates, 219, 220; training summer Bible school counselors, 220–221; untapped resource of faith community, 210–211; youth mental health promotion, 220

Family-driven treatment: Alaska Youth Initiative, 177; Blended Funding program and clinical services in community, 171–173; *Building and Evaluating Family Support Initiatives* (Dunst et al.), 163; case examples in King County Blended Funding Project (BFP), 170–171, 174, 180, 185; Child and Adolescent Functional Assessment Scale (CAFAS), 177; choosing measurement tools, 176–178; Community Connections Questionnaire (CCQ), 178, 179; Comprehensive Mental Health Centers Act, 171–172; confidence in family member effectiveness, 184–185; creating a model of change, 174–175; dialectic behavior therapy (DBT), 172; disseminating results, 178–180; evaluation of Blended Funding Project, 174–180; families as full partners, 183–185; family-centered mental health services model, 164–165; Federation of Families (FOF) in Blended Funding Project (BFP), 169, 171, 173–174; Fort Bragg Evaluation, 177; history of family support movement, 163–164; identifying relevant outcomes, 175–176; impact of

managed care, 166; implementing evaluation design in the field, 178; implications of participatory research for care of children, 180–181; individualized education plan (IEP), 171; King County Blended Funding Project (BFP), 163, 169–186; "leap of faith" with funding, 184; Needs Met Questionnaire, 180; Oregon Partners Family Empowerment Scale, 176; Oregon Partners Project, 177, 178; outcomes and summary of Blended Funding Project, 181–183; participatory research model, 167–169; psychiatric consultation, 173–174; Service Fit Questionnaire, 178; Vermont System for Tracking Client Progress, 177; wraparound process, 165–167, 169–170
Fine, M., 196
Flaherty, L., 40
Fort Bragg Evaluation, 177
Foster, S. L., 91
Frank, R. G., 130
Freud, Sigmund, 212
Friedman, R. M., 19
Friesen, B. J., 165, 167, 169, 180

Garza-Guerrero, C., 49–50
Ghuman, Harinder S., 9, 10
Gold, S. J., 44–45
Goldman, S. K., 130
Gooloshian, H., 196
Gordon, N. J., 163–164, 165
Grealish, E. M., 115, 117
Guidance counselors, in history of ESMH programs, 21–22, 24

Hall, E. T., 45
Han, Yu Ling, 4
Harris, J. R., 50
Health Care Financing Administration (HCFA), 172
Hebeisen, Thomas, 10
Henggeler, S. W., 120, 121
Hoagwood, Kimberly, 177
Home-and community-based mental health services: acute versus chronic mental disorder care, 9; Child and Adolescent Service System Program (CASSP), 115; family as collaborators of care, 10; Geel, Belgium, 114; history, concepts and models, 113–128; home-based family-centered services (HBFCS), 118–120; Homebuilders Program, 118, 119–120; Maine Model for Home-Based Services, 118; Multiple Impact Therapy, 118; Multisystemic Treatment (MST) model, 120–123; Nashville Comprehensive Emergency Services, 118; Saint Dymphna, 114; social ecology, 118, 120; *special population,* 9; "strength chat" in wraparound approach, 116; variables influencing setting of care, 113–114; wraparound approach, 115–117; Yale Intensive In-Home Child and Adolescent Psychiatry Services model (YICAPS), 123–125. *See also* Family-driven treatment; Mobile crisis response systems; Narrative family therapy approach to acute services
Home-based family-centered services (HBFCS), 118–120
Homebuilders Program, 118, 119–120

Immigrant children: elementary school program serving immigrant and minority children, 39–56; in history of ESMH programs, 21, 22; *Improving Quality of Health Care for Children: An Agenda for Research* (AHSR), 96

Individuals with Disabilities Education Act (IDEA), 59; of 1990, 24; Amendments of 1997, 78–81; in school-based mental health programs, 77–80

Johns Hopkins University (JHU), 20, 28, 31
Johnson, A., 211
Joshi, Paramjit, T., 9

Kaleidoscope program, 115
Kaplan, D., 41, 45
King County Blended Funding Project (BFP), 163, 169–186
Knitzer, Jane, 2, 19
Koroloff, N. M., 165, 167, 169, 180

Lichenstein, R., 9
Linkages to Learning model, 8, 42–43, 44
Lutheran Family Services, 210, 215

Maine Model for Home-Based Services, 118
Making the Grade, 60
Managed care, 33, 69; in family-driven treatment, 166; impact on setting of mental health care, 10; third-party revenue model, 58–60
Maryland State Department of Health and Mental Hygiene (DHMH), 19
Maternal and Child Health Bureau, 7
McClowry, S. G., 41
Media outreach and working to improve child and adolescent mental health systems: being responsive to the media, 231–233; bridging, 232–233; childhood depression and DSM-IV, 226; community as resource to media, 235–237; concise language and using statistics, 232; connecting media awareness to child/adolescent mental health, 233–234; developing a multimedia campaign (MC), 234–237; limitation of current programs and development of reforms, 227–228; Littleton, Colorado, incident at Columbine, 225, 235; poor understanding/social stigma of mental health care, 226–227; prevention and mental health promotion, 228; public education and increasing awareness, 227, 228–229; quality improvement and evaluation documentation, 228; Rolland, Kayla, shooting of, 235–236; working with media to raise awareness, 230–231
Mental Health Association, 19, 145
Merrick, Tom, 19
Minority children, elementary school program serving immigrant and minority children, 39–56
Mobile crisis response systems: administration and leadership in CMT, 161–162; capacity and composition of mobile crisis team, 134; case management by CMT, 159; challenges and risks in CMT system, 160–162; Child and Adolescent Functional Assessment Scale (CAFAS), 153–154, 155, 156; child mobile team (CMT) administration, 152–155; child mobile team (CMT) members, 152–155; child mobile team (CMT) principles and model, 150–152; child mobile team (CMT) referral process, admission criteria, and intake procedure, 155–158; child mobile team (CMT) staff recruitment, orientation, and supervision, 152–153; City of Baltimore crisis response system, 131–146; collaboration with emergency rooms, 140–141; collaboration

with existing child/adolescent crisis response systems, 142; collaboration with public agencies, 139–140; coordination and administrative structure of crisis response system, 138–139; core values of, 145; crisis beds-group care, 137–138; crisis beds-therapeutic foster care, 137; crisis hotline, 133; dealing with youth and family resistance and dysfunction, 160–161; dependable relationship versus dependency on clinician, 160; fragmentation of service delivery, 130; individualized treatment plan (ITP), 137; in-home intervention, 136; insurance coverage for, 157–158; interventions, 132–138; linkage to ongoing mental health treatment, 141–142; mobile crisis team, 134–135; one-to-one supervision, 136; outcomes, 143; partnership organizations, 131–132; response at location of crisis, 134–135; response to emergency room, 135; sensitivity to cultural and individual needs, 143–145; staff's countertransference and feelings of hopelessness, despair, frustration, revulsion, and insecurity, 161; team leader, role in CMT, 153–154; team meetings in CMT, 154–155; team psychiatrist in CMT, 154; therapeutic versus case management needs, 160; treatment services by child mobile team (CMT), 158–159; University of Maryland Walter P. Carter Clinics (WPCC) child mobile team (CMT), 150–162
Mordock, J., 160
Multiple Impact Therapy, 118
Multisystemic Treatment (MST) model in home-based services, 120–123
Myers, C. P., 103

Nabors, L. A.,103
Nader, Ralph, 130
Narrative family therapy approach to acute services: assessment, 198–199; changing the approach to change, 200; client as the expert/stories of client's lives, 193; crisis unit, 196–197; externalizing problems, 194; family expertise with a "unique outcome," 193–194; intervention, 199–200; management versus treatment, 203–204; narrative therapy, description of, 192; out of the box with narrative thinking, 201–202; philosophy and core elements, 192–193; problems versus solutions, 203; residential and day program, 201; restoring safety and promoting change in 30 days, 197–198; stepping back and viewing the problem, 195; team collaboration and strength, 202–203, 204; teamwork and supervision, 195–196; Terry Children's Psychiatric Center narrative family therapy approach, 191–205; treating a child in a crisis bed, 199; triage, 198; use of language in communicating with families, 193–195, 202, 203
Nashville Comprehensive Emergency Services, 118
National Alliance for Mentally Ill, 145
National Assembly on School-Based Health Care (NASBHC), 41
National Association of State Boards of Education, 63
National Committee for Quality Assurance (NCQA), 96

National Conference of State Legislature, School Health Finance Project, 59
National Defense Education Act, 23
National Education Association, 22
National Institute of Mental Health (NIMH), 177; Child and Adolescent Service System Program (CASSP), 2, 115, 130

Office of the Assistant Secretary for Planning and Evaluation, 59
Office of Faith-Based and Community Initiatives, 11, 209
Office of Health Maintenance Organizations, 96
Office of Juvenile Justice and Delinquency Program, funding for violence prevention programs, 8
Office of Technology Assessment study, 2, 18
Oppenheim, Jennifer, 8
Oregon Partners Project, 176, 177, 178
Osborne, Nancy, 220
Osborne, Tom, 220

Parents Involved Together, 145
Patterson-Dehn, C., 41
Paul, T. W., 138
Pew Littleton Charitable Trust, 225
Piacentini, J., 99
Plante, T. G., 218
President's Advisory Commission on Consumer Protection and Quality in the Health Care Industry, 95
Principles providing proactive delivery of mental health services: Annie E. Casey Foundation, 2; broad systems of care, 4; CASSP guiding principles, 3; Child Mental Health Service Program, 2; cross-cutting issues, 11; elements of community-change programs, 8; factors promoting school-based programs, 6–7; faith-mental health partnerships, 11; family as collaborators of care, 10; launching of CASSP program, 2–4; mental health programs in homes and community, 8–10; narrative therapy approach, 10; Office of Faith-Based and Community initiatives, 11; proactive and preventive care in community, 1–2; public awareness of child and youth mental health, 11; Robert Wood Johnson Foundation, 2; school-based mental health programs, 3–4, 4–8; settings for child and youth mental health care, 10; *special population,* 9; State Comprehensive Mental Health Services Plan Act, 2; Substance Abuse and Mental Health Services Administration, 3; *Unclaimed Children* (Knitzer), 2; "waiting" for patients, 1; World Conference on Mental Health Promotion, 11–12
Prodente, Christine, 11
Project Wraparound, 115
Pumariega, A. J., 99

Quality improvement (QI), and expanded school mental health, 103–106

Religion/religious organizations. *See* Faith-based organizations (FBOs), children's mental health partnering with
Reynolds, W. M., 99
Risk factors/behaviors, 6, 18, 40
Robert Wood Johnson Foundation, 2, 39, 42, 60
Robin, A. L., 91
Roth, S., 194
Rowland, M. D., 120
Ruffin, J. E., 141–142

Safe Schools Health Students Initiative, 7
Salvation Army, 210, 215
Saxe, L., 2
School-based health centers (SBHCs), 17–18, 27, 28–29, 31
School-based mental health programs: advisory board, 63; assessment and consultation with teachers, 91; barriers-to-learning framework, 4–5; *Building Support for School Health Programs: An Action Guide,* 63; *Cardinal Principles of Secondary Education* (NEA), 22; Challenging Horizons Program (CHP), case example of, 83–87; changes after World War I and World War II, 22–23; Child and Adolescent Service System Program (CASSP), 19–20; cognitive-behavioral therapy (CBT), 88–89; collaboration, 60–63; confidentiality, 81–83; continuing education for staff, 70; crisis planning and management, 67–68; developing partnerships, 60–61; developing program structure, 65–68; DSM–IV eligibility criteria for special education, 78; Education for All Handicapped Children Act of 1976, 23–24, 25; education time, 90–91; evaluating needs, 64; expanded school mental health (ESMH) programs, 5–6, 7, 8, 17–18; factors promoting school-based programs, 6–7; family therapy, 91; field of school mental health, 72; funding for, 7, 23, 58–60; group therapy and skills training, 88–89; guidelines and recommendations for, 57–74; hiring staff, 68–69; history of, 17–23, 20–24; Individualized Education Plan (IEP) documentation, 77, 80–81; Individuals with Disabilities Education Act (IDEA), 77–81; Individuals with Disabilities Education Act (IDEA) of 1990, 24; in-school observation, 91; introducing the program, 68; Making the Grade, 60; managed care, 69; Medicaid revenues, 60; need for expanded mental health programs, 18–20; needs assessment and resource mapping, 63–65; orientation and training, 69; planning committee, 61; prevention programs, 6; professionalization of social and psychological services in schools, 23; program routine, 87–88; program structure concerns, 65–67; public law 105-17: IDEA Amendments of 1997, 78–81; quality assurance and evaluation, 70–71; recreation time, 89–90; referral procedures, 75–77; resource mapping, 64–65; Robert Wood Johnson Foundation, 60; role of guidance counselors, 21–22, 24; selecting a school, 63–64; Smith-Hughes Act, 23; special education regulations, 77–81; staffing, education, and training, 68–70; stakeholder involvement, 61–63, 65; supervisors/supervision of staff, 69–70; *A System of Care for Severely Emotionally Disturbed Children and Youth* (Stroul and Friedman), 19; third-party revenue models, 58; *Unclaimed Children* (Knitzer), 19; "visiting teachers," 21; Vocational Rehabilitation Act of 1973, 79, 80. *See also* Baltimore City school mental health programs; Elementary school program serving immigrant and minority children; Evaluation and quality improvement

Search Institute, 211
Shafer, M., 9
Shoenwald, Sonja, 177
Skinner, B. F., 212
Sluzki, Carlos, 193
Smith-Hughes Act, 23
Spaulding, Frank, 21
Special education regulations, in school-based mental health programs, 77–81
State Comprehensive Mental Health Services Plan Act, 2
Stoep, Ann Vander, 10
Stroul, B. A., 19, 130
Summer Treatment Program, 83
A System of Care for Severely Emotionally Disturbed Children and Youth (Stroul and Friedman), 19

Tashman, N. A., 6, 103
Taylor, L., 98, 227
Terry Children's Psychiatric Center narrative family therapy approach, 191–205
Turner, A. J., 138
Turner, J., 196

Unclaimed Children (Knitzer), 2, 19
University of Maryland: Baltimore (UMB), 20, 28, 31–32; Walter P. Carter Clinics (WPCC) child mobile team (CMT), 150–162
U.S. Department of Education, 42; school–based mental health program funding, 7, 8; Special Education and Safe Drug Free Schools, 7
U.S. Department of Health and Human Services (DHHS): Center for Mental Health Services, 3; on mental health care, 225–226; school-based mental health program funding, 7; Substance Abuse and Mental Health Services Administration, 3, 8
U.S. Surgeon General's Report on Mental Health in 1999, 11

VanDenBerg, J., 9–10, 115, 117, 165, 177
Van Vlaenderen, H., 167–168
Vermont System for Tracking Client Progress, 177
Violence in schools, prevention programs, 7
Vocational Rehabilitation Act of 1973, 79, 80

Walker, P., 137
Warner, B. S., 40
Weist, Mark D., 9, 40, 95–110
Western Psychiatric Institute and Clinic (WPIC), 83
White, M., 192, 193, 194, 202
Williams, D., 211
Windermand, P., 196
Woodruff, D. W., 48, 49
World Conference on Mental Health Promotion, 11–12
Wraparound approach, 115–117, 165–167, 169–170

Yale Intensive In-Home Child and Adolescent Psychiatry Services model (YICAPS), 123–125
Youth Self Report (YSR), 102

For Product Safety Concerns and Information please contact our EU representative GPSR@taylorandfrancis.com Taylor & Francis Verlag GmbH, Kaufingerstraße 24, 80331 München, Germany